The FIDDLER'S ALMANAC

by Ryan J. Thomson

© 1985
Captain Fiddle Publications
Newmarket, New Hampshire

For my Parents

Grateful acknowledgement is given to Roundup Records for permission to reprint record reviews, Matt Fichtenbaum for contributing information on Swedish fiddling, Linn Schulz for all sorts of helpful suggestions, The Division of Continuing Education of the University of New Hampshire for allowing me computer access time, Paul Mangion for the photograph of the author, Cheryl Cizewski for invaluable criticism of early drafts, Sarah Reynolds for proof reading and suggestions, and Barbara Sullivan for contributions of original art work.

typesetting by Linn S. Schulz
book design, cover art and paste-up by Ryan J. Thomson

Library of Congress Catalog Number: 84-73053
International Standard Book Number: 0-931877-00-8

Copyright © 1985 by **Captain Fiddle Publications**
4 Elm Court
Newmarket, New Hampshire 03857

205

Contents

Preface

I AM AN INVETERATE COLLECTOR of all types of practical information concerning the many activities that I'm involved in. Consequently, when I became interested in fiddling, I began filling boxes and bookcases with music books, catalogues, schedules, magazines, and all sorts of information relating to that subject. As a graduate student I was fortunate to have access to a university interlibrary loan service from which I was able to locate many obscure articles on fiddling. In my travels from coast to coast in the last dozen years, I've collected a wealth of printed material and field recordings from fiddlers and fiddling events in many states.

At first I used the collected information to improve my own fiddling. Later, as I began performing and teaching music, I recognized the need to organize and consolidate the information in order to share it with other folks.

The present volume has evolved out of this process, and more directly, from the short courses on fiddling that I have taught at the University of New Hampshire for several years within the Division of Continuing Education.

In the course of writing this self-published book I discovered that I had much more material than I could possibly fit in, and so I drew the line at a reasonable place. I have, however, included a number of topics which I know will be useful to beginning and seasoned fiddlers alike, and also to those who are perfectly content just to listen to fiddle music.

Since there is so much more to be said about fiddling than what I've included in this book, I'm already in the process of organizing a second volume to cover other areas and topics about fiddling.

I've enjoyed working on this project, and I'm happy to be able to share my information and experiences with you.

THE ENCYCLOPEDIA tells us that the violin is a stringed musical instrument, played with a bow, which assumed its present form about the beginning of the 16th century. Its Anglo-Saxon name was "fythel," from which "fiddle," was derived. The fiddle and the violin are one and the same instrument. Players of classical music usually call their instruments violins, but occasionally fiddles. Players of other types of music on the instrument seem to use "fiddle" more often than "violin," but one might make the distinction that "violin" is the more formal of the two names. When asked the question about what the difference is between fiddle and violin music, Allan Block, a fine New England fiddler, replied, "The person who plays it."

Fiddles generally have four strings with various exceptions. Some Asian folk fiddles have only one or two strings. My two-stringed Asian fiddle is made from bamboo, gourds and animal skin. I've danced contra dances where New Englander Dudley Laufman called the dance, played a three string "kit" fiddle solo, and danced—all at the same time. The three strings are all that is needed for most dance tunes. Five string fiddles are becoming popular among some fiddlers in bluegrass, jazz, and rock. These fiddles generally have a lower C string added to the G, D, A, and E strings already present.

Some European fiddles have sets of sympathetic strings which are not fingered but vibrate along with the strings that are fingerd. Other fiddles, such as the "Nyckel harpa" or keyed fiddle of Sweden, aren't noted with the fingers but have keys or buttons which are pressed to obtain notes.

All instruments in the violin family produce tones by the same general principle, though: a bow made with fiber strands is drawn across the strings, causing them to vibrate. The vibrations are transmitted to the body of the instrument, which in turn sets air molecules moving to carry the sound to our ears. Different notes are achieved by altering the length of the portion of the string that is allowed to vibrate. When a finger presses down on a string, it limits the length of the vibrating portion of the string. By allowing less string to vibrate, the tone is higher. At the same time, a string that is loose produces a lower tone than a string that is taut.

Fiddle music is played in many different countries of the world, often for dancing. Though modern recorded music is common throughout most of the globe, people still gather to dance, sing, and listen to live fiddle music. Fiddling traditions are carried on by local customs, ethnic groups, and young people interested in maintaining and reviving those customs and traditions. Folk dancing to fiddle music continues in the Tatra Mountains of southern Poland, small villages in France, and the Canadian provinces. Mexican folk musicians perform on fiddles hand carved from native woods. In New England, a continuous tradition of country dancing to fiddling has been alive for over 200 years in places like the Nelson Town Hall in New Hampshire.

In the days before rapid mass communication, local fiddlers often had styles distinct to their regions, and music was transmitted from region to region by wandering musicians, troubadors, and travelers. Very little of this music was written down and most players learned new material by ear, as it was passed person to person. Fiddles are small and easy to carry and immigrants from many countries found their music welcome in the new world. Many small and relatively isolated communities fostered particular styles of fiddling. The Cape Breton area of Canada is home to a continuing tradition of Scottish fiddling which spans many generations. The French influence was wide ranging as it spawned the vigorous country dancing and fiddling of Quebec, the New England states, and Cajun styles in the gulf coast area of the U.S.A. Irish fiddling traditions were strengthened and maintained in urban centers such as Boston and Chicago. In the southeastern section of the U.S.A. various European influences contributed to the evolution of the new styles of "southern" square dance and "bluegrass" fiddling.

In the pre-Civil War United States many Black slaves were fiddlers, and some made fiddles as mentioned in this August 18, 1768 ad in the *Virginia Gazette*: "Run away, a black Virginia born Negro fellow named Sambo, about 6 ft. high, about 32 years old. He makes fiddles, and can play upon the fiddle, and work at the carpenter's trade."

Various peoples of other backgrounds such as Polish, Scandinavian, Lebanese, etc. also retained the music of their ethnic origins as they settled in North America. Even though there was some blending of styles in the great "melting pot," many ethnic fiddling styles have remained distinct.

I was sitting on a bench on a beautiful New England afternoon fiddling the "Fisher's Hornpipe" while several people munched on sandwiches. A passerby stopped briefly to listen and then began an animated conversation with a seated diner. The discussion turned to fiddles, and the passerby claimed authoritatively that fiddles and violins were two different instruments, constructed differently, played differently. He couldn't describe the differences exactly, but just knew deep down that there was a difference. I played on, enjoying the sun's warmth, and the vibrations of the fiddle on my collar bone. At the time, fiddling away the afternoon seemed more important than entering the conversation.

I have never found an entirely satisfactory answer to the question about the difference between fiddle and violin music. In some respects there are some general differences which seem to hold up much of the time. Fiddle music, for example, seems to incite toe tapping, knee slapping, and frenzied hand clapping which would be out of place in the concert hall performance of a classical violinist.

I once attended a performance of a leading Irish traditional folk band, the Chieftains, in the Los Angeles Civic Auditorium. Amid the many patrons in formal evening wear from the classical music series were other folks informally attired in jeans and flannel shirts. As the band played medleys of Irish tunes, the crowd seemed confused as to whether clapping was appropriate. Occasionally spontaneous clapping would burst out of sections of the audience followed by the shushing sounds of others in attendance. Throughout the concert was the clicking and snapping sounds of tapes being replaced in portable cassette recorders.

John Burke, fiddler for the Old Hat Band, in a program for the San Diego State Folk Festival, explained that "the technical disciplines of fiddler and violinist are both quite demanding being dictated in the case of the fiddler by how he feels about a tune, and in the case of a violinist by how he understands what he is playing." Both fiddlers and violinists would argue that their music has depth of emotional feeling, but an observer of fiddling would find listeners expressing their emotions by dancing and shouting while the auditors of violin music can often be heard in intellectual discourse concerning the esoteric significance of a particular score.

Some cynics attempt to show that folk and fiddle music have been traditionally the music of the "lower classes" and the simple country folk, while classical music is the higher art form of the "upper crust." That may be partly true, but why then is the current revival of fiddle music well infiltrated by highly educated folks from middle and upper middle class backgrounds? Why are world class violinists such as Yehudi Menuhin and Itzhak Perlman cutting albums of jazz fiddle music? The more I learn about both fiddling and violin playing, the more the distinctions between them seem to blur.

The first time I listened to a Paganini Caprice, I immediately noticed a similarity of his violin music to fiddling. The music wasn't in a strict dance tempo like most fiddle music and was technically more demanding; however, there was a feeling to the music of wild and crazy abandon that is common to the sound of "hot" trick fiddling. I had to find out more about this character. Sure enough, I found ample biographical information in the library about Paganini.

He was born in 1792, composed his own tunes, and developed a stage presence designed to cause fainting and great awe in his audience. He essentially wrote the rest of the orchestra into his scores as a backup band to his virtuoso fiddling.

Nicole Paganini

Paganini would come out on stage dressed all in black with deep sunken eyes and incredibly long fingers which could contort to reach seemingly impossible sequences of notes. He would play a few pieces and then get down to serious business. A string would break on his violin, then another, and then a third (all by prearrangement, of course), and he would proceed to complete an immensely difficult passage on one string alone.

Ladies in the audience would swoon at his feet and rumors spread that he was in league with the devil. A doctor's report of a physical examination of Paganini was published to dispel the notion that he had cloven hooves rather than feet. There's not a whole lot of difference between his antics on stage and that of some hot bluegrass or trick fiddlers I've seen.

I suppose that one of the biggest differences between classical violin and fiddle though, is that violinists are usually bound to their music stands and printed score while fiddlers are bound only by their imaginations. Only rarely do I encounter a violinist who can play more than a few isolated fragments of various pieces without fixating on sheet music, while the average fiddler can play all afternoon without repetition by memory alone.

Fiddlers have much more freedom to improvise while playing than violinists. One of the hallmarks of a great fiddler is an ability to continuously vary the melody line in such a way that the essence of the tune remains intact. But then, great "classical" musicians and composers such as Paganini and Bach also improvised while they performed. However, the violinist of average ability today is usually discouraged by his or her peers and music teachers for improvising on classical pieces while the converse is true for most fiddlers.

Fiddlers revel in altering tunes in ways which suit their tastes. One fiddler might play a tune with a highly ornamented melody line while another fiddler might take the same tune, remove many of the melody notes, "flattening" the melody, and adding rythmical bowing patterns. On this point, Delores ("Fiddling De") DeRyke, from Lincoln, Nebraska, wrote that, "To today's old time fiddler, the most precious part of his art and skill is his right to be original and inventive in his renditions of his fiddle tunes. To him this makes all those hours of practice worth the effort and the sweat — and the painful criticism by non-fiddlers who do not understand and can never understand the feelings of the fiddler toward his art and skill. Nor can they understand his even more treasured love and devotion to freedom and originality, which are the very roots of his legacy as an old time fiddler as well as his American citizenship."

Even within the folk fiddling tradition though, there are cliques of musicians who play together in a narrowly defined style, possibly in emulation of a particular traditional fiddler or fiddlers, from a particular historical period and geographical location. Since there are scores of distinct fiddle styles around the world which have been distinguished by the folk music scholars, one might expect to find the proponents of each, and one does. At most folk festivals around this country one will find small clusters of musicians playing in such diverse styles as Irish "Sligo," New England "Contra Dance," North Carolina "Round Peak," Texas "Contest," or a variation of "Bluegrass" fiddling. And these styles may be so different from each other that there is little interchangability between them.

"The main person who was an influence on my particular style was the most amazing fiddle player ever, Benny Thomasson. He had every kind of music combined in his playing, and any kind of music I've played since I started playing Texas fiddle music has been greatly influenced by that."
— **Mark O'Connor, winner of several National Championships** (*Frets*)

In recent times there has been an explosion of global traveling, recordings of fiddling, and written music. Fiddle bands can be found in California that specialize in French or Irish music, while "old timey" American fiddling is very popular in Great Britain and Australia. Japan has numerous bluegrass clubs, and fiddle music is taught in the public school system in the Shetland Islands.

It is very important to some fiddlers and fiddling organizations to maintain the traditional playing styles distinctive of their regions, while others blend styles freely and even create new styles. A particular organization may claim that the style of playing that its members play is "authentic old time fiddling," while another organization may have different standards.

This diversity of folk fiddling styles is what makes folk fiddling so exciting and different from "classical violin," in which the standards of performance are far more rigid and structured, even between different regions and countries. A Texas-style melodic fiddler, for example, may describe highly rhythmic Virginia or North Carolina dance fiddling as "scratching away on the fiddle," and an Irish fiddler may wonder why the New England-style players leave out the embellishments and ornaments from their Irish tunes.

Most communities in the United States have fiddlers, although few are available to the public eye. Square dancing, although still popular, has often gone the route to record players and more modern music, as it is often cheaper to play records than hire a band. There are still pockets of intense traditional dancing to live fiddle music though, and this is growing as New England contra dancing spreads to the West Coast and Europe. More and more rock and popular bands seem to be using fiddles. Once people get a taste of fiddle music and like it, they want to hear more, and often develop an interest in the more traditional roots of the music.

Every state in the Union has fiddle contests, and bluegrass and folk festivals have grown in number in recent years. Classical violin students are urging their instructors to show them some fiddle or jazz tunes. This interest is extending deep into classical music circles as famous violinists such as Yehudi Menuhin and Itzhak Perlman record albums of jazz-style fiddle music. Menuhin also professes a liking for folk fiddling and has studied with Shetland Islands fiddler Tom Anderson.

"You know, young people coming up, learning to fiddle, they want to do everything they can. . .in more modern ways, you know. Time changes. And I think . . . that as time changes, music should change to fit the playing now and 30–40 years from then, I couldn't even touch 'em, see. Well, I like that, I mean that'd be fine."
— **Benny Thomasson at the 1974 Old Time Fiddle Contest, Weiser, Idaho interview by D. Garelick, M. Mendelson, & N. Dols**

As jazz music developed early in this century in the United States, the style was taken up by fiddlers. Early pioneers of jazz fiddling such as Joe Venuti in the U.S. and Stephane Grappelli in France continued the improvisational swing styles of American jazz players. Their recording careers have both spanned over fifty years.

Jazz greatly influenced the playing of fiddle-based western swing dance bands of the 1930s and 1940s such as Bob Wills and the Texas Playboys, and Milton Brown and His Musical Brownies. It has a continuing influence on bluegrass fiddling, the developing backup rhythm accompaniment to Irish fiddling, and recently, in the "New Accoustic" music of performers such as the David Grisman Quintet, Mark O'Connor, and others.

Fiddle music certainly has its heros and leaders, and they provide the inspiration for new generations of fiddlers who will continue to keep the music alive and well in its various forms.

"I listen to a lot of music that Kenny Baker turned me on to, jazz violinists like Stephane Grappelli, Joe Venuti, musicians like that. Some of it is a bit over my head at the present. I can understand what Venuti's playing a lot better than what Grapelli plays."
— **Blaine Sprouse**
  The Bluegrass Band (*Frets*)

"I heard Stephane Grappelli and Joe Venuti on this TV show and I thought it was great. I always liked that kind of music. The guys I liked best in the jazz scene were Stuff Smith and Svend Asmussen, more so than Grappelli...I figured if I could learn a little bit of bluegrass fiddling, that would be a starting point."
— **Tim O'Brien**
  Ophelia Swing Band,
  Hot Rize (*Frets*)

Within any fiddle style there may be fiddlers who alter their music enough from the mold to stand out, in spite of the danger of alienation from their peers. Tommy Potts (*The Liffey Banks*, Claddash Records, CC13) is one of these. In an interview by Larry Sandberg he explained that "in my mind I liked the fiddle. The music itself was stereotyped and there was a lack of development. There was no variation or composition. I wouldn't go across the room to hear those musicians who played all the same, the one thing is just the same as the other to them. What made it frustrating was that for the purists, the ultra-nationalists, everything outside of the same notes all the time was wrong. You were anti-Irish. This has been said about me quite a lot. It doesn't bother me; I'm happy with my gift." (*Oak Report*, Winter 1981)

The clash between the "purists" who advocate a particular style, and the innovators such as Tommy Potts in Irish fiddling, Vassar Clements in bluegrass, or Jean Luc Ponty in jazz, is what keeps fiddle music alive and growing.

Fiddling is a dynamic and vastly expressive art form with all of the trappings of other art forms. There are old standards, new trends, conservatism, economic and social considerations.

The title of "fiddler" has been ocasionally one of dubious distinction. Herbert Halpert interviewed fiddler Dean B. Winifred Merrill, formal Dean of the Music School at Indiana University. Dean Merrill had this to say about the social aspects of fiddling: "When I was eighteen, I had two students: one was a Presbyterian minister and the other was a Congregationalist. The Congregationalist minister told me that in his ministerial life it so shocked some of his parishioners that he played the violin, that he was obliged to play it to himself, and he urged me not to let it be known that he was taking lessons; and the Presbyterian minister said the same thing. One of them said, 'Not that there's anything wrong in playing the fiddle, but you know people will talk.' As for a girl to play the fiddle! She was on the way to perdition." (The interview took place in 1942, *Hoosier Folklore Bulletin*)

One has only to attend an "old timey" music jam session in order to experience first hand the hold that the "devil's instrument" has on impressionable minds. The musicians, usually several fiddlers, banjoists, and guitar players, hunch together, thrashing away on their instruments, now and then hollering a verse to some old time tune. The tunes themselves are short, usually about sixteen measures, and yet the musicians play them over and over, continuously, with variations so subtle, that only initiates to the art can pick them out.

Often the intensity of the playing reaches a feverish pitch, and an almost nirvana-like state is reached by the participants, as they settle into the repetitive groove of hypnotic-like melodies. Non musicians who witness such scenes are often aware that something profound is happening to the active participants, although the feeling may not be shared by the observer.

The musicians report experiencing a "musical high," in some ways similar to the highs experienced in driving fast cars, sky diving, or love making. While in this state they are often unaware that the sun is about to rise, that their spouse or companion is waiting to go home, or that their body has been urging them to visit the rest room. No wonder that the dictionary includes definitions for fiddle such as

"to trifle, waste time, etc." You can be certain that these meanings were brought to common usage by non-fiddlers in the company of those possessed by the "fiddler's fix."

There is a positive note though, as one who is in perfect health is described as "fit as a fiddle." The fiddler also knows, of course, that his fiddling is not trifling, but is a way to bring life and vitality to many other lives. The Scottish fiddler John Hay Delldonald was described as playing "so lively that even cripples while listening to his playing, were induced to throw away their crutches and dance." Robert Burns similarly commented on fiddler Mayor William Logan in 1786: "Thairin-inspirin, rattlin' Willie!... Hale be your heart! Hale be your fiddle! Lang may your elbuck jink and diddle." (*Rantin' Pipe and Tremblin' String*)

"Folk players just took it for granted that you weren't supposed to do certain things outside the regional styles, or the traditional style in general: not to play in the third position, for example, they'd say it was too flashy. We've stuck our neck out a few times, and I think people now realize that there is such a thing as innovation, without twisting the whole thing inside out."
— **Martin Fay**
with the Chieftains (*Frets*)

BELKNAP'S MARCH,
AND
OTHER DANCE MELODIES
Including
JIGS, REELS, WALTZES,
~and a~
HORNPIPE.
COMPOSED BY
BILL WELLINGTON.
with Piano Accompaniment, by
JANET MUSE.

The last great fiddle revival in this country took place in the 1920s and an anonymous article on "Aged Fiddlers," graces the pages of the classically oriented music publication *Etude* in 1929:

During the past season the country fiddler has "come back" as never before. The whole country, from Maine to Texas has resounded to the merry lilt of "The Turkey in the Straw" and "Money Musk," much as it used to do when the country fiddler had the monopoly of furnishing the dance music for the back-woods of America. There have been contests galore for the "country fiddler" championship of township, county, city, state, and section. The papers have been filled with pictures of aged fiddlers, and not a few have secured engagements at high prices in vaudeville. Anyone who can saw off a few bars of "The Arkansas Traveler" and "Pop Goes the Weasel" is in great demand for concerts and entertainments.

The remarkable part of this revival is the age of these old chaps. They are mostly in their sixties, seventies and eighties, and one old fiddler is still going strong at ninety. Youth has the call for almost every other form of entertainment, but in this instance the public wants its country fiddlers "old"— the older the better. The young country fiddler must wear a white wig and an "old" makeup if he expects to get by with it.

We often hear old and middle-aged people say that they cannot play the violin because their fingers have grown too still, but here we have the spectacle of these old country fiddlers sawing off rapid jigs, reels, "hoe-downs of all kinds, which, however little merit they have from a musical-student's standpoint, at least require great fingering ability. Most of these country fiddlers do very little in the way of position work, artistic shifting, and the various solo graces of violin playing, but what they do excel in is strongly marked rhythm and perfect evenness of rapid technical passages. Many an advanced violin student who is studying Kreutzer, Rode and the concertos cannot play these old time rapid dance tunes with the vigorous rhythm and lilt which the humble country fiddler gives them.

How is it that the fingers of these old fellows have not grown too stiff for all this rapid fingering? The answer is that they have been playing for dances all their lives, and their fingers have not had time to get stiff. Continual exercise has kept them supple. It will be found that most of these old men are hale and hearty and have excellent health and good nervous systems, an important consideration in playing these rapid dance tunes in which there must be a perfect coordination between finger and bow, each stroke of the bow attacking the string when the proper finger is on it. To have bowing and fingering thus synchronized, the nervous system and the brain of the performer must be in the finest working order, a condition unattained, often, even by violin students who have devoted much time and practice to the art.

However, let not the aged man who has never played the violin imagine he can start at the age of sixty or seventy and become a proficient performer. It cannot be done. Here we have a case not only of genuinely stiff fingers and arms, but of stiff brain and stiff nervous system as well. The old man who commenced playing the violin in childhood, and has kept it up ever since, has much of his old time power because he has a life-time of practice and playing behind him. Brain, muscles and nervous system are trained for the art; and, if he escapes certain forms of muscular rheumatism, he can continue his fiddling as long as he lives.

"Finished" violinists naturally sneer at the humble country fiddler, but one thing is certain. He has done his share in making the violin popular in the United States and has given millions of people unbounded pleasure, for, whatever its shortcomings, his playing radiates gaiety, good humor, and clean, wholesome fun.

Was the author of the *Etude* article a classical violinist? The article was one of the very few anonymously written stories in that issue. Regarding the article, it probably would be very difficult for an elderly person with no experience in any aspect of music to learn the fiddle. However, I know of a person who began fiddling in his sixties who does a credible job of dance fiddling. Of course he had the benefit of many years of square dance calling and listening to fiddle music. I started fiddle at age 24, which hasn't seemed to slow me down any. If you set your mind to it, all kinds of things are possible!

Let's go back another thirty years to 1899. Robert Tayler, who had been governor of Tennessee from 1886 – 1890 and again from 1896 – 1898, had made national headlines by entering fiddle contests while still in office. He wrote the following letter to all fiddlers:

En Route, April 24, 1899.
My Dear Fellow — Sawyers:
Experience teaches us that first impressions are the more lasting. Next to the impressions which I received from a dogwood sprout or twig of a weeping willow when I was a barefooted boy, are the impressions which were made upon my young mind and heart by the fiddlers. The tunes they used to play got tangled in my memory and the incidents

and happenings of the happy days gone by.

I can see Polk Scott and Sam Rowe just as plainly now as I actually saw them when I was a ten-year-old lad at the old log schoolhouse that stood by the bubbling spring. They played at the "exhibitions" at the close of our school; and I have never heard any sweeter music since. Sam's big brown whiskers rolled and tumbled in ecstacy on his fiddle, as he rocked to and fro, with half-closed eyes, and, with whizzing bow, reveled in the third heaven of "Arkansas Traveler." Polk's black mustache swayed and flopped like a raven's wings, as he soared amid the grandeurs of "Natchez Under the Hill."

They were the "Paganinis" of the mountains; they were the "Ole Bulls" of our humble society; they were the royal "Remenyis" of our rural, rollicking festivities; they were big hearted and genial; they were noble fellows, and so are all fiddlers to this good day. Their melodies were the echoes of nature's sweet voices. In every sweep of the bow there was the drumming of a pheasant or the cackle of a hen or the call of Bob White or the trill of a thrush. Sometimes I could hear a whippoorwill sing; sometimes a wild goose quack, and the music was always mellow with 'moonshine.'

When I grew a little larger I used to slip out from under the smiling roof of "home, sweet home," and cut the pigeon wing with the rosy-cheeked mountain girls, until it seemed that my very soul was in my heels. I still have fond recollections of every fiddler who played at the old-time country dance; and when I hear those sweet old tunes, even now it is difficult for me to keep my soul above my socks.

So far as I am concerned, I am a worshipper at the shrine of music. The classics of Mozart and Mendelssohn are grand and glorious to me, but I cannot be persuaded to turn my back on the classics of the plain country fiddlers. The old country tunes were handed down from the days of the revolution, and every one of them breathes the spirit of liberty; every old jig is an echo from the flint-lock rifles and shrill fifes of Bunker Hill; every 'hornpipe' is a refrain from King's Mountain; 'Old Rattletrap' is a declaration of Independence; 'Jennie, Put the Kettle On,' boils over with freedom; 'Jaybird Settin' on a Swingin' Limb' was George Washington's 'favorite,' and 'Gray Eagle' was Thomas Jefferson's masterpiece; 'Leather Breeches' was the Marseillaise hymn of the old heroes who lived in the days of Davy Crockett.

Hungarian gipsy by Joseph Pennell

"Kato Havas, in her valuable monograph on the causes and treatment of nervous affections in violin playing, posed the interesting question why it is that Hungarian gypsy-players appear to be immune to such disorders. She said that the reasons are manifold, but 'first of all they are not burdened with the responsibilities of our social system. They do not have to do better than their fellows in order to succeed. In fact, they would be hard pressed to understand why anybody wants to succeed at all. Secondly, their sole interest is the pleasure of the listeners. They are free from all obligations, except the one and only obligation — to communicate.'"
— Music and the Brain
by MacDonald Critchley

No wonder the fiddlers are so patriotic and brave. I never saw a real genuine fiddler who would not fight; but mind you, I have quit fiddling.

When I grew large enough to cast sheep's eyes at the girls, when love began to tickle my heart and the blood of the violets got into my veins, I began to draw the bow across the vibrant strings of the fiddle to give vent to my feelings, and I poured my spirit out through my fingers by the bucketful. I swapped spirit for smiles at the ratio of sixteen to one; I exchanged clogs for compliments, and jigs for sighs and sentimental exclamations. No ordinary mortal ever felt the raptures of a fiddler; the fiddle is his bride, and the honeymoon lasts forever.

I fiddled and I fiddled and I fiddled, until youth blossomed into manhood, and still I fiddled and I fiddled. Politicians sneered at me as a fiddler; but the girls said it was no harm, and the boys voted while I fiddled, and the fiddle won. There is always some old sour and tuneless hypocrite abusing and denouncing 'us fiddlers.' I have heard them say that they never saw a fiddler who was 'any account,' and I have known good men who sincerely believed that fiddlers were dangerous to communities. There never was a greater error of opinion. There is no harm in wiggling the fingers than there is in wagging the tongue, and there is a great deal more religion in a good, law abiding fiddle than there is in some folks who outlaw that devine instrument. There is infinitely more music in it than there is in some hymns I have heard sung by old dyspeptics who denounce it. Music is music, whether it be the laughter and song of the fiddle or the melodies of the human voice; music is the hallelujah of the soul, whether it comes through fiddle strings or vocal chords. Happy is the home in which fiddles and fiddlers dwell, and nearest to heaven is the church where fiddlers and singers blend their music in hymns of praise to Almighty God.

I have heard cultivated musicians laugh at the country fiddler, and call his tunes 'rag music'; but the law of compensation governs in this realm, as well as any other, for the country fiddlers laugh just as heartily at the sublimest efforts of high-class musicians. Neither can understand the other. To the noteless and untutored fiddler the grandest efforts of the greatest orchestra are the senseless hieroglyphics of sound; to the cultured ear the simple melodies which dance out from the bosom of the fiddle and the soul of the fiddler are but the ridiculous buzzings of the bumblebee discord.

But there is no reason why the virtuoso and the fiddler should fall out. Let the nightingale sing in his realm, and let the cricket sing in his. We will all play together on golden fiddles in the "sweet by and by."
Yours truly,
Robert L. Taylor
(This article was uncovered by Charles Wolfe, *The Devil's Box*)

Fiddlers are everywhere. I've carried my fiddle with me from one end of the continent to the other, from California to Washington state, Vermont to Mississippi, to Canada and everywhere that I've heard of fiddlers and fiddle music being played. I've met and played with other fiddlers from all sorts of backgrounds and lifestyles. The one important thing that we shared was love of fiddle music. One of the quickest ways of discovering other fiddlers that I've found is to take out my fiddle at the local park. Besides the gaggle of children that collect will be musicians, friends of musicians, and would be musicians. Many people find fiddles and fiddlers objects of great interest. It's surprising to discover the large numbers of people who have never had a chance to see a fiddle played close up.

"While I was in [New] York I took lessons on the violin of Mr. Phile, and of Mr. Hoffmaster, a dwarf, a man about 3 foot, large head, hands and feet; his wife of the same stature. A good musician, he composed the following hornpipe expressly for me, which is become well known in America, for I have since heard it play'd the other side of the Blue Mountains as well as in the cities."
— **John Durang, born Lancaster, Pennsylvania, 1785, professional hornpipe dancer (*National Folk Festival Program, 1976*)**

The way that the sound is produced is a mystery. The performing fiddler can use this factor as an important feature of the act. The old vaudeville routine goes something like this: "Everyone knows that fiddle strings are made of catgut. What you may not know is that the bow hairs are made of horse tails. Well, the poor kitten inside of the fiddle is terribly upset about the fate of her mother. (Pointing at the strings.) So when you drag the horse's tail across the cat's guts the sound comes out the F holes. (Demonstrating with the bow.)"

Some fiddlers have taken advantage of the mystique of the violin to benefit themselves with logos and bumper stickers such as "Take a Fiddler to Lunch." If you want attention in a crowd of people, take out a fiddle and you've got it. Before long someone will come up to you to exclaim, "My uncle Bill plays the fiddle and is always looking for someone to trade tunes with." And then it's off to uncle Bill's house for an evening of fine fiddle music.

Fiddlers love to get together and exchange licks, lore, and the enthusiasm from mastering their latest tune:

A. "I got this here old fiddle from my granddaddy. Isn't she a beauty?"

B. "That's not bad, nice curly maple on the back; here, try mine. It's a real Stradivarius; see the label?"

A. "You know, 'Strads' are nice, but I've never seen nor heard a fiddle as good as made by this old guy that I used to know, name was Clem, Clem something. Boy, did he make a pretty fiddle. And he could play the warts off a frog's back!"

B. "Have you heard this tune, 'Woodchuck Up a Tree'?" (Plays it.)

A. "Now that's a good one. Show me how that first part there goes. It reminds me of an old recording of the Toothless Twins."

My first experience with actually holding a fiddle came when a friend showed me her violin that she had taken lessons on when in grade school. I was in my early 20s and fascinated by the instrument. I borrowed it and kept it for several months, now and then taking it out to draw the bow across the strings lovingly, but not even knowing how to tune it up.

During this time I used to go down to the city park on weekends to watch all the interesting people. In southern California, during this period of the late 1960s and early '70s, there were many interesting people to watch. There were hippies, flower children, Hell's Angels on motorcycles, street musicians, and costumed members of strange religious sects. Everyone was vying for public attention.

I found myself drawn particularly to the music of "old time" string bands. There would often be a fiddle, banjo, guitar, bass, and mandolin. The music wasn't like anything I had ever heard before. There was nothing quite like it on the radio, or TV, or what I had studied in my piano lessons. It was different than the music of "folk singers," or string quartets. They would play old fiddle tunes such as "Soldier's Joy," or "Over the Waterfall," often singing humorous verses.

The music was rough and unpolished, unlike popular music on the radio, or symphonies that I had attended. And yet it was good. I would leave the park humming the simple tunes and feeling refreshed. Furthermore, it was obvious that the musicians were having a good time and the crowds of people that were watching would be caught up in the infectious enthusiasm, often tossing folded bills into the open instrument cases, the old "green paper airplane flying contest."

After asking where I could hear more of that music, I was directed to coffee houses, and in particular, the weekly contra and square dances, where all of the traditional musicians for miles around would congregate. I started attending the dances regularly and was soon swept up by the old time country dance fever. A group of students from New England had brought traditional country dancing to southern California and it caught on in a big way. Some friends of mine from a local rock band even put down their electric instruments and took up banjos and fiddles.

Through a large but close knit group of folk musicians I met many players of widely different musical styles. At times the contra dance "orchestra" would exceed twenty members, with everyone playing together: bluegrass pickers, old time fiddlers, New Englanders, and the classical musicians with their music stands. The overall sound was wonderful, and the dancers couldn't be happier. Much of the best music, however, took place in the jam sessions in the corridors outside of the dance hall. Musicians would exchange their latest tunes and show off new instruments.

At weekend parties we would locate a house (and willing occupants) with a large living room or kitchen, and clear out all of the furniture for dancing. This old fashioned country dancing inspired new musicians, dancers, and many marriages. Offshoots from this group went on to establish regular contra dances up and down the west coast in the early '70s. I was one of the few who eventually made it back to New England to explore the roots of the music.

My mother, who also lived in San Diego, had bought an old banjo at a yard sale, and upon seeing it for the first time I was determined to learn to play it. I borrowed it for several months, took a handful of lessons, and locked myself away for hours at a time in my apartment learning tunes like "June Apple," "The Rose Tree," and "Colored Aristocracy." After a few months I felt confident enough to play at the weekly dances and at the park on weekends.

One day I was hitchhiking home from Balboa Park in San Diego with my banjo, when a Volkswagen van pulled up. I hopped in and noticed a lot of instrument cases. The occupants eyed my banjo and then asked me what band I played with. When I replied that I was "just learning, really," they mentioned that they were forming a new band and although they already had a banjo player, they needed a guitarist. I lamented the fact that I knew but three chords on a guitar, but I was immediately offered an intensive crash course on guitar. I readily accepted and was soon being introduced into the world of old time fiddle tunes.

Our fiddler, David Brown, although self taught by ear on fiddle tunes, had originally received violin instruction from Curt, the brother of the famous Isaac Stern. The banjo player, Pamela Ostergrend, had been active in the folk music movement of the

covered that certain types of fiddle tunes were very difficult to play on the banjo, although I was getting good enough on the banjo to win contests. A friend loaned me an old fiddle and I began scratching away on tunes that I already knew on the banjo, or had heard at the country dances. It never occurred to me to take any violin or fiddle lessons, since I had heard that traditional fiddlers were self taught and learned tunes by ear. Among the folk fiddlers I knew, written music was generally taboo, except to some of the New Englanders who had to resort to recruiting classical violinists to fill out their band. I watched and listened to other fiddlers a lot and took note of the differences between styles.

I was exposed to some of the best fiddlers in the world as they passed through town, such as Aly Bain of the Boys of the Lough, who played Irish and Shetland tunes in concert. I noticed that after the concerts, in late night picking sessions, Aly played jazz and American tunes. Tommy Jarrell, the master of southern fiddling, and the Highwoods String Band, were exciting to watch and learn from, because of their highly rhythmic playing.

1960s in Ann Arbor, Michigan, and had recordings of her playing in Library of Congress collections. Within a short time we were playing several times a week at the beach, in parks, pizza parlors, and eventually performing almost full time at Old Town State Park in San Diego, which was a reconstruction of the frontier town that had existed there in the days before California was a state.

In this period of the early 1970s, traditional folk music was still relatively popular with the general public. San Diego State University, through the efforts of Lou Curtis, annually hosted what was billed as the "largest folk festival west of the Mississippi." Many of the finest fiddlers and folk musicians from around the United States and Canada were brought in for the week long extravaganza. Some of them stayed around the area or visited regularly, and I picked up a lot of folk lore and tunes. I soon dis-

I spent many hours at a festival following Benny Thomasson (the King of Texas Fiddling) around and marveling at his melodic techniques. At this time he was simultaneously National Open Division and Senior fiddle champion. At another fiddle festival I observed Mark O'Connor as *he* followed Benny around, trying to pick up new licks. This was after Mark had already won several national championships.

Martin, Bogan, and Armstrong performed in San Diego as the first all black jazz string band that I'd heard. Their bluesy style was an inspiration to my own blues fiddle playing.

I was at an informal jam session when someone mentioned to Kirk and Sam McGee (of Grand Ole

Opry fame) about Benny Thomasson's fine version of "Billy in the Lowground," and Kirk proceeded to play his version, just as spirited, but in a very different southern style. I was learning that widely different fiddling styles could be equally as exciting in their own way when played by masters.

Clarence Langen performed in San Diego and provided my first heavy dose of French and Canadian fiddling. A friend later tipped me off about the incredible techniques of Jean Carignan and I practically wore out my copy of his record. A visiting fiddler/student from France passed through town and we had a first hand source for French folk tunes. French Canadian fiddlers, New England fiddlers, violinists turned fiddlers, all of these and more were grist for the mill of my fiddling experience.

It wasn't long after I started playing fiddle that I discovered the advantages of cassette tape recorders, fiddle contests, folk festivals, and picking parties, for inspirations to my continued improvement on the fiddle.

I spent a number of summers traveling from one festival or contest to the next, from one region of the country to another, seeking out other fiddlers and musicians, sharing tunes, meals, and a gypsy-like life style. (Gasoline was inexpensive then.) I always found it challenging to try to balance my music with my jobs or school studies. For a time I shared a house at the beach in California with a group of other folk musicians. From my unfinished loft in the attic I could listen through the ceiling to my roommates as they practiced various styles of music.

I had to climb up a wooden ladder from the utility room to reach my niche. It was a good place for a beginning fiddler, as I went through the inevitable stages where every note sounds like the result of pulling the cat's tail. I caught on quickly, however, but it seemed like I never got enough time to practice. The great satisfaction gained by mastering a difficult passage after a couple hours of practice always made me wonder how much could be mastered after even more practice.

After trying out various professions and graduate school, I finally was taken in by the "devil's instrument." I succumbed to its pleasant seduction and presently make music my job and occupation.

My fiddle demands a lot of attention. It lies in its case and seems to look up and say, "Teach me something new." I remember that just after I started learning fiddle I mentioned to a fiddling friend that I only wanted to learn some "basic fiddle," and he replied that there was no such thing. I'm beginning to see what he meant.

As I've gradually made music a bigger part of my life, I remember fondly the many milestones along the way which have made the time spent sawing away worth it: my first recognizable tune, my first duet with another musician, my first paid performance, winning my first fiddle contest, performing in my first folk festival, playing in Nashville, etc. My goal is to become the best musician that I can be and have the opportunity to share my music with as many people as possible.

Although one of my biggest pleasures is making music with other musicians in public performances, there are a lot of other ways to enjoy fiddling. Many folks get great satisfaction from playing by themselves in the privacy of their own home. Others look forward to regular picking sessions with their friends, along with socializing and exchanging new tunes. One doesn't have to play at the level of a professional musician in order to have a good time. I had just as much fun when I only knew a dozen tunes as I do now after ten years of playing.

I see no end in sight of being completely satisfied with my fiddling. I relish the thought of continuing to improve on my knowledge of music and playing ability. I take occasional lessons from classical violinists, jazz violinists, and other fiddlers and often exchange my knowledge in the process. The fiddle is an endless source of enjoyment and challenge.

I often find that in teaching my own students, I learn as much as they do. I can sense in some of them the same intense feelings about fiddling that I had when I was first learning. A phone conversation that I had today started out like this:

"Ryan, I've got a problem with my fiddle."

"What kind of problem?"

"Well, you see, I just drove my car into a lake..."

This drawing shows three examples of the Viola da Gamba (1, 2, 3), a Viola Bastarda (4), and a Viola da Braccio (5), circa 1619, which were ancestors of the modern violin family.

FIDDLES ARE RELATIVELY EASY to find if you know where to look. If money is no obstacle and you need a fiddle right away, seek out an established violin dealer. Check the Yellow Pages for "Violins." If you can't find a violin category in the phone book, look for a "Music" category. Call the firms listed and ask about purchasing a fiddle or violin. Most cities have violin dealers, and many of them operate out of their homes rather than stores. Many music stores obtain their used fiddles from a local person who works at home or comes in part time to do instrument repair.

Contact the music department of your local school or college — they will be able to refer you to the right person to contact. You should, of course, seek out local fiddlers and violinists and get their advice.

Another good source of fiddles, although somewhat rare, is a shop that specializes in folk or bluegrass music, since the personnel there are often aware of the needs of the amateur fiddler, as opposed to those of the professional classical violinist. A fiddler will often settle for an instrument of lower cost, and of different quality than that demanded by the violinist.

Alternate sources of fiddles are pawnshops, antique stores, junk dealers, newspaper ads, flea markets, and yard sales. It is with these sources that you stand the chance of either landing a real gem, or losing your shirt. Most antique shops or flea markets that I've attended either underprice or overprice old fiddles. It's not unusual to see two violins side by side, each selling for $100, but with one worth $150 and the other $20. One flea market dealer explained to me that he never sells them for less than $35, because that's what he gets from people who make lamps out of them.

Some antique shops hire someone to evaluate and repair their musical instruments before sale. The knowledge of these "experts" can vary widely. One shop that I visited had a repair person so bad that the fiddle strings ended up crossed inside the pegbox and attached to the wrong pegs. At a pawn shop, all incoming fiddles were routinely stripped of their original finish, and a shiny new coat of clear plastic was applied to the entire instrument with a spray can. This, of course, destroyed the monetary value and tone of the fiddles.

An advantage of buying a fiddle from a professional dealer is that the quality of the instrument is more assured and proper service will be easily obtainable. In addition, you will usually get what you pay for from an established dealer. Prices may range from $100 for a used factory-made fiddle, to $10,000 or more for a symphony-quality instrument. I do recommend buying used fiddles rather than new if you are looking in the $50 to $500 range (1984 prices), since you can often get a better instrument for the price.

When you go shopping for a fiddle, take along a friend who plays violin or fiddle. Better yet, take two friends so that you can stand back and hear the differences between fiddles, and get several comments. Have your friends bring along their own favorite instruments to compare with the ones that you are trying out. After the final selection, take your friends out to lunch to celebrate.

> Antonius Stradiuarius Cremonenſis
> Faciebat Anno 1713 (AS)

A situation may arise in which you locate a fiddle that seems very reasonably priced and appeals to your fancy. The problem may occur that the person selling it knows absolutely nothing about fiddles and cannot vouch for its condition or value. Similarly, you may not have the proper knowledge yourself to judge the instrument's condition. If you don't have a knowledgeable friend handy, the solution to this dilemma would be to put a deposit down on the instrument and take it to an established dealer.

You may get varied reactions to your visit to a professional dealer. It turns out that appraising the value and origin of fiddles is a difficult task and takes years of experience. Many fiddles have imitation labels placed in them and many rare and valuable fiddles have been copied frequently with varying degrees of success. It takes an expert to sort out the different instruments. Because fiddle experts are more accessible than doctors, lawyers, or business consultants, people often assume that they will be happy to spend hours of their time giving out free information.

One fiddle maker and dealer that I've met will not even look at an instrument until $10 is placed in his hand. He claims that unless he follows this policy, people come into his shop all day long and pester him about the old fiddles that they've found in their attics and he doesn't get any fiddle making done. You will get along better with most dealers if you just ask a few important questions and resist the temptation to chat at great length.

Less difficult and time-consuming than assessing the origin and value of a fiddle, is to look it over carefully to see if it is well made and in playable condition. Instead of asking how much an instrument is worth, you might ask, "This instrument is being offered to me for $125.00. Is that a fair price?" If the fiddle needs repair work, then you can get an estimate and still find that the purchase price is reasonable, even considering the cost of repairs.

On the other hand, if you ask about the value of a fiddle, an expert will expect to be paid for an appraisal which brings to bear many years of experience and study. Verbal or written appraisals generally run from $20 to $50. A written appraisal can be useful when you sell or trade your instrument, or for insurance purposes.

A fiddle expert that I know in California who deals mostly in instruments valued $5,000 and up, has given up formal paid written appraisals because of the "controversies, law suits, and great difficulties of positively identifying origins of violins." He was willing, by appointment, however, to give me a free verbal evaluation of my fiddle, because of his general interest in the subject.

Another source of information which you may be lucky enough to find is the serious amateur violin maker. Some amateur makers craft instruments fine enough to rival those of the professionals. Since the amateur's income does not depend upon the sale of instruments, skills, and knowledge about fiddles, he may be much more willing to spend hours demonstrating and explaining the whys, wherefores, and how-tos of fiddles.

In the following section I'll discuss some of the physical features of a fiddle which help determine its quality. This isn't meant to be a do-it-yourself guide to searching out valuable violins, but merely an aid to your general knowledge. For more detailed information, refer to the books that I've listed in the "Sources" section of this volume.

Hundreds of years have gone into the design and construction of fiddles. During this time, tried-and-true techniques of construction have been devised which will give a fiddle a good resonant sound. Newer techniques are always coming along. Some will be improvements while others will be failures. When in doubt about a construction or repair technique, traditional methods will always be satisfactory. If a fiddle is well constructed along traditional European lines, it will sound good, hold together well, and be relatively easy to repair. The key word here is *repair*.

All fiddles will need repair work at various times during their lives. Unlike many other instruments, well constructed fiddles will not lose their tone quality, and will even improve over time if properly maintained. However, it is normal for certain parts to wear out: the fingerboard gets indented from the rubbing of fingertips and strings; the pegholes become larger as the pegs are turned; the bridge warps and has to be straightened or replaced; glue dries out and joints separate; the belly of the fiddle often developes cracks which may buzz when the fiddle is played. Many books have been written on violin building and repair. Some of them are listed in the "Sources" section of this volume.

There is, of course, more than one way to complete many repairs, but this choice is better left to the experts in the case of fiddles. I would advise anyone contemplating even a minor do-it-yourself repair to their own instrument to consult a professional before proceeding. The bane of the fiddle is the amateur woodworker who attempts to repair it with cabinet-making or furniture-repairing techniques. A fiddle is not built like a table or chair, with sturdy bracing and strong glues meant to hold it together indefinitely. A fiddle is purposely built to be able to come apart again for repair, with glue that is no stronger than the wood itself. I mention glues particularly, because some of the worst damage to fiddles that I have seen has been done by otherwise knowledgeable woodworkers who have used "white" or "super" glues improperly on fiddles, unaware of the mechanical stresses on stringed instruments. The results are often splintered wood and separated joints which then become very difficult and expensive to repair properly.

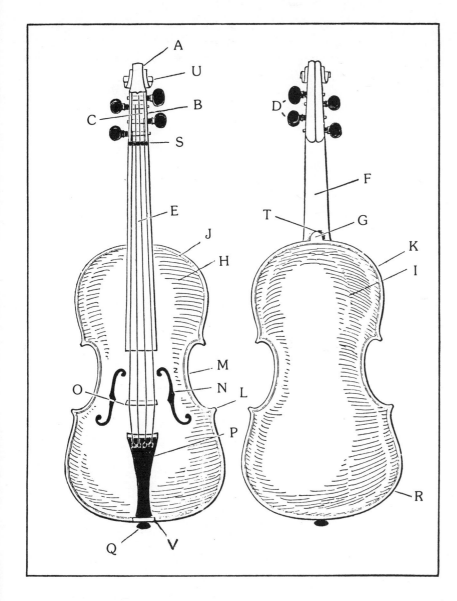

Parts of a Fiddle

A. Scroll
B. Side of Scroll
C. Peg box
D. Pegs
E. Finger-board
F. Neck
G. Button
H. Belly/Top
I. Back
J. Purfling
K. Edges over Ribs
L. Corners
M. Center Bouts
N. F-holes
O. Bridge
P. Tailpiece
Q. Tail Button/Pin
R. Lower edges
S. Nut
T. Shoulder/Heel
U. Eyes of Scroll
V. Saddle

The techniques of fiddle construction are also related very importantly to the acoustic or tonal properties of the instrument. Tom Hosmer, a violin repair shop owner and expert fiddler, relates the story of a fine cabinet maker from New York who made fiddles in his spare time. As Tom says, this man "made instruments that were as clean on the inside as anything you would see from the nineteenth-century Paris shop of J. B. Vuillaume. Every joint was perfect. He was a cabinetmaker, and constructing violins was a busman's holiday for him. Unfortunately, his instruments were acoustic disasters, and lacked greatly in tone and volume."

So what do you specifically look for in a fiddle? You can assume that unless the fiddle is new, it has probably been worked on occasionally since it was made. The first thing then, that I look for in a fiddle, is quality workmanship and materials. Let's take a look at each part of the fiddle. Remember that there are exceptions to these rules of thumb, but the purpose of this checklist is to give you some general guidelines for quality:

Back - Most fiddles have two pieces of maple wood joined very accurately. Many of the better quality fiddles have one-piece backs although this isn't essential for good sound. Cracks in the back are usually more difficult to repair than cracks in other locations.

Belly - This is always made of spruce in good fiddles. The surface should retain the original carved shape and not be warped. Generally speaking, cracks in the belly of the fiddle can easily be repaired. Look for cracks running from the saddle up under the tailpiece, directly above the soundpost, running from the openings in the F holes. Older cracks will be dark from accumulated dirt.

Bridge - This is easily replaceable if it is damaged or missing. The bridge should have no bends or warps, although the front surface (toward the fingerboard) is normally curved slightly from hand carving. Look at the edge of the bridge closely. The lines in the wood should be straight from top to bottom. If they are curved, the bridge will most likely warp in the direction of the curvature.

With the strings under tension, hold the fiddle up to a light and look at the corners of the bridge feet where they contact the belly of the fiddle. There should be a perfect fit with no light showing under the corners. A poor fit can easily be corrected, however.

The bridge is never glued on, but a correctly fitted bridge is absolutely essential for the tone of lthe fiddle. Although most bridge feet are handcarved to fit the fiddle, some bridges come with self adjusting feet to aid in the fitting process.

F-holes - These should be symmetrical and the same distance from each side of the fiddle on better fiddles. On cheaper fiddles one F-hole will often be noticeably closer to one side than the other.

Fingerboard - The best fingerboards are made of ebony, although the ones on cheaper fiddles may be made of other softer woods. Sight down the top of the fingerboard and look for grooves made by fingers and strings.These will need to be planed out at some point, as they affect proper intonation. Run your finger down the neck of the fiddle on the joint where the fingerboard is glued to the neck. On better fiddles this joint is an almost perfect fit with no gaps or overlap between the two pieces of wood. Amateur repair work often shows up here as a poor fitting joint. this may be a sign that the fiddle has been poorly treated in other ways. Light colored wood on the fingerboard next to the glue joint may indicate that the black dye has rubbed off and that the fingerboard isn't really ebony.

Finish - New instruments will, of course, have a nice glossy finish which may have various color tints depending upon the whims of the maker. Used fiddles are a different story. If the finish looks old and mottled, good. If it looks freshly finished with furniture

oil, polish, or spray shellac, consider passing it by since these materials can detract greatly from the tone and value of the instrument. A good used fiddle should rarely be refinished as it may lose the effect of many year's of aging which has improved the tone and increased its monetary value.

Hieronimus Amati Cremonensis
Fecit Anno Salutis 1640

Label - Probably more than 90% of all fiddles have labels which do not indicate the actual maker of the fiddle. Most fiddles have labels in them which say "Stradavarius," or "Copy of Stradivarius." Other common names are Guarnarius, Amati, Bergonsi, Maggini, etc. This just means that the fiddle was copied after the maker named. Sometimes the label will appear to be very old, yellowed, with frayed edges and a signature scrawled in fading ink. Labels such as these were often ordered by mail in mass quantities to slap into factory-made instruments of varying quality. Only the experts can tell for sure and even they often have trouble. Remember that even if a fiddle isn't a real Stradivarius, it may still be a fine playing instrument. It all boils down to this: labels mean very little in fiddles.

Neck - Check to see if the neck-body joint of the fiddle is loose. If so, it can be easily reglued although don't try it yourself unless you have the proper glue and know where it is supposed to be clamped. The portion of the back of the neck between the peghead and the heel should be varnish free to reduce friction while playing. A varnish coat here can indicate lower quality construction or repair, although the varnish can be easily removed with fine steel wool.

Nut - The nut is preferably made of ebony with evenly spaced notches for the strings. It should be exactly perpendicular to the strings rather than at an angle. (Each string must be the same length between the nut and the bridge.) A missing nut can be easily replaced.

Pegs - These are made of ebony in most of the best fiddles, but other hardwoods are used occasionally, such as boxwood and pear. A matched set is best and they should fit perfectly with no wobble. Newly fitted pegs don't stick out past the peg hole opening but fit flushly. As the pegs and pegbox wear, the pegs begin to stick further and further out the opposite side of the pegbox. Eventually larger pegs must be fitted or the pegbox holes reamed and rebushed. Beware of pegs made of soft woods stained black to resemble ebony, as they will eventually splinter and chip. Properly operating pegs are essential for keeping your instrument in tune.

Emmett Lundy, born 1864, Grayson County, Virginia, when asked about his first fiddle, "Well, it was a canteen my oldest brother carried through the army ...and was struck with a mini-ball and mended...and when he brought it back home and left it there and went west, I put me a neck to it and made me a fiddle and learned to play on it with horse hair strings."

— Devil's Box

Pegbox - In better fiddles the sides of the box are symmetrical with an equal thickness of wood on both sides. Look for cracks radiating out from the peg holes.

Purfling - These very thin alternating light and dark lines around the edges of the belly and back are strips of wood which have been inlaid into the fiddle. Their purpose is to help prevent cracking of the belly and back. Cheap or homemade instruments often have these missing altogether or painted on.

Scroll - The way that this part of the fiddle is built or looks won't affect the sound of your instrument. A devil or bull's head may look nice although most of the best makers stick to the traditional design. All fiddle parts can be ordered separately from catalogues and some builders have merely added on a mail order machine-made scroll and neck. A better fiddle will show hand working on the scroll which will also be very symmetrical rather than lopsided. You can assume that if a maker took the time to make a fine scroll, he also took care in constructing the rest of the fiddle.

Saddle - This should be ebony and shouldn't fit too precisely but have a very small space between each end and the body of the fiddle. Since it contracts and expands at a different rate than the body of the fiddle, cracks will often occur in the belly at this point.

Sides/Ribs - These should be symmetrical and attached firmly to the belly and the back of the fiddle. If the joints have separated, they can usually be reglued easily.

Soundpost - The sound post ideally should be one half of the diameter of the post away from the bridge foot under the E string side. In cheaper fiddles it may have to be moved around more in order to improve the tone. Since it remains in place by friction alone, it can be reset if found rattling around inside the fiddle. Resetting is hard to do without proper tools, but can be learned easily from someone with experience.

Tailbutton - If you see light colored wood in a chipped area, it isn't ebony. If it was ebony, it probably wouldn't have chipped. Some tailbuttons have a built-in pitchpipe.

Tailpiece - These are usually ebony but are sometimes made from other hardwoods or metal with built-in fine tuners. The tailpiece should not be touching the body of the fiddle, but should be hanging suspended between the strings and the tailgut. Nylon is the preferable material for tailguts.

Keep in mind that if a fiddle meets all of the above guidelines, it may cost several hundred dollars in a retail shop. However, you can still make fine music on a fiddle with a few small cracks, a stripped finish, a finger board that is not ebony, or other minor construction lapses and errors. We must all keep within our budgets, and an inexpensive fiddle is better than no fiddle at all! In addition, many of these faults can be corrected at relatively low cost. It may be worthwhile to invest in an instrument which is basically sound but in need of an overhaul. I just want to make sure that you know a little bit about fiddle construction and repair in order to aid you in judging the quality of an instrument.

Fiddle Bows

FIDDLE BOWS ARE USUALLY constructed of varieties of "Brazilwood." Over the years this type of wood has proved to be superior to any other wood for bow construction. "Pernambuco," named the same as a seaport in Brazil, seems to be the best of the lot. Most classical violinists use pernambuco bows, which are also the most expensive.

A good generic Brazilwood bow is adequate for part time fiddlers, although most professionals use pernambuco bows. The cheapest bows are made of other types of wood, metal, or fiberglass. Years ago, bows made of a banded wood called "snakewood," were in vogue, and some of these with ivory frogs are valuable simply as collectors items, although most of them don't play particularly well. Imitation hand-painted snakewood bows also abound. I would advise avoiding all materials except Brazilwood and purchase a used bow from a reputable dealer, rather than a new one, if you have less than $100 to spend on a bow. If money is no object, better quality new bows start at several hundred dollars.

Look for genuine horse hair rather than nylon or fiberglass, as you'll get a better tone. Higher quality bows also have a frog made of ebony wood with pearl and abalone inlay rather than plastic. Expensive bows often have silver or gold wrapping and fittings, while inexpensive bows use leather and plastic. Some very good playing pernambuco bows can be found, however, with plain leather grips and simple trim. The proof of the pudding is in the stick itself and the nature of the trim and other decorations are secondary in terms of a bow's playability.

Good modern bows are not carved into their final curved shape, but are made straight and then carefully bent through the use of heat. This puts a spring-like tension and resiliency into the wood which affects the ease of playing and tone of a fiddle. Bows can lose this tension, and start to straighten out or warp due to age, inferior wood, or failure of the owner to loosen the hair when putting the bow away. The result is a bow that is harder to play with, and produces a poorer tone. Bows can have the proper curve put back into them by experts, but there is a chance of breaking the bow in the process. It's therefore a good idea to find a bow with a good amount of spring already in it.

Bows are somewhat fragile and can easily break if sat on or dropped on the tip. Bow hair can break through vigorous use of the bow, old age, or a certain type of insect which sometimes infests fiddle cases. Typical 1984 prices for various repairs by professionals in my area run as follows:

Bow rehair . . . . $20 - $25
New nickle-silver grip $18
Sterling silver grip $22
Splicing a broken stick $80
Bow stick rebending . . . . $15 and up

Well made bows are usually easier to repair and rehair than cheap bows because of the better materials and construction. Some repair shops charge more to work on cheap bows than on quality bows. Serious repair work on valuable bows should definitely be entrusted to the experts and not to the handyman. Many mistakes are irreversible.

When going to buy a bow, take along a knowledgeable friend, if possible. Check that there are no cracks in the bow or frog, that the hair loosens and tightens easily, and that the bow retains some curve and spring even when tightened up to normal playing tension. Some cracks are easily repaired, others very difficult to remedy. Hair is easily replaced by someone with the proper tools and training. However, it is hard to judge the playability of a bow without the hair being in place.

With someone else playing, stand back and listen to the tones that different bows will produce on the same fiddle. Play several bows and try to feel the differences between them. Some bows will feel too heavy or light, or too wobbly.

When you find one that plays well for you and is constructed well, buy it, even if it is not the most expensive one or as fancy looking as some of the others. At a later date when you find a bow that plays even better, you can keep the old one for use as a spare. When you find a still better bow, you can trade in or sell your original bow.

"But a fiddle's as important as a wife, sure, because it's something you love and cherish all your life long. And they're as important as a wife because there are days when that fiddle will pick you up when probably the whole rest of the world just fell on you! But your fiddle comes through and kinda saves you!"
— **Joe Dominick, fiddle maker from Winchester, New Hampshire**

A Time to Dance by Richard Nevell.

If you can't decide right away after trying out several bows in the shop, give yourself a couple of days and then go back. Some dealers will let you try out a bow for a week or two after leaving a deposit. A bow maker taught me a useful technique when I was trying out one of his bows. He advised me to play only the bow that I was interested in purchasing for a week or so, and then, after being warmed up during a practice session, to suddenly switch back to my old bow: this sudden switch, rather than a simultaneous comparison, will often show up the true differences between the bows. This technique helped me discover that a new bow that I thought was better than my old bow really wasn't better, and I used the method again to find a truly better bow.

Oftentimes a fiddle is sold together with a bow and case, which will save you the trouble of searching out separate items. Bow prices can range from $25 to $75,000, and bows are as different from each other as people are.

As you get better on the fiddle and learn new techniques, your needs will change and you may want to look for either a new fiddle or bow. One thing that is nice about well-constructed fiddles and bows is that their value rarely goes down, and often goes up over time, unlike products such as automobiles, typewriters, or refrigerators. If you pay $200 for a fiddle or bow worth that much, and play it for a couple of years, and then decide to move up in quality, you should be able to get your $200 back again, provided you've kept your instruments in good shape.

A Fiddler's Accessories

Rosin - I prefer the dark colored rosins which are harder and less crumbly. Better rosins often come in small cloth bags which help prevent breaking or chipping, since the piece is protected. Broken rosin can be gathered up, however, and reused by melting it down in a mold within a double boiler. Some good brands are Hill, Thomastic, and Hidersine.

Chinrests - These come in many shapes, in case a particular one is not comfortable. They may be wood or plastic. Some people become allergic to them, particularly wooden ones, due to the constant contact with the skin. In such a case, one should change to a chinrest made of a different material or place a handkerchief between the chin and the chinrest.

Mute - Any object that can be temporarily attached to the bridge will cut down on the volume of the fiddle. This is useful for practicing without disturbing others. Clothespins will work in a pinch, but the heavier and denser the mute, the more that the volume is reduced. My favorite kind can be bought in a music store and is a metal cylinder filled with lead which makes the fiddle very quiet.

Shoulder rest - Some players of both classical violin and fiddle music find that a shoulder rest helps them support the fiddle under their chins. Some rests are semi-rigid and clamp onto the fiddle. Others are soft, fabric covered sponges that attach with rubber bands. Some people make their own shoulder rests by folding up washcloths or other materials to the desired thickness.

Humidifiers - These are useful to prevent excessive dryness in the air from drying out the glue joints and wood in the fiddle and causing cracks. They can be bought at music stores or constructed from plastic containers and sponges. My favorite brand is "Dampit."

Tuning gears - Some fiddles have tuning gears fitted to them rather than wooden pegs. These can work acceptably well, yet many players feel that they detract from the appearance of a fiddle.

Strings - Each type of string material has its advantages and disadvantages. For beginners I recommend medium to low priced steel strings. For more experienced players I'd advise trying out various types. My own favorite strings are "perlon core" Dominant strings.

Gut strings give the nicest tone and put less stress on a fiddle because they are low in tension. On the other hand, they are greatly affected by humidity and can be hard to keep in tune in harsh climates and when playing outdoors. Fine tuners won't work with gut strings. Many classical players favor them.

Steel strings are louder, harsher sounding, easy to keep in tune, and work well with fine tuners. They also put more strain on your fiddle than strings made of other materials. Most country fiddlers favor them for their bright sound.

Synthetic core strings are a happy medium for many players, more expensive than steel strings, but not affected by humidity and with a softer tone than steel. Fine tuners work well with them. They are more fragile than steel strings and may wear out sooner.

Fiddle case - Make sure that your bow and other loose objects are secured within the case or they will easily damage the fiddle if free to move around. Nice cases have bow holders and pockets for accessories.

Learning to Play the Fiddle

THERE ARE TWO MAJOR approaches to learning traditional fiddle tunes. One involves learning tunes by ear, and the other requires learning how to read music. Both techniques of learning fiddle tunes have their advantages and disadvantages, depending upon the abilities and proclivities of the learners. Simply put, some people tend to learn more easily by ear, while others prefer memorizing tunes from the printed page.

Neither technique is "best" for learning traditional tunes, although there are proponents of each approach. To beginners who are unsure of which technique to use after reading this section, I suggest that you try both methods. You'll soon discover that one or the other of the techniques seems easier, and you may also find that using them both together is a great help.

There are many excellent fiddlers around, including professionals, who do not read music, but many of the best players read and write music to some extent, and also have the ability to learn by ear. In my own case I taught myself how to play by ear, and after a few years, discovered the advantage of also learning how to read music.

In order to learn tunes either by ear, or by reading music, one must first know enough of the basics about playing the instrument to be able to produce musical notes, if only in a rough manner. To obtain this preliminary knowledge and skill, I suggest that a beginner consult other fiddle/violin players, teachers, or instructional books. It is certainly possible to learn to play the fiddle without a teacher, as I have done, but I would recommend to others that they take at least a few lessons.

It is very helpful to have a knowledgeable person point out the various standard ways of holding the fiddle and bow, and to give feedback concerning your developing playing skills. The best teachers are appreciative of all styles of fiddle and violin playing and are also familiar with both techniques of learning by ear and using written music. On the other hand, many teachers use one or the other method exclusively with good results. Check around and try out different approaches until you find a teacher and method with which you are satisfied.

Regardless of the methods that you use to learn fiddle tunes, it is in your best interest to listen voraciously to as much fiddle music as you can, of all styles. This will help develop your "feel" for fiddle music, and give you ideas about how to structure your own playing.

Learning by Ear

The oldest and most often used technique of learning traditional folk and fiddle tunes involves listening to them often until they are familiar enough enough to be imitated on one's own instrument. This method of learning by ear is tried and true and was in popular use long before written music was invented: one person plays a tune, another person hears the tune and learns it, and then passes it on to a third person, and so on.

The basic process of learning a fiddle tune by ear involves the following steps:

1. Listening to the tune until it is familiar enough to be sung, whistled, or played back in your mind.
2. Finding the notes on the fiddle and memorizing the fingering as you go.
3. Trying out various bowing patterns until the tune flows smoothly.

Beginners often start with ear training exercises such as finding simple meolodies on the fiddle that they have known from childhood such as "Mary Had a Little Lamb" or "Twinkle Twinkle Little Star." Since I had been a country dancer before becoming a fiddler, I started out by learning tunes I was already very familiar with from dances. Many old time country fiddlers grew up listening to fiddle tunes from an early age and so had a head start in learning by ear.

Nowadays though, because of record players, tape recorders and video players, we can listen to tunes over and over as many times as we like, which probably compensates for not growing up with the tunes. Some tunes are much more difficult to learn by ear than others, however, so once again I recommend that beginners get guidance from an experienced fiddler, teacher, or book.

"You've got to get the tune on your mind and then find it with your fingers. Keep on till you find what you want on that neck. But keep that tune in your mind just like you can hear it a-playin'"
— Hobart Smith,
  Old time southern fiddler,
  (*Beginning Old Time Fiddle*)

When tunes are learned by ear they are likely to be changed somewhat in the process. These changes may be inadvertent or purposeful, dependent upon the learner. Melody notes may be added, altered, or deleted, keys changed, and bowing patterns modified. As a consequence of this influence, fiddle tunes are constantly evolving as new variations become popular and older variations are rediscovered.

Folk music scholars label this effect the "folk process," and feel that it is important in maintaining the "living tradition" of folk music. Other people sometimes feel that this is a disadvantage to learning by ear since it results in everyone playing the tunes somewhat differently. This issue also spawns arguments about which version of a tune is the "best" version.

One of the major advantages to learning by ear, however, is that the learner can bypass the time-consuming, and for some, laborious, process of learning to read music. Learning by ear is also conducive to improvisation, as one is not bound by a written version of the tune. Aside from traditional fiddle tunes which are standardized to a certain extent, other styles of fiddle playing demand a large amount of improvisational ability. For example, many of the best bluegrass, jazz, blues, and rock fiddlers play completely improvised solos. This skill evolves out of a great deal of playing by ear.

In support of traditional ways of learning to play fiddle was Earl Johnson, a prize winning fiddler at the large Atlanta, Georgia fiddle contest in 1926. He describes his own experiences:

> Back when I was younger I got the idea that the violin might be better music than the fiddle, so I gave it a good try. I studied several months under a well-known teacher, and the longer I worked, the more I realized that the fiddle furnishes the superior type of music. The violinist doesn't play his own music, he just translates somebody else's ideas. And he concentrates so hard on getting his notes, his rests, and all the other details the way the composer wrote them that he can't put himself into the music. But a fiddler can cut loose, and if he doesn't like the tune as he learned it, he can improve on it.

This point of view illustrates the feelings of many fiddlers that written music is for "violinists," while playing by ear and developing personalized versions of fiddle tunes is an admirable ability and goal in fiddling. Of course, there is no reason why a fiddler couldn't first learn a tune from written music, and then personalize it with improvisational skills learned by playing by ear. In fact, many experienced fiddlers utilize all possible resources for learning tunes. The ability to play and learn by ear is just one valuable and useful skill for beginners and professional players alike.

In order to develop the skill of playing by ear, it is necessary to do it often. Some of the situations in which you can practice it are as follows:

1. playing with other musicians in jam sessions.
2. playing along with records and tapes.
3. trying to repeat a short passage on fiddle that another musician has just played.
4. sitting in with the band at square and contra dances.
5. finding the melodies on your fiddle of any songs or tunes with which you are familiar.
6. learning the same melody in different keys.

Written Music

One of the major advantages of using written music to learn fiddle tunes is that it eliminates much of the trial and error process that accompanies learning by ear. This is especially valuable for trained violinists who may already be competent at reading music. In addition, two musicians who learn from the same source can be assured of playing identical versions of a tune.

On the other hand, written music presents other difficulties, particularly with traditional fiddle styles. Some fiddlers and people who study fiddle music are interested in maintaining traditions and argue that the use of printed music is not traditional and may be harmful to the folk process. An example of this point of view is stated by George Emmerson who studied the history of Scottish dance music:

> When the tune is 'frozen' on the printed page by its creator, it is no longer the property of the folk, nor so violently exposed to the vagaries of oral transmission. It is in a sense no longer a living organism subject to growth or change. Thus, strictly speaking, it is not 'traditional' although it may in every way conform to the traditional pattern and be couched in the traditional idioms.

We are fortunate, though, that over the years various persons have attempted to capture on paper the wonderful tunes that they heard being played around them by musicians who often couldn't read or write a note. Many fine tunes might have been lost forever if it hadn't been for the efforts of scholars and tune collectors.

The major difficulty in collecting these tunes and committing them to paper has been noted by many scholars and is typified by the Gows of Scotland in the *Complete Repository of the Original Scots Slow Strathspeys and Dances*, in which they noted that "in every part of Scotland where we have occasionally been, and from every observation we were able to make, [we] have not once met with two professional musicians who played the same notes of any tune." [1802]

It also turns out that good players improvise quite a bit while playing, and any particular version of a tune that is written down leaves out the many other possible variations. This point was illustrated quite well by Francis O'Neill when he collected tunes for *The Dance Music of Ireland* (1907). O'Neill couldn't write music himself but was assisted by a trained violinist who would attempt to reproduce a particular musician's version in musical notation and then play it until it sounded "right" to the musician. The final agreed upon version was recorded on paper. The following account illustrates the difficulty of recording the playing of a particular musician:

> It seems that on this particular occasion Touhey (a piper) wanted to learn a tune from McFadden (a fiddler). He had McFadden play it for him several times and then tried his own hand at it. Of course McFadden had to play it again, pointing out several 'errors.' This happened a number of times until Touhey finally gave up, for McFadden was playing the tune a little differently each time through!

Another consequence of written music is the controversy over which versions of a tune are definitive. Oftentimes I have been in the company of fiddlers who argue that their particular version of a tune is the "right," or "true," or "standard version" of a tune because they had located a printed version of it in so and so's "old" book of fiddle tunes. If the composer of a tune is indicated, then I suppose that one could argue correctly that the printed version is the "true" written version. However, many thousands of tunes which appear in written music are not listed by composer, and in fact the composers and original versions are not even known since the tunes originated via the folk process.

To compound this problem, printed versions of traditional tunes often vary significantly from one book to another. Note the page of five different versions of the tune "Soldier's Joy" from five different fiddle tune books, that I've included in this volume.

Notice the similarities and differences between them, and one of my own variations.

Most printed sources for fiddle music include little or no information about rhythm variations and slurring notes with the bow, and this problem is illustrated by professional fiddler John Burke who explained that:

> The fiddler is his own 'rhythm section,' and it is this characteristic which most readily distinguishes him from his 'high falutin' score-bound cousin, the violinist. Violinists are not trained to produce rhythm and melody simultaneously. This is why violinists never sound 'right' when playing fiddle music. Even when they read the tune perfectly from the score, half the music is missing.

Finally I'd like to note the thoughts of Miles Krassen, who edited the "new and revised" O'Neill's *Music of Ireland*:

> In a work of this size it is only possible to go through each tune once. This precludes the possibility of including many fine variations. Yet, it is the subtle art of variation that makes the playing of Michael Coleman and other great players so consistently exciting.

Using Ear Techniques and Written Music Together

As a professional player, I now have a vast library of printed music, field recordings, and commercial records of fiddle tunes. I find these aids indispensible for improving my own playing. Let's imagine that for some reason I need to learn a particular traditional tune quickly. I will try to find a printed version in my library, and at the same time I will search out several different recorded versions. From among these sources, and considering my technical abilities on the fiddle, I will put together a workable version of the tune.

The key to my ability to synthesize a fiddle tune in various different styles results from years of listening very carefully to fiddle playing, and to as many different players and styles as possible. Any distinct traditional style of fiddling tends to have playing techniques of rhythm and melody that are fairly common throughout many tunes within that style. There are stereotypical bowing patterns, double stops, and beginnings and endings.

After deciding about the style that I wish to play a tune in, I go about constructing the tune in a methodical way. If I will be playing it in an ensemble such as a contra dance band. I may leave out extra embellishments in order to keep the melody line simple and distinct. However, if I am the only "lead" or main melody instrument, I may "fancy up" the tune. For "southern," or square dance tunes I might add rhythmical bowing patterns. For bluegrass, Irish music, or performance-oriented situations I might add embellishments to make the tune "flashy" or "tasteful" according to the style desired.

But if I don't have to learn a tune in a hurry, the way I prefer to learn it is to gradually absorb it during weeks or months of listening to various versions. By listening to fiddle tunes many times over a long period of time, they eventually become so familiar that they are easy to learn by ear. Oftentimes a familiar tune will just pop into my head, in its entirety. This might happen at a lunch break or at three o'clock in the morning. Fortunately, my fiddle goes most places that I do, and so I can immediately sit down and commit the tune to memory while experimenting a bit with the fingering and bowing.

After I've played a tune for several years I gradually acquire numerous variations of the melody line, bowing patterns, and phrasing. This happens a lot with tunes that I play for country dances. It's not unusual for a particular square or contra dance figure to go on for 10 minutes or more. During this time I may play a particular tune through a couple of dozen times. Now and then the bow slips, or the mind wanders, and *voila!*, I accidently play some notes that are different than usual, but that sound agreeable to my ear.

The next time that the tune comes around I may try the new "lick" out again to see if I can repeat it. On other occasions I may experiment with new variations out of boredom, or in response to some interesting lick that I hear one of the other musicians playing.

In this way the tunes evolve both in the way that I play the melody notes, and in the rhythms that I create with the bow. Sometimes I may be playing at a dance where there is a strong "back up" rhythm section of guitar, piano, and bass. In this case I might play versions of tunes that have elaborate variations on the melody but simple rhythms. The other musicians are taking care of the rhythm, so I am freer to play fancier notes as the lead instrument. At other times I might be playing a duet with another lead player or have a weak rhythm accompaniment, and so must alter my playing to strengthen the beat, to make the music more danceable. I'll then change to more rhythmic bowing and a simpler melody line.

On one occasion I was playing very fast southern tunes for a clogging team from Virginia, when suddenly the rhythm instruments dropped out of the public address system due to technical problems. I immediately shifted to my most rhythmic variations of the tunes and was able to keep the dancers going for several minutes until the other instruments came back on.

A written version of a tune can often supply the basic framework of melody upon which rhythm and embellishment can be draped. Knowing something about the traditions and lore surrounding particular fiddling styles along with time spent listening to other fiddlers play them can often aid in this method. For example, southern Appalachian fiddling evolved in the mountains where there were no guitars for rhythm accompaniment and the fiddle had to play melody and rhythm simultaneously for dancers. This style of fiddling is thus characterized by strong driving rhythms. Some of the bowed rhythms within the southern USA tradition are very intricate and require many years to master. Other styles of fiddling require vastly different techniques. Texas style fiddling, for example, is accompanied by other instruments playing rock solid backup rhythms, which leaves the fiddle free to play soaring melody lines in many variations.

In summary of this section I'd like to make the following pronouncements:

1. There are no universally accepted versions of any traditional fiddle tune.

2. A printed version of a tune is just one person's biased idea of how a tune should go (or went).

3. It is not necessary to have the ability to read music to be a good fiddler.

4. An experienced fiddler will play any particular tune with several variations.

5. Individual taste determines which version of a tune is the most meritorious.

6. It's perfectly proper to use any combination of various learning techniques to learn to play the fiddle.

Written Variations on the tune "Soldier's Joy"

1001 Fiddle Tunes

Fiddler's Tune Book

Appalachian Fiddle

O'Neill's Music of Ireland

Beginning Old Time Fiddle

A Variation I Might Play

Jana Jae, 1974 Ladies National Champion, National Old Time Fiddle Contest, Weiser, Idaho, when asked what an aspiring fiddler needs to do to advance professionally: *"Taking lessons is definitely a big help. If you can learn the correct fingerings, the correct vibrato techniques, and the correct shifting patterns, it makes everything so much easier, because it helps you know your instrument . . . On the other hand, I don't think that you have to hold your instrument a particular way, because there are a lot of great fiddlers who hold their fiddle 'wrong.'"* (Frets)

When interviewed by Matt Glaser concerning Stephane Grappelli and improvisation, "From my earliest years I was trained to study already-written works. I'd love nothing more than to have or to develop the talent to improvise. But the nearest I can get is to play with people who do, so at least I bask in their glory."
— Yehudi Menuhin,
classical violinist
(*Oak Report*, Summer 1980)

"The way they teach violin nowadays is no good because they don't teach you chords. If you don't know chords you can't play behind anybody because the notes don't mean anything."
— Joe Venuti, jazz fiddler
(*Sing Out*)

"Improvisation, it is a mystery. You can write a book about it, but still by the end no one knows what it is. When I improvise and I'm in good form, I'm like somebody half sleeping. I even forget there are people in front of me. Great improvisers are like priests: they are thinking only of their god."
— Stephane Grappelli, with
Django Reinhardt and the
Hot Club of France (*Frets*)

Although modern records are recorded at either 33 1/3 or 45 RPM, early fiddle records were recorded at 78 RPM. These records can still be found at flea markets, yard sales, or through newsletters and magazines that cater to collectors. Many, but not all, of these have been reissued on modern LP albums. In order to play the original 78s, however, you must try to locate the type of record player that was made up to the early 1960s, with 4 speeds: 16, 33 1/3, 45, and 78 RPM. Another advantage of this type of record player is that you can play modern LPs at 16 RPM, which is about half speed, which slows down fast fiddle tunes enough to aid in learning them by ear.

Fortunately however for most of us, there are hundreds of modern LPs available with fiddle music which we can play on present day turntables. There are some features of modern turntables which are useful to fiddlers. "Variable speed" controls allow you to change the speed of the record to match the tuning on your fiddle or other instruments. "Multiple repeat" controls allow you to repeat a particular tune endlessly, without having to manually replace the tone arm.

Most records of fiddle music probably won't be found in your neighborhood record store, since the market for them is not nearly as large as for popular music. Therefore you will have to search them out. If you do find fiddle records in a commercial record store, they are often in the "Folk," "Country," "Ethnic," or "Bargain" bins. If you are lucky, you may live close to a record store that specializes in "folk" type records and which may have many records of fiddling. Most record stores will be happy to order any records that they don't have in stock. Used record stores are also often a good bet. The alternative to stores is to order records through mail order companies. I have listed a number of reliable mail order companies in the "Sources" section of this book.

Although there are scores of recordings of excellent fiddlers and bands with fiddlers in them, I will list just a few of my favorites in several catagories of fiddle styles. All of these are available through folk record stores and mail order distribution companies:

Bluegrass
Kenny Baker, Scotty Stoneman with the Kentucky Colonels, Byron Berline, Blaine Sprouse, Vassar Clements.

British Isles
Tommy Potts, Kevin Burke, Bothy Band, Tom Anderson, Aly Bain, Boys of the Lough, Chieftains, How to Change a Flat Tire, Tommy Peoples, Michael Coleman, De Danann.

Canadian
Jean Carignan, Graham Townsend, John Campbell, Ben Guillemette.

Country, Jazz and Swing
Stephane Grappelli, The Hot Club of France, Joe Venuti, Eddie South, Stuff Smith, Svend Asmussen, Emelio Caceres, Johnny Gimble.

New England
New England Chestnuts Album, Allan Block, Arm and Hammer Stringband, Strathspey, Canterbury Country Dance Orchestra, F & W String Band.

Old Time
Highwoods String Band, Tommy Jarrel, J.P. Fraley, The Skillet Lickers, Franklin George, Red Clay Ramblers, New Lost City Ramblers.

Texas
Benny Thomasson, Dick Barrett, Mark O'Connor, Vernon Soloman, Terry Morris, Texas Shorty, Johnny Gimble, Herman Johnson.

Hard to Classify
Marie Rhines (many styles), Fiddle Fever (jazzy old time?), Darol Anger (New Acoustic Music).

There are many other types of fiddling than those I have listed. For example, I enjoyed hearing traditional Chinese bowed fiddles at the Smithsonian Institute in Washington, DC. The one recording that I obtained of a "Nan-hu," or Chinese two-stringed fiddle is on the Nonesuch label, number H72051, and is entitled *China, Shantung Folk Music & Traditional Instrumental Pieces*. For other styles of fiddling mentioned in this volume, see the article contributed by Matt Fichtenbaum in which he lists recordings of Swedish fiddling. The "Record Review and Description" section of this volume lists records of Mexican, Cajun, Ukrainian, and Polish fiddling. The additional lists of jazz and blues fiddlers and recordings are in the "Sources" section.

Your two best bets for locating some of the rarer ethnic fiddle recordings are to order the catalogues from the mail order companies listed in this volume, and to contact ethnic organizations, clubs, and musicians directly. Many cities have "International Houses," or "Centers" at which various ethnic groups have meetings, dances, and information on folk arts and music.

Some fiddlers produce and sell their own records directly to the public at performances, which may be the only place to obtain them. Many such records on small independent record labels go out of print, but may often be located through used record stores or by mail order through record collecting newsletters. I have listed some of these publications in the "Sources" section.

The actual process of learning tunes from a record involves listening to the record many times until the tune is extremely familiar. Keep in mind that many of the tunes on records may be very difficult to reproduce note for note by the average fiddler since they were recorded by professional musicians playing fancy and intricate versions. Don't be discouraged if, after a hundred listenings, you still can't figure out how virtuoso fiddlers such as Vassar Clements or Kevin Burke play a particular passage. Remember that it took them years to learn to play like that. Instead, work toward simpler versions of tunes at first which are more in line with your present abilities on the fiddle.

It helps very much to have several versions of the same tune to listen to. It helps also if you have a way to slow the tunes down. A written version can give you ideas about how to fill in places where the techniques involved are beyond you present ability. Most written versions of traditional tunes are much simpler than what the professionals play in actual performances. Another help is a fiddling friend or fiddle teacher who may know a version of the tune already, and can help you through the tough spots.

Oftentimes it is difficult to pick out the fiddle part on a record in which there are also many other instruments. Keep an eye out for records in which the fiddle is the prominent instrument in all of the tunes, and where the other instruments keep to the background. Some fiddle records are recorded with the fiddle on one channel, and the other instruments on another channel, so that you can tune them out for the purposes of learning the fiddle part. After learning the fiddle part, you can tune it out of the record and play along with the rest of the band on the other channel.

Tape Recorders

Tape recorders are very useful for the modern fiddler as an easy way to store fiddle tunes for learning at a later time. Portable cassette recorders can be carried easily to wherever the music is being played. For recording music I recommend that you buy a medium or better quality recorder. The best portables (and the most expensive) are stereo and can be hooked up directly to your home stereo system for excellent sound.

Some portable models offer two speed operation. If you record a fiddle tune at the higher speed and play it back at the low speed, the tune will be half as fast and exactly an octave lower in pitch. That is, an "A" or any other note will remain the same note but be just lower in pitch. This two speed feature can be used to record both records and live fiddlers. The same technique can be used with a two speed reel-to-reel tape recorder. At half speed, it is much easier to detect when the bow changes direction and other subtle playing techniques.

At slower speeds, everything will sound much different and takes some getting used to. Low bassy sounds will predominate and make it a bit difficult sometimes to pick out the fiddle from the other instruments. This problem can be partially corrected by making the initial recording with treble controls set to maximum and bass controls set at minimum. Use of a graphic equalizer is even better for this purpose.

My fancy home cassette deck has a feature called "programmable repeat," which is extremely useful for learning tunes. With it I can endlessly repeat any portion of a tape, whether it be ten seconds or thirty minutes. I can listen to a particular passage over and over until I can figure out how it is played.

Another useful feature is a variable speed or pitch control which can be used to speed up or slow down a tune so that it matches the tuning on your own instrument. This is usually easier than retuning your instrument to match the recording.

Sixty minute cassettes have stronger and thicker tape than longer cassettes and will hold up better under constant rewinding and playing. they will also last longer in your car stereo and resist jamming. For long cassette life buy medium quality or better tapes and avoid "budget" tapes.

Radio Programs

Most areas of the country are served by radio stations affiliated with the "National Public Radio" network. These are listed in newspapers along with their broadcast schedules. By writing to an NPR station directly, you can obtain detailed monthly programming information. Many shows feature fiddling, bluegrass, oldtime country music and related topics. My own show featured live music, interviews, and selected recorded material. As "Captain Fiddle" I always joined in with the guests and fiddled a bit. Public Radio stations are always responsive to personal letters. If they don't already feature some folk music programming, they may be likely to do so on the basis of personal letters from interested listeners. The hosts of many shows are often open to phone-in requests for fiddle music.

Some commercial and college stations also offer programs with fiddling and folk music. Bluegrass and folk music newsletters list these stations.

Music Stores

In this volume I've listed some of the mail order music stores and retail stores which cater to fiddlers, but almost any music store can order many of the supplies that fiddlers need. A music store is also a useful clearinghouse for information about all kinds of music and musicians. If you let it be known that you are interested in fiddling, the word will be spread and you may soon have contacts with people who have similar interests.

Most music stores have a bulletin board for musicians to exchange information. I once encountered a handbill with printed letters several inches high spelling out "fiddlers," which listed a telephone number. I called the number and became "picking partners" with the person who had posted the notice. You might leave such a sign yourself if you are having difficulty locating other musicians in your area. An ad in the local paper can also accomplish the same result.

"As soon as I had the scale on the fiddle, I was playing Irish tunes...I knew all the tunes already from dancing, so even though I was playing classical music in class, I'd be playing jigs and reels for myself."

— Eugene O'Donnell
Derry, Ireland (*Frets*)

The Eighth
San Diego State
Folk Festival

Festivals

Lots of fiddlers spend time at festivals. In fact, many serious amateur fiddlers almost make a career of traveling from festival to festival to see old friends and learn new tunes. It is generally true at most festivals that the best music isn't on the main stage with the featured acts, but off to the side at jam sessions or at the midnight-to-dawn picking parties which always follow the festivals. Keep your ears open for the location of these parties.

I might mention at this point that it is common courtesy at festivals to be unobtrusive while taping. Some musicians don't like being taped, while others love the attention. It's always a good idea to ask first, or observe what the other people around are doing, and note the reactions of the musicians. At some concerts and festivals taping is encouraged. At the National Fiddle Contest in Weiser, Idaho, a special room is set aside for people with tape recorders to hook directly into the main sound system for the best possible recordings. At another concert featuring Doc Watson, I saw tapes confiscated and erased by security guards. You should at least appear to be abiding by whatever rules are present if you do intend to tape.

"Bluegrass" and "Folk" festivals are often quite different. Folk festivals tend to feature more traditional styles of fiddling such as old timey, Irish, and other ethnic styles. Bluegrass festivals, on the other hand, rarely feature traditional fiddling, but concentrate on more modern styles.

Some festivals focus upon a particular ethnic style. In the Northeast we have Scottish, Irish, French Canadian, Scandinavian, "International" and other folk dancing and music festivals. These types of festivals are good for learners who wish to go right to the source of traditional folk arts.

Some festivals encourage jam sessions and provide places for these activities, while others would rather have just listeners. Look for festivals that offer workshops in fiddling and other types of music. I usually only attend events where there is a place where I can take out my own fiddle and play a bit when the mood strikes.

marLborough FoLk FestivaL

Junior High School · Union St. · Marlborough, Massachusetts

Sunday · August 24 · 1:00 · 6:00 pm

In Concert - Banjo Dan & the Midnite Plowboys · Joe Val & the New England Blue Grass Boys · Tony Saleten · Rick & Lorraine Lee · Music for Contras·Squares & Folk Dancing · Cambridge Folk Orchestra · Timber Salvage · The New Caledonians · Last Chance String Band · Dance Demonstrations

Tickets · Ticketron · OCA

B Sullivan

LAST CHANCE STRING BAND.
from NH's seacoast, features Paul Mangion on banjo, Ryan Thom son on Fiddle, and guitarists Charlie Nolan and Jim Marks. These four musicians are all vocalists who together produce a unified sound and exhuberant style. Paul will lead banjo workshops and Ryan will head up the fiddling.

Country Dancing

Country dancing to live fiddle music presents another great opportunity to meet people interested in fiddling. I've been dancing and playing for dances for twelve years or so and it has become an important part of my life. In my area of New England, there are dances four or five days a week within an hour and a half drive from my house. I learned my very first fiddle tunes by hearing them played at country dances.

You'll find that dancing itself will help your playing as you will pick up a feeling for the rhythms and melodies. Besides, it's a lot of fun! Many New England dances have steps and figures which closely match the structure of the tunes themselves.

Many dance musicians encourage other visiting musicians to "sit in" with the house band, even if the visitors are beginners. Courtesy dictates that a guest play quietly or not at all if he or she does not know the tune in progress. Even if the tune is known quite well, one does not "hog" the stage unless invited to by the host musicians. By common custom, guest musicians may be invited to play the entire dance if they wish, but it is generally recognized that they won't be paid, even if the hired musicians take off a little time to dance. Feel free to take along your cassette recorder to tape tunes you like.

Serious dance fiddlers often keep a notebook in their fiddle case with the list of tunes that they know, tunes that they have in common with other musicians and bands, and tunes they wish to learn, etc. Once one knows more than a couple of dozen tunes, it becomes easy to gradually forget the ones that are not played often, unless the list is around as a reminder. After my own tune list exceeded 150 tunes, I found that it was difficult to keep all of them in good practice, but at least I have them noted so that I can go back and practice the ones that I need to. Besides the tunes on my list, there are probably another 200 or so that I am familiar enough with that I can play them along with someone else who knows them well.

It is not uncommon for fiddlers who have been playing many years to have several hundred tunes in good playing shape. I imagine that I will go on learning new tunes for the rest of my life. You'll find that the more tunes you know, the easier it is to learn new tunes.

CONTRA DANCE
~ TO ~
TRADITIONAL NEW ENGLAND AND APPALACHIAN TUNES
given spirited expression
~ BY ~
CAPTAIN FIDDLE'S COUNTRY DANCE ORCHESTRA
CHIP HEDLER CALLING
2ND & 4TH Fridays at 8:30 pm
NEWMARKET TOWN HALL

HALLOWE'EN CONTRA DANCE
COSTUMES IF DESIRED
CAPTAIN FIDDLE'S BAND
WITH
MARY DESROSIERS
CALLER
OCTOBER 28
NEWMARKET TOWN HALL
8:30 PM ~ 12:00 AM $3.00

"Kissing appeared to have been an essential part of most English dances, a circumstance which probably contributed not a little to their popularity. This custom, according to Mrs. Lilly Grove, author of Dancing—a renowned work—still survives in some parts of England, and when the fiddler thinks the young people have had music enough, he makes his instrument squeak out two notes which all understand to say 'kiss her.' At the end of each strathspey or jig a particular note from the fiddle used to summon the rustic to the agreeable duty of saluting his partner with a kiss, that being his fee or privilege according to established usage."

— (from *The Elements of Traditional Scottish Dance Music*)

Getting Together With Other Musicians

When you are learning fiddle, it helps to have other musicians around from which to learn. People tend to learn the most from other players close to their own level of ability or slightly better, although sometimes more advanced players will take the time to slow down a bit and help beginners. Try to seek out those players who are the most helpful toward you. Remember that sooner or later you will be a much better player and in a position to help others.

After you've located a few other fiddlers or musicans, you might organize regular meetings or picking sessions. They could be as often as once a week, or monthly, and could rotate around at different homes. Other likely locations include community centers, parks, schools, town halls, and churches. Often restaurants or bars will make a room available on a regular basis to pickers. In return for a place to play, the establishment receives the benefit of extra business in food and drink. I've started picking organizations at a couple of universities that I've attended. Colleges will generally provide a room, advertising in school publications, and sometimes even sound systems for mini-concerts, dances, or performances.

"Me and Bill used to ride along in the car, in fact when he wrote 'Roanoke' we'd just worked Roanoke, Virginia. Bill always kept his mandolin inside the car and he got foolin' with 'Roanoke,' and we stopped the car and I got my fiddle out of the trunk and tried to work out the fiddle part."
— Gordon Terry
played with Bill Monroe
(The Big Book of Bluegrass)

"That's how to play — work off the chords. Learn the chords; work riffs around them. If a song is in A, learn the I–IV–V chords (A, D, E) and you'll know where to start. Use the chords to back up the vocal and the riffs to fill in the gaps and imitate the voice."
— Fats Kaplin, blues fiddler
(Sing Out)

Practice

All of us would like to learn to fiddle better and learn as quickly as possible. Fortunately, there are some rules of thumb which make the learning process more efficient. There are a few things to keep in mind, though. All individuals are different in their various abilities. Some people find bowing easy and fingering difficult while others encounter the opposite situation. You will find that some techniques on the fiddle come more naturally than others.

There are some facts about practicing which, if followed consistently, will help you to learn faster. Scientists have found that the brain works more efficiently under certain conditions. For example, it is better to practice in short repeated sessions than a long continuous session. Two separate forty minute sessions a day are better than a two hour continuous session. Beginners often profit with two twenty minute sessions a day, once in the morning and again in the evening. Some people find that three separate sessions are even better. The best length of a practice session is different for everyone depending upon stamina, previous experience, and day to day routines.

Fifteen minutes every day is better than an hour straight every three days.

I suggest practicing often in front of a mirror to observe your style. This way you can check if your bow is perpendicular to the fiddle, how much of the bow you are using, whether your bow strokes are smooth, whether your body is in good posture, etc. An advantage of practicing in a small room or stairwell is that the sound of your fiddle is amplified and sounds better, no matter what your ability, sort of like singing in the shower! A contrasting situation would be to play in a large carpeted room which might make your fiddle sound thin. This type of practice situation might help because you must work harder to get a full tone.

In order to get the most out of a playing session, you must be refreshed and relaxed. Many fiddlers and violinists alike have found that they play better when relaxed. I find that yoga and stretching exercises work best for my own playing.

Try to remember the first few times that you tried to dance, skate, or ride a bicycle. If you were like most people, you found that your muscles were tense and you felt somewhat clumsy. Later on the activity became easier and you found it more enjoyable. If you continued long enough at it, you found that you could learn to move gracefully and efficiently. Your muscles were no longer tense and you didn't get tired as easily because you were only using the muscles that were needed, when you needed them.

With fiddle playing, you don't build up strength as you learn to play better, but instead use less strength than when you are beginning, but in a more efficient way. You learn to use only the muscles that you need, when you need them. If your left hand is clamped down on the fiddle, knuckles white, as you struggle to get the right notes, you are wasting energy and tiring yourself out. This tension will creep lup into your arm, jaw, neck, and back and you will begin getting aches and pains. Now, I want to emphasize that everyone will experience some tension and strain during practicing and learning the fiddle. But if you are aware of this muscular tension, you can do quite a bit about it.

"My parents decided that they wanted me to play the fiddle, before I had any say in the matter. They thought the best way was for me to learn the mechanics of the instrument from a classical teacher. At first I couldn't see any difference between playing a scale and playing a reel, and I wasn't that keen on either of them."
— Keven Burke, Bothy Band Ireland (Frets)

"I only use a few inches of my bow, therefore I have better control — like a trumpeter controls his breath. When I desire a staccato effect I naturally play on the frog of the bow, strong enough as if I were fiddling on a washtub."
— Stuff Smith, jazz fiddler (Sing Out)

First of all, try to avoid clamping down on the fiddle, either with your left hand, or with your jaw and collar bone. Of course, you don't want to relax so much that you drop your instrument, but you do want to find a happy medium. Ideally your fiddle should be balanced, delicately, yet firmly. If you constantly think "relaxed," you will gradually get better at it. Why is it so important to be relaxed? Besides making it easier to play the instrument and allowing you to play for longer periods of time, your playing will sound much better! If you are stiff and tense, your playing will sound scratchy. If you are relaxed, your bowing will be stronger and more rhythmic on a fast breakdown or reel, and richer and more vibrant on a waltz. In addition, your fingers will be able to move more rapidly and with greater accuracy.

I should note here that a fair number of fiddle players hardly ever "practice" the fiddle in any systematic way. Rather, they just get out their fiddles and play the tunes that they know whenever the mood strikes them. This may suit those who play only a particular style, where constant repetition of tunes serves as a source of practice. However, if one is interested in learning more diverse styles, or improving tone and bowing, a little self discipline is needed. The easiest way to practice is to play all of the tunes that one knows best. A more profitable way to practice might be to concentrate on the tunes or techniques which one finds most difficult yet wants to learn.

I mix both easy and hard tunes in my practice sessions, but spend at least three quarters of the time on very difficult or new pieces. I save the tunes that I know well for playing with my friends or for performing purposes. I find that practicing the difficult pieces increases my ability to play the easier ones better, without actually practicing them. In addition, I gradually overcome the difficulties of the tough tunes.

There is something else that you should know about practicing. Generally, the more often and harder that you practice, the faster that you will improve. Many people are not aware of the fact that improvement does not come at a regular rate, even if one practices regularly. Improvement comes in leaps and bounds with occasional spells of no obvious improvement. Sometimes it may even seem as though one is falling behind. This has something to do with the way that the brain processes information coming to it. In a typical situation, you may improve rapidly for awhile and then enter a "plateau" in which you don't seem to get any better no matter how much effort is exerted. However, if you persevere, you will eventually overcome the barrier or difficulty. The brain sometimes has so much information to process that it takes a long period of time to make all of the right connections. Although regular practice always pays off in the long run, it may help to take a day off now and then, particularly after a long period of intensive practicing.

Another characteristic of how your brain works is that as the brain processes information that you have learned, the incorrect actions tend to be eliminated from the correct ones. An example is the situation in which you are attempting to play a difficult passage and you keep trying and trying but not succeeding even though you know what you are doing wrong. Then, the following day, you pick up your fiddle and all of a sudden you can play the previously difficult passage easily. Your brain has made the correction automatically while you were sleeping. This may seem pretty amazing, but then human beings are amazing in other ways. In order for this process to best take place, however, the initial hard work is necessary.

I believe that many people who try to learn a reasonably difficult skill such as playing an instrument often get frustrated and quit during a plateau in which they are seemingly at a standstill in their playing. If they just worked a little harder or longer they might suddenly be over their hurdle and rapidly improving again. Keep at it; you can only get better!

If you are considering a professional career in music, then practicing can take the form of a full time job. Lynn Shaw, a North Carolina fiddler, played rock and acoustic guitar for nine years before playing fiddle: "I didn't consider myself listenable until after a year of practice at twelve hours a day. I had a few good friends that stuck around but most of them left," he said in an interview.

When I was on the road with a professional band, we played six four-hour performances a week, three to four two-hour band practices a week, plus my own personal practice schedule of one to two hours a day. You can bet that my playing improved rapidly! On the other hand, any regular practice at all is cumulative, and just twenty minutes a day will lead to steady improvement.

"When I first saw Doug, I thought Jeez, what is this? The bridge on his fiddle is flatter than a classical player would want, but not as flat as on a hoedown fiddle. He'll put his right hand thumb on the bottom of the frog, as opposed to the notch. He uses a very relaxed tension on the bow, and varies it with his little finger as he plays. A classical player would disparage his technique, but it's effective, very effective."
— **Edward Warner**
in charge of Doug Kershaw's
instruments (Frets)

"There's no end to what you can do with the instrument, no end. Don't kid yourself just because it has four strings and it's small. There's nothing you can't do with it if you put your mind to it."
— **Doug Kershaw**
Cajun fiddler (Frets)

A Bit About Fiddle Techniques

A factor which enters into the picture is your preference for particular fiddle styles or tunes. Some styles seem to require a "classical" approach to technique and thus are easily learned from a book by any violinist who can memorize. Other styles may involve playing techniques which trained violinists often have little experience with, and thus the time spent listening is critical to learning the style properly.

In most cases it helps to actually observe the person playing a particular style, to note bowing motions and fingerings. The sounds of certain southern USA styles, for example, are difficult to reproduce unless the bow grip is altered from classical technique, so that the bow can be both held, and "rocked," across the strings at a point closer to the center of gravity, in other words, farther up the bow.

Southern and bluegrass fiddlers often flatten their bridges also to facilitate double stopping and bow rocking across two or more strings. Classically trained violinists often shy away from southern style fiddling because they don't relish the idea of altering the bridges on their expensive violins or changing the way that they hold their bows. Some fiddler/violinists solve this problem by having two fiddles, one adapted for southern fiddling, and another for other styles.

Contrary to the opinion of some classical musicians, holding the bow "southern style" is not a bad habit which violinists should avoid, but rather should be considered as a new technique or tool to add to one's bag of fiddle tricks. Just as it is possible to be skilled at both tennis and golf, one can learn additional ways to holding and playing the fiddle.

V. S. Skamser, in *Violin Science Reports*, number two, describes and ilustrates various bow grips, from "Old German," "French-Belgian," "Russian," to "Advanced Russian," which he recommends. He describes the advanced Russian technique as a "high speed, three or two finger bow hold," which "many great violinists" use, "especially in passages demanding speed and brilliance." I was amused and interested to note that the "advanced Russian" grip was almost identical to that which southern style self taught fiddlers use in playing fast breakdowns.

Some fiddlers find that holding a fiddle at chest level is comfortable, particularly if they have long fingers. Folks with short fingers seem to do better with a more standard "violin" approach. When in doubt, classical violin techniques will solve most problems in many (but not all) fiddle styles. I suggest that you experiment, and watch other players of all styles. Ask lots of questions and find out which techniques work for other players. Keep your mind open to trying out new ideas.

There is, of course, no "right" way to hold or play the fiddle. I personally use a fairly "classical" approach to holding the fiddle which I adapted through trial and error. It seems to work best for my body structure, although I do shift my playing techniques for different styles of fiddling. If a fiddler is able to achieve the kinds of sounds that he or she desires, then it doesn't seem to matter much whether the techniques used match up to any kind of standard method.

"Nobody learning to play the fiddle, no young person, should pay any attention to what I do, because I do everything wrong. I hold my bow wrong, I hold my fiddle wrong, I mash too hard on the bow when I play...a lot of things people would in no way associate with good fiddle playing. But it suits me."
— **Charlie Daniels**
   The Charlie Daniels Band
   (*Frets*)

"My training is entirely the folk training. I have a good deal of knowledge about the classical methods, though, and I befriended a number of excellent teachers in Toronto. Whenever I needed to know something I'd go to them and say, 'Listen, I don't want to learn the whole repertoire and do boring Kreutzer exercises, but show me how to do this.'"
— **Ben Mink**
   from the Canadian
   "heavy metal" trio, FM
   (*Frets*)

41

Tuning the Fiddle

LEARNING TO TUNE your instrument quickly and precisely will add greatly to your enjoyment of playing. Tuning is a skill which anyone can acquire with practice. The most common technique of tuning a fiddle is to compare and adjust the pitch of the strings to a standard. A standard reference pitch may be obtained from a tuning fork, electronic tuning device, pitch pipe, or from another musical instrument.

A few people have what is sometimes called "absolute," or "perfect," pitch. That is, they have developed the ability to produce any given musical note on demand, from memory, or can perhaps name any given note that is played on an instrument. they may know exactly what an "A" string at the standard pitch of 440 Hz. is supposed to sound like, and can easily tune their string to the correct pitch without an additional reference. Most of us don't have this ability and must use other means to tune. However, anyone can learn to develop what is called "relative pitch." That is, once a standard of any pitch is set for one string, they can determine the proper pitch of every other note or string in relation to the standard.

The most accurate way to tune to standard pitch is with an electronic tuning device or a tuning fork. Electronic tuners are far more expensive than tuning forks, but have several advantages. For example, you can use them in a noisy environment so that you don't have to depend solely upon your hearing. When playing on stage I often use an electronic tuner which is wired directly to my fiddle. By plucking any one string, the tuner lights up with two red arrows if the string is in tune. If the string is out of tune, the corresponding sharp or flat red arrow flickers or goes out, indicating what direction and how much to tune the string. This sytem is quick and easy, as I don't even have to touch the tuner.

In less noisy situations a tuning fork also serves perfectly well, although it lacks a visual indication of proper tuning. It can be rapped against a firm but slightly cushioned surface such as the heel of a shoe and then placed, handle end down, on the top of the bridge to produce a clear tone. This is repeated while the fiddle string is tuned to match the pitch of the tuning fork.

Pitch pipes can be purchased which produce either one tone, usually A440, or all four tones required by fiddle strings: G, D, A and E. Blowing

> *"If you've ever played tunes with Mr. Oppor Knockity, you might know that he has perfect pitch and a fiddle that stays in tune. I've heard it often said that 'Oppor Knockity only tunes once.'"*
> — *(Devil's Box)*

into them produces an audible reference pitch to which the strings are matched. There is a disadvantage in tuning to pitch pipes. That is, the pitch of a tone produced by blowing changes with how hard one blows, the shape of the mouth, and the placement of the tongue within the mouth. It is therefore very difficult to get a tone which is consistent from one person to another, or one time to the next, unless the pipe is blown into in exactly the same way each time.

The same problem occurs if one attempts to tune a fiddle to a flute or penny whistle. Unless the flute or penny whistle player is an experienced musician, the tone will vary noticeably up and down in pitch. One may tune the fiddle string precisely to the penny whistle only to find later that the whistle note doesn't match the fiddle string because the player is now blowing harder, or easier, or playing the note in another octave. In addition, wind instruments change pitch as they become warmer from the player's breath. Experienced wind instrument players are aware of these variations in the pitch of their instruments and correct for them by breath control and the position of the instrument relative to their lips.

A fiddle can be tuned to a piano quite easily if the piano has been well maintained. The most common practice is to tune the "A" fiddle string to an A minor or A major piano chord. The other fiddle strings are then tuned to the "A" string. Some pianos are out of tune, however, which makes tuning to them difficult. When a piano goes out of tune from neglect it often follows a particular pattern. The notes in the center two or three octaves tend to stay in better tune in relation to each other than the very high, or very low notes. Also, the overall pitch of a piano often drops as much as a whole note. The "A" key when struck may actually produce a G or G sharp or somewhere in between.

Many piano tuners, when retuning old pianos, don't even try to tune them up to the standard A440 Hz, but try instead to get all of the notes in good tune with each other at a lower overall pitch. If you have no choice but to play with an out of tune piano, try tuning to the chords in the center of the keyboard. Chords at the extremes will probably be too far out of tune. If you don't wish to tune your fiddle too far down to match the piano, find out if the piano player can transpose to a higher key.

Tuning to other stringed instruments such as guitars or mandolins should follow a similar procedure. The fiddle can be first tuned to individual strings to get into the ballpark, and then fine tuned to blend in with the sound of a chord on the other instrument.

As you begin to develop your ear to hear various subtleties in tuning, other tuning "tricks" will come to your attention. If you approach a group of musicians who are playing a fiddle tune in the key of G, for example, you can tune your D and G strings so they will blend in with the overall sound of the other instruments when played as a double stop. Your A and E strings can then be tuned to the D and G.

If you find yourself without a tuning fork, your fiddle can be tuned by locating a music station on the radio and tuning your strings so that they blend with the sound of the music. This often works best with classical music rather than other types, since it is usually recorded at strict standard pitch. Of course, if you are trying to learn a fiddle tune from a record, it is useful to tune to the record even if it is not at standard pitch.

Knowledge of the mechanical aspects of fiddle pegs and strings will also aid in tuning. Your strings are attached at one end to the tailpiece, and at the other end to the pegs. The only thing which keeps the pegs from turning is the friction between the two dissimilar pieces of wood; the pegs and the peg box. Fiddle pegs must be able to do two seemingly contradictory jobs: on is to stay in place when set, and the other is to be easily turned when tuning. To solve this problem a mixture of Ivory or similar soap and ordinary blackboard chalk is applied to the area of a contact between the pegs and pegbox. If the pegs are too slippery, add more chalk. If they stick too firmly, add a bit more soap.

Often times a peg will keep coming loose even when pushed in very tightly into the pegbox. It is possible that the peg does not fit properly and needs to be reshaped or replaced. There is a trick, however, which will help keep the peg in place. Wiggle the peg from side to side slightly, while pushing it in, and it will stick in further, much in the same way that a key is wiggled to fit into a dry or rusty lock.

A little bit of graphite, or number two pencil lead rubbed into the grooves in the nut and bridge will allow the strings to slide more freely for easier tuning. Get in the habit of putting the graphite in the string grooves every time that you replace your strings.

Why is proper tuning of the fiddle so important? Let me give you an example. The fingers of a fiddler becomes accustomed to always returning to the same exact spots on the finger board in order to achieve a certain tone. This is similar to the ability of a typist to accurately hit the proper keys to form words. Imagine that you have been playing fiddle for a while and your fingers have become very good at always hitting the correct notes. Every time that you want a G, your finger goes immediately to the proper place. The many previous hours of playing and practice have paid off.

Suppose you pick up your fiddle one day and attempt to play a G but every time that you place your fingers in what you have learned to be the right place, a wrong note comes out of the fiddle! What is causing this? Your fiddle is probably out of tune. What this means is that the strings are either too tight or too loose. Remember that if you move your finger only a fraction of an inch on the string it changes the note produced. Changing the tension on the string has the same effect as moving your finger; the note produced is either higher or lower than it should be when you place your finger on the correct place on the string.

The solution to this problem is to always maintain your strings at the exact same tension from one playing session to another. Why couldn't you just move your fingers to the new "correct" place? After all, your fingers and ears have become good at this skill. Let's look back at the typewriter example for a clue. Suppose someone shifted the keys around so that every time you pushed the "S" key an "O" was typed. Sure, you could learn all over again how to type, but wouldn't it be a heck of a lot easier if you just put the keys back in the right places? The same thing is true of fiddle strings! If your fiddle is tuned up properly, then you will only have to learn one set of fingerings. If your strings vary in tension from one playing session to the next, the job of learning the correct placement of the fingers becomes almost impossible.

Proper tuning is especially important to the beginner who is learning the proper finger placement for the first time. Trying to learn to play fiddle on a poorly tuned instrument is like walking uphill on a sand pile, falling back two steps for every three steps forward.

There are other good reasons to be careful about tuning. If any one string is played on your fiddle, the motion of that string will set the other strings vibrating slightly and add to the total sound produced. This additional sound is most pleasing to the ear when all of the other strings are in proper tune to each other. Another reason is a practical one. If a fiddle is always tuned up to the same tension, it won't need tuning as often. Fiddles are designed and constructed to sound best when the strings are at a certain tension, just as your car runs best when the engine is tuned properly. For example, fiddles tuned too low often lack brightness, and fiddles tuned too high may sound tinny.

Playing in Tune

A major difference between a fiddle and its other stringed cousins such as the guitar or mandolin is that it has no frets. This characteristic has both advantages and disadvantages. An advantage is that one can move fingers around on the smooth fretboard very rapidly. It also makes available an infinite rainbow of different tones since even a fraction of an inch of finger movement noticeably changes the sound of a note. The same amount of movement on a fretted instrument has much less effect. The disadvantage is that there is no immediately obvious guide for placement of the fingers. Frets serve this function in other types of instruments by limiting the overall length of the portion of the string that vibrates. The distance between frets has been mathematically calculated by instrument builders to give the correct notes of a musical scale when a finger is placed behind the fret of a plucked string.

The fiddler doesn't have these specially placed guides but must rely upon the ear and previous experience to place the fingers in the proper place to achieve a particular note. A finger must be placed very precisely since only a tiny deviation may produce a note that's too high or too low.

An accomplished fiddle player has several different tricks up his sleeve to aid in placing his fingers properly. Through fiddle practice, his brain has learned to guide his fingers rapidly to the approximately corect region of the fingerboard, much in the same way that a typist can place fingers on the proper key without looking. If the fingers are used regularly to practice, they develop good flexibility and muscle tone. As the fiddler plays a note, the brain senses the note through the ear, and then compares that sound with a memory of how the note is supposed to sound. If the note sounds incorrect, the brain sends a message back to the fingers to move a tiny bit to correct the error.

Besides playing along with other musicians, tapes, and records, there is another practice technique that is very useful for learning to play in tune. That is to practice scales to a constant drone. The drone is a musical tone produced by a mechanical or electronic device. Some electronic tuners produce all twelve different musical tones and electronic keyboards will produce both individual tones and chords. The procedure is as follows:

1. Set the droning device so that it produces one of the twelve possible tones within the middle range of your fiddle.
2. Practice scales, arpeggios, or tunes that are in the same key as the drone note.
3. Listen carefully to the sound that the fingered fiddle notes make as they mix with the drone and strive for a smooth harmonious blend.
4. Repeat with other drone notes and keys.

As one practices the fiddle, the ability to correct errors while playing becomes gradually better and better. The ear gets better at detecting wrong notes, and the fingers get better at correcting them. Although no one is born with the ability to hear in-tune or out-of-tune notes, many inexperienced musicians have gradually become expert at tuning their own instruments.

One cannot learn to tune from a book. "Hands on" training with an instrument is a must. Feedback and instruction from a knowledgeable person can also be very useful.

"What do a sailor and a good fiddler have in common? They can both handle high Cs."

— (Devil's Box)

Up until the advent of radio and phonographs, most fiddlers learned by ear from other musicians. There were, of course, some printed collections of tunes from British Isles sources and dance music volumes, but the average fiddler didn't read enough music to take advantage of these. Many musicians learned mostly from their neighbors and relatives. In order for a fiddler to learn a tune by ear, it was necessary that he or she be present while other musicians played.

Fiddle music got a tremendous boost in the 1920s. As radio and recorded music began to become popular, fiddlers now had much greater exposure to music. If a fiddler purchased a 78 RPM record of fiddle music, it could be played over and over again to learn a tune. Many radio stations began presenting programs of live country music. Henry Ford was crazy about fiddling and sponsored fiddle contests all over the country. As the recording industry discovered this public interest, they sought out country musicians to record.

Frank Walker, a Columbia record pioneer in this era, describes the recording of early country music:

> As the business grew, we made periodical trips to the South, and at least two trips a year. In those days, recordings were done on solid wax and you had to bring containers of the waxes you used. So you were very careful and very choosy.... We recorded in dozens and dozens of different places, all the way from San Antone to Houston and Dallas, and Johnson City, Tennessee, and Memphis, and Little Rock and New Orleans and Atlanta and everywhere.
>
> But that's the way we built up in advance — getting word around that a certain time of the year we were going to be there. And these people would show up sometimes from eight or nine hundred miles away.... They never asked you for money. They didn't question anything at all. They were just happy to sing and play, and we were happy to have them. Most of them we saw had something to go back with.... You brought in a little of the mountain dew to take care of colds or any hoarseness that might happen, and also to remove a little of their fears of strangers doing this sort of work.

Some folk music scholars argue that the record companies recorded only songs and tunes they thought would "sell" to the public, and so the records weren't truly representative of average fiddling. Other scholars feel that these early recordings do represent authentic old time fiddling in a relatively pure form before it was "contaminated" by mass communication.

In any case, the debate goes on about what is "authentic old time fiddling," and the scholars and tune collectors continue to dig out the oldest and most "backwoods" type fiddlers they can find to get the oldest and most "original versions" possible. In fiddling circles, one often hears stories about how some one has recently discovered old "so and so" who is 84 years old and lives in a two room shack in some isolated locality, preferably in the mountains. This person's brain is picked for tunes learned from his old grandfather. The learner then proceeds to learn this tune with, of course, some "minor" changes in bowing, drones, meter, etc. and passes it off as a "real old time" version.

There are, of course, serious scholars who try to record actual performances of tunes as precisely as possible for posterity. Some fiddlers strive to play these tunes just like the old timers, while others are moved to create new styles and traditions. Just as in most other areas of human endeavor, there are conservatives who are attempting to maintain things the way they were, and uppity newcomers who want to adapt, change, and blend.

In any case, it is interesting to look back into the fiddling heyday of the 1920s and to the lives and music of some of the early recorded fiddlers. Eck Robertson was one of the first fiddle players and country musicians to be recorded commercially. He fiddled "Sally Goodin" and "Arkansas Traveler" for Victor records in 1922.

"Blackberry pie and huckleberry puddin'
I'd give it all up just to see Sally Goodin."
— **traditional verse to tune**
of "Sally Goodin"

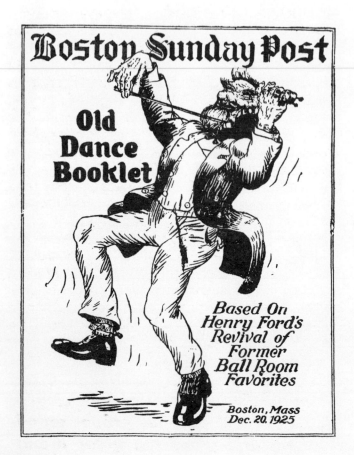

Boston Sunday Post

Old Dance Booklet

Based On Henry Ford's Revival of Former Ball Room Favorites

Boston, Mass Dec. 20. 1925

Earl Spielman interviewed "Eck" (Alexander Campbell) Robertson in 1969 when the fiddler was 82 years of age. Eck considered himself a Texas style fiddler and was familiar with other well known fiddlers such as Clayton McMichen, fiddlin' John Carson, and "Uncle" Jimmy Thompson. When asked how he first got to meet somebody who was in the recording business, Eck replied, "I met lots of musicians and lots of fiddlers and lots of lady musicians then, even. They all taken a liking to me like a hungry boy eating plums. Damn, I was the most popular dang fiddler ever was on the road. I could book any damn town I came to, didn't make any difference where it was." Eck described some experiences on the road: "You've got to have something about you that's different than the average fiddler does. Do everything that's in music. And show yourself up as being an expert. I've had people gather around me in crowds, where there'd be fifty people in one damn bunch in little towns I'd be in. I'd be playing the fiddle sitting out on the sidewalk, and they'd just keep gathering

together till there'd be maybe a hundred there. Quit their damn business, lots of them did, just to come and stick around me while I was playing, watching and listening to me play. Making records of my playing, some of them would."

Early recorded country music was termed "old-time music" by the radio stations and recording companies of the early 1920s according to National Archive researcher Guthrie T. Meade, Jr. The label has persisted to the present time for this kind of music which predates bluegrass styles. Even in the 1920s this music represented an earlier era but sprang from such diverse sources as British popular ballads, age old fiddle tunes, and songs comtemporary to the times. Much of it was drawn from minstrel and music hall songs of the late nineteenth century.

Following the first western recordings of Eck Robertson and Henry Gilliland were those of OKEY records in Atlanta with Fiddlin' John Carson and A. A. Gray in 1923. Columbia recorded Gid Tanner of "Skillet Licker" fame in 1924. The record companies began seeking out musicians who were well known in their communities and so recorded in many locations around the country.

A few of the fiddlers recorded in the early 1920s were past 70 years of age when they came into the studio. Examples are "Uncle" Am Stuart (born 1851), "Uncle" Jimmy Thompson (ca. 1843), Col. John A. Pattee (born 1844), Henry Gilliland (born before 1850), and Mellie Dunham (born 1853). Folk music researcher Norman Cohen points out that the fiddling of these older recorded performers, "represent our only direct documentation of what American folk fiddling sounded like prior to the urbanization and industrialization that commenced in earnest during reconstruction."

While writing the previous paragraph, I was moved to pull out my old scratchy 78 record of Uncle Am Stuart (Vocalion 14919). On the record were the tunes "Nigger in the Woodpile" and "George Boker." The accompaniment sounded like plectrum banjo rather than clawhammer or finger picking. From a traditionalist point of view, it would be reassuring to note that "Nigger in the Woodpile," a common dance tune, is played very similarly today by many fiddlers. Many musicians, however, have changed the name due to its connotation as a negative racist stereotype. While listening to the recording, I had an eerie sense of being taken back in history before the days of TV, radio, records, or electric lights. I felt a certain kinship to Uncle Am, having learned the tune the same way that he did, by hearing other musicians play it.

"Uncle" Jimmy Thompson was already around 80 years of age when he first performed on the month old radio station WSM in Nashville in 1925. Charles Wolfe describes what the scene was like:

> As Uncle Jimmy sits before the huge microphone with his flowing white beard and plays "Tennessee Waggoner":

> The switchboard lights up as calls for more flood the studio. Hay (of WSM Barn Dance) realizes that this rustic native of Martha, Tennessee, whose repertoire dates from the Civil War, has touched a nerve with the hill folk of Tennessee. Uncle Jimmy plays on and on, answering request after request. After an hour, Hay is afraid Uncle Jimmy is getting tired. But the fiddler replies, "Shucks, a man don't get warmed up in an hour."

He was an experienced fiddler at the time, having performed in vaudeville and numerous contests and had spent ten years in Texas absorbing the "long bow" style of playing. Only six recorded 78 RPM sides exist of his playing.

In 1925, Mellie Dunham of Maine, a favorite of industrialist Henry Ford, challenged Uncle Jimmy Thompson to a fiddle contest which was never held. A Boston newspaper article concluded: "The Maine fiddler takes exception to the crowning of Thompson as America's champion barn dance fiddler following a contest which lasted eight days in Dallas. 'He may have defeated 86 opponents in the Dallas contest,' declared Dunham today, 'but they were all southerners and they don't know as much about barn dance fiddling in that section as they do "down in Maine." I'm ready to meet any and all of them, but I'd rather like to meet Uncle Jimmy Thompson, who claims the title, first.'" Uncle Jimmy's famous reply to the challenger was that: "If Mellie Dunham will come down. . .I'll lay with him like a bulldog." Mellie (Alanson Mellen Dunham) was a farmer and snow shoe maker besides being a fiddler. Judging from the 78 RPM record I have ("Lady of the Lake" and "Mountain Rangers," Victor 19940) his playing is similar to much of present day contra dance fiddling with piano accompaniment.

Folk music scholar Paul Wells says of Mellie:

"Quite frankly, he was a fiddler of only average ability, and many other musicians felt that his fame was undeserved and that they could do as well or better." But fame he did have. Mellie Dunham, the maker of snow shoes used by Commodore Robert Perry in his North Pole expedition, played extensively around the eastern United States. After winning the title "Champion Fiddler of Maine," he visited Henry Ford in Michigan and embarked upon a series of vaudeville tours in Boston, New York City, and in other New England states. In appearance, he was described as a "sawed off Mark Twain," which was perfect for the part.

His fiddling brought attention to the New England fiddling tradition and he made four records for Victor in 1926. Other New England fiddlers to record on 78s soon afterward included Joe Shippee of Connecticut and John Wilder, Calvin Coolidge's uncle and leader of the "Plymouth, Vermont Old Time Barn Dance Orchestra."

When asked his age at an interview in 1930, "82, and I've got grown grandchildren, and great big great grandchildren runnin' cars and trucks yet, and a playin' the fiddle yet. And I love to look at a pretty woman just as much as I ever did."

— "Uncle" Jimmy Thompson
Tennessee Fiddle Champ 1926
WSM star (Devil's Box)

Uncle Bunt Stephens had been fiddling for almost 40 years in 1925 when word reached him about the series of fiddle contests being put on around the country by Henry Ford through his many dealerships. After winning a local contest, he joined twenty-five other local Tennessee champions to compete in Nashville. Uncle Bunt was one of the three finalists, placing third after Jimmy Thompson, second, and Marshall Claiborne, first, a one armed fiddler who held his bow between his knees.

These fiddlers went on to a contest in Louisville, Kentucky to meet state finalists from Kentucky and southern Indiana and to determine the "Champion of Dixie." These finalists, including Uncle Bunt, went on to Detroit where Uncle Bunt was given the title of "World Champion Fiddler." His masterpiece tune was "Old Hen Cackled," and his neighbors said he could make a cackling hen ashamed of herself when he imitated her with his fiddle. Henry Ford presented Bunt with a new Lincoln car, $1,000, a broadcloth suit of clothes, paid for his dental work, and entertained him in his house as a personal guest for a week.

Uncle Bunt appeared on the Grand Ole Opry and went to New York to record for Columbia. He recorded four sides, the only known recordings of his playing. The Columbia advertisement for his records read as follows:

> This is "Uncle Bunt" Stephens, champion fiddler of the world. The old adage warns us that uneasy lies the head that wears a crown. But not so "Uncle Bunt's." His heart is as light as the bright mountain dance music he plays. "Uncle Bunt's" title was recently won in a contest staged in Detroit by Henry Ford. An almost unbelievable number of fiddlers competed — one thousand, eight hundred and sixty five! "Uncle Bunt" is an exclusive Columbia artist. He makes his Columbia New Process Records with the fiddle that won him the championship.

"Fiddlin'" John Carson recorded nearly 150 selections for OKEY records between 1923 and 1931, including two dozen for RCA Victor. He was born in the Blue Ridge Mountains of Fannin County, Georgia in 1868. He was a race horse jockey in his teens, but as he became huskier he went to work for the Exposition Cotton Mill. After working there for twenty years, he became foreman, and then later worked as a house painter. During this time he was establishing a reputation as a fiddler, playing the fiddle that his grandfather had brought over from Ireland in a flour sack.

He was a frequent winner of the annual Atlanta contest, winning first place seven times between 1913 and 1922. He was one of the first country performers on radio and in 1922 after a performance on WSB, the Atlantic Journal commented:

> "Fiddlin'" John Carson, champion southern bowman, fresh from Fannin County and keyed up for the oldtime fiddler's convention in the auditorium September 28 and 29, is an institution in himself and his singing of "The Little Old Cabin in the Lane," and the playing of "Turkey in the Straw," "Old Joe Clark," and "The Old Hen Cackles," by Fiddlin' John and his four cronies. . .was enough to put any program over with a rush.

"Goin' up the road,
  whoopin' and a hollerin'
I got drunk on four cent cotton.

Woke up this morning,
  feeling kind of rotten,
I'd been drunk on four cent cotton.

Times is hard,
  they're getting kind of rotten,
Everybody's selling four cent cotton."
— **from the Skillet Lickers' tune**
"Four Cent Cotton"
County 506

Tip McKinney was a member of a String Band called "Pope's Arkansas Mountaineers," which was recorded in Memphis, Tennessee in February of 1928. He was interviewed in 1973 by Julie Hager and Jim Olin. Tip said that although he had known the other members of the band for a long time, they had only played together for "about 7 or 8 days," before the recording session. When asked about the tuning used on his guitar and mandolin picking on the records, he replied:

> We played in what they call "Italian" tuning, you know, where they tune 'em up. It was an altogether different tuning from what I ever done before. Guitar, fiddle, banjer, everything; all the instruments were tuned like this.
> We all tuned 'em up with the violin. And the feller that knowed about it, feller by the name of Sparrow. He knowed how it was tuned up. And my brother had quite a time tuning the banjo up with it. Some way or other Sparrow showed him how to do that. And the way we played nearly all of the pieces was in that Italian tuning. But it would sound out all right. That man that recorded those records said that was music like he had never heard. That's what he said.

Learning to Fiddle

Tip described some of his early experiences with music:

See, they'd have an old "stomp down," they'd call it. That's an old square dance. Come by and holler, "Are you all comin' out to the stomp down tonight at so and so's house?" That's the way it was. They'd go for miles and miles around, don't you see.

It was kind of amazing to watch 'em when I was just a boy, but after I got to be a pretty good-sized young fella, I learned to call sets and things like that and I learned to dance.... Some of the fiddlers was "jig' fiddlers," you know. They cut their music up a whole lots. I call them "jig' fiddlers." Then they got some that's good smooth violin players. That's the kind of man that plays the violin right, like it ought to be played—any time....

The best violin players that we had in this here county could make a violin. They made their own violins. Make as good a fiddle as you ever looked at. There was a feller by the name of Jim Manis. He could play "Leather Breeches" and put four parts to it:

"Leather britches, leather britches,
buckled on behind
wife kicked me out of bed
cause I had my leather britches on..."

...That's the way the old tune went, you know. Well, he was the only violin player I ever heard that could put four parts to that tune. Every one of them Manis's could play the violin—and the girls, too. Them girls could rear down on a violin and make it talk.

There were, of course, many other colorful characters in the early days of recorded fiddle music. I've included just a small sample. Within the last few years, many of these early recordings on 78 rpm records have been reissued as anthologies on modern $33\frac{1}{3}$ rpm albums. Check my record review section for more information.

Charles Wolfe has studied this period of fiddle music extensively and readers interested in learning more should read his articles in *Devil's Box*, his *Tennessee Strings* book, or various record album liner notes, such as those for "Nashville—The Early String Bands, Volume 1 & 2" on County Records, numbers 541 and 542.

B. Sullivan

Swedish Fiddle Music
by Matt Fichtenbaum

Matt Fichtenbaum is an authority on traditional Swedish music, a fine instrument builder, and an accomplished musician in the Boston area. I've listened with interest to his workshops and radio broadcasts, and have danced to his playing at Swedish and New England country dances. The following article is a composite of two pieces he wrote for the Eisteddfod and New England Folk festivals.

TRADITIONAL SWEDISH FOLK MUSIC, going back to the 1500s, is primarily fiddle music. The keyed fiddle, or nyckelharpa, is most associated with the Swedish province of Uppland, north of Stockholm; other folk instruments found in Sweden include the cow's horn, the spilåpipa (a wooden flute resembling the pennywhistle), and the clarinet. This folk music is largely workers' and peasants' music: it was important for the weekly dances in the farm and industrial societies; and for various ceremonial events—weddings, midsummer, Christmas, etc.

At the beginning of the 1900s the old folk music became less popular: people moved to the cities and became more interested in band music played by professionals, and less interested in their own music. Nowadays interest in the old musical traditions is strong in Sweden, and many people participate in this revival, learning to play instruments and forming musicians' groups to play at festivals and for folk dances.

Two hundred years ago, the *spelman* was the center of Swedish music. On the farms and in the villages, he provided the music for Midsummer and Christmas celebrations, for parties and weddings, for church services and Saturday night dances. The village fiddler's position was a respected one, his profession was his music, and he sometimes did not take kindly to amateurs making music. Nonetheless,

music was the avocation of many a farmer or blacksmith, and a worker who was quick with his instrument was often encouraged to play for his fellow workers rather than help out.

There was always something magic and supernatural associated with the good fiddlers. Some had learned their fiddling from the Devil himself, by a stream under a bridge at midnight. Others carried some long-dead musician's finger bone in a little bag at their waist, or used it for a fiddle sound-post. Legendary keyed-fiddler Byss-Kalle encountered another fiddler at a wedding; the other, taking offense at the competition, played a few notes and all the hair fell from Byss-Kalle's bow. Fortunately, Kalle had a spare bow along, and when he then played, the other's keyed fiddle broke into pieces and fell to the floor.

Even some tunes have magical qualities—best known is Horgalåten, said to be the devil's tune. If played long enough, this polska puts dancers and musicians alike under a spell, and they cannot stop dancing and playing. Unless someone comes in and cuts the fiddle strings, the unfortunates will dance and play themselves to death. In the village of Horga, which gives the tune its name, there is a mountain with a ring-shaped gully in the rock. This is all that's left of the dancers' last long night.

Tune Types

There are several different tune types, among them gånglåt (pronounced GONG-lote) or walking tune, polka, schottis, vals (waltz), and polska. The name "polska" really denotes two different dances: the eighth-note, or hambo, polska with strongly marked 3/4 beat; and the sixteenth-note polska (slängpolska, or turning polska) with a more even beat. (Don't confuse either form of polska with the polka, which is a 2/4 rhythm.) Some tunes are associated with special occasions, such as the brudmarsch (bridal march), and the skänklåt (gift-giving tune, pronounced SHENK-lote), both associated with weddings.

The origins of the tunes are as varied as the tunes themselves. The shepherdesses' old horn-calls provided inspirations. Classical music from the European continent was overheard by folk musicians and incorporated into their repertoires in the familiar dance-tune form. Fiddlers might wake with a tune in their heads, or hear some sounds in nature and preserve them in a ganglat. When younger people spent time with an old spelman to learn to play they'd also learn his tunes, and thus a rich musical "oral tradition" developed.

Styles

Playing styles depend on both the type of tune and the particular region in Sweden from which a tune comes. Regions, and even individual villages, have their own musical and dance "dialects," and the rhythmic subtleties and musical ornamentation for the same tune as played in two different villages can be very different. It is believed that, in olden times, each village had its own "great fiddler," and this fiddler's individual style, emulated by other local fiddlers, became that village's style. These style differences are most evident in rhythm (when the "2" beat comes in a polska, for example), and bowing.

Bowing

Some bowing patterns are characteristic to the various tune types. The duple-meter "shuffle" pattern has groups of four sixteenth-notes, with the first two slurred and the next two individually bowed; this is common to walking tunes and sixteenth-note polskas. The eighth-note hambo polska rhythm, a 3/4-beat pattern, consists of a down-bow on "1," an up-bow on "2," and both a down-bow and an up-bow on "3." The result is a down-bow on the first and third beats, bringing the rhythm forth very clearly. Different regional dialects of this polska have different rhythmic emphases, one very common variant makes the "3" beat a little long, which makes the final up-bow very short.

Harmonies

Fifty years ago, when two or more fiddlers played together, some would play melody while the others accompanied, using the fiddle to play chords. This simple accompaniment brought out the music's rhythm and gave a fullness beyond that of the melody alone. In more recent tradition, the harmony or "second" part is no longer chording but instead is a melody in its own right. This second part is almost always improvised, not composed or arranged in advance. Harmonies typically include thirds, sixths, and octaves from the melody; arpeggios on the appropriate chord, occasional unisons, and fragments of counterpoint. Whatever the notes of the second part are, the bowing, and thus the underlying rhythm, closely follow those of the melody.

Tunes usually consist of two, three or four sections. Commonly each section is played twice, and the whole tune is repeated two or three times if played for the music, or as long as necessary if played for dancing.

Some Swedish fiddle and keyed-fiddle records are available in the U.S. These are:

Folk Fiddling from Sweden - (Nonesuch H-72033) Björn Ståbi and Ole Hjorth came to the Newport Folk Festival in 1969 and recorded this album while here. Lots of twin-fiddle harmonies, but not as lively as some of the other records.

Authentic Swedish Fiddle Music from Boda Village - (Vanguard SRV 73016, also available as Sonet 740.) A Vanguard release of a Swedish record (jacket text in English). Two, three, or four fiddles; and a zither. Excellent. (Also found in Swedish, as "Latar fran Laggar Anders Kök.")

Fiddle Music from Sweden: Uppland - (Philo 2017) Two keyed fiddles, although you'd never know from the title. A Philo release of a Swedish record, and about the only keyed fiddle music available here.

The American Swedish Spelmans Trio - (Rounder 6004) Edwin Johnson, who emigrated from Sweden in 1919, and two of his descendants play tunes in an older style (chording harmonies, etc.).

The Dancing Bow - (Sonet 201) A good two-record anthology of music from Sweden's different provinces, compiled from other records (i.e., the keyed fiddle music comes from the Philo record). Distributed through Rounder.

Three Swedish Fiddlers - (Shanachie 21001) An excellent, listenable collection of tunes for two or three fiddles. this is a Shanachie release of a Swedish record called "Tre Spelmän." Buy this one!

Gathering at Delsbo — the Swedish Fiddlers - (Folkways 8471) A Swedish field recording from a "Spelmansstämma," or fiddlers' festival. Good music in an informal atmosphere.

Bockfot! - (Musical Heritage MHS 3571) This is a release of a Swedish record recorded live at a coffeehouse in Stockholm. The jacket text is in English and the commentary on the record is in Swedish. Björn Ståbi and Pers Hans play outstanding one- and two-fiddle music. Musical Heritage Society is in New York City, and distributes its own records.

Norsk Ltd., 800 Linden Avenue, Boulder, CO 80302 sells, by mail order, a good selection of Swedish and Norwegian records, and will furnish a list upon request (of course, the jackets are in Swedish or Norwegian). Roundup Records (the mail-order division of Rounder), P.O. Box 147, East Cambridge, MA 02141, carries many of the smaller labels. Alcazar, RD #2, Box 82, Waterbury, VT 05676, also distributes a number of them, including some of the records of the Faeroese group "Spaelimenninir i Hoydølum."

Pronunciation

    å o as in *boat*, without the diphthong
    ä e as in *get*, or somewhat more open
    ö o as in *work*, without the r
k or sk before e, i, o, ä is pronounced *ch*.

Tunes

The following pages include a selection of dance tunes—schottis, hambo, långdans (long, or walking dance), waltz, walking tunes, and ceremonial tunes. Where bowings are indicated, they are suggestions that help bring out the tune's rhythm. Keep in mind that the written music gives only the skeleton of a tune, and that the character is best learned through careful listening. Happy fiddling!

Långdans from Sollerön, Dalarna (Swedish)

Svensk — Anna's Waltz (Swedish)

Skänklat from Dala-Järna — Gift Giving Tune (Swedish)

Långdans from Småland (Swedish)

Schottis efter Storbo Jöns (Swedish)

Reinlander (Norwegian)

Karis Pers Polska — Hambo (Swedish)

Gånglåt efter Hjort-Anders — Walking Tune (Swedish)

Rättvikarnas Gånglåt — Walking Tune (Swedish)

Slågpolska from Småland (Swedish)

Vårvindar Frisca — Hambo (Swedish)

Fiddle Contests

IT'S SUMMER AND TIME for the country fair. The announced events include a fiddle contest and you eagerly make your way to the staging area. Not having been to many fiddle contests before, you are going now with a new perspective. You are learning to play fiddle and so are attending an event where you know that there will be other fiddlers to watch and learn from. Getting yourself a seat close to the stage, you can see several fiddlers to the back and sides of the stage warming up.

The M.C. welcomes the crowd and announces the start of the contest, and explains the rules: There will be two categories, Junior and Open. Each contestant is to play a waltz, a hoedown, and a tune of choice. First are the juniors. An eleven year old sets up on the stage and plays her three tunes, slow and scratchy, but trying hard. Her sister, a year older, plays her tunes faster and smoother. A fifteen year old boy plays very fast and fancy, better you think, than most fiddlers that you have heard before.

Several different people in the open division play. The first contestant plays at a relatively slow pace, and with much vibrato, like a violinist. Another plays with much shuffling of the bow, not as smooth as the first, but the music makes you want to tap your feet. The third person plays a fast tune, and a fancy waltz, and ends with "The Orange Blossom Special." The crowd goes wild; you find yourself clapping hard while the folks next to you are yelling for more. A couple of seemingly average fiddle players follow.

A bluegrass band comes on the stage to do a set so that the judges can tally up the score. Finally the band ends up with a gospel number and the M.C. calls out the names of the winners and asks them to the stage. The prizes are presented. In the Junior category, first place goes to the older of the two sisters. The persons behind you whisper that the fifteen year old played much better, and why didn't he win? In the open division, first place goes to one of the last fiddlers to play, someone whom you hardly noticed, and the person who played "The Orange Blossom Special" and brought the crowd to its feet only got third place. Did the judges make a mistake? How did they reach their decision?

For the answer, let's look inside of fiddle contests. For a start, the criteria which judges use in a contest vary widely from contest to contest. Why is this? Isn't it fairly easy to tell the really good fiddlers from those who are not so good? The simple truth is that if you ask several different people who their favorite fiddler is, you will probably get several answers. If you press them a bit for who they think is the "best," their answer may change and be qualified with a comment like, "if you mean, who can play the fanciest, I guess X would qualify, but then I don't know anyone who can keep time like Y."

Experienced fiddlers themselves disagree about what is "good" fiddling. What it finally gets down to is that fiddling has no universal standards. Because there are so many diverse styles of playing, there is no "right" way. But wait, you say, if there is no right way, how did the judges select the winners? Simple,

the judges had their own personal standards and likes which they applied in determining the winners.

They may have been biased against fast tunes such as the one that fifteen year old played in the Junior category, or "bluegrass" tunes such as "The Orange Blossom Special." They may have given top honors to those fiddlers who played in the best "danceable" style. That is, the type of tune and style of playing best suited for country dancing. In another contest a different set of winners might have come away with the trophies.

Lynn Shaw, a fine fiddler from North Carolina who has won many fiddling awards, has retired from competition because "you can't judge a style of music.... Fiddling contests are becoming a place for trick fiddlers who pack a song full of notes and lose the melody line," Shaw said. "In a race you can tell who won, but in a fiddler's contest there are a million ways to play the notes.... Fiddling is an art form, like painting," he added, "Could you imagine a painting contest between Leonardo DaVinci and Michelangelo?"

That sums up one opinion pretty well, but there are other sides to the issue. Various fiddling organizations work diligently at maintaining a sort of "quality control" over the type of fiddling they promote. Anyone who has traveled around the country to different fiddle contests or events has seen and heard the wide differences in styles. There are large regional differences in styles, and within these, accepted ways to play. Where in one area extra melody notes are penalized, in another they may be necessary to win a contest.

All of these differences of opinion help keep fiddle music exciting and lively. I was once witnessing an argument by two fiddle players about which of two styles was "better" fiddling. A third person, a non fiddler, stepped in and exclaimed, "It's all fiddle music regardless, and I like it all."

Most styles of traditional fiddling developed as music for dancing. As you know, there are many styles of dancing, and so the fiddling follows suit. Waltzes demand a slower tempo, and a particular 3/4 time beat. Hornpipes used to be played slower than most fiddlers play them today. That's because they were originally played for people who were dancing hornpipes.

Hardly anyone dances hornpipes today, and so these melodies became faster and thus suitable for square and contra dancing, and more recently even faster and fancier still for bluegrass bands. Reels, hoedowns, or breakdowns, whichever you wish to call them, have always been played rapidly, but the speed often increases when they are played for listeners rather than dancers. In fact, one of the major distinctions between "traditional" fiddling and the more modern "bluegrass" fiddling is that bluegrass is primarily "listening" music, whereas traditional fiddling was (and is) primarily used for dancing.

Of course both fiddling and dancing are evolving and changing as time goes by. Appalachian style "clogging", "buckdancing," or "flatfooting" to traditional square dance tunes is recently evolving into much fancier team style exhibition dancing which is done primarily to bluegrass style music. Bluegrass music got ahead of the dancers for a few years, but is now becoming the music of choice as clog dancing traditions evolve. Unfortunately for fiddlers, however, some of the more progressive clogging teams are bypassing traditional music in favor of rock and popular music.

Bluegrass fiddling itself is evolving as more players are adding techniques from jazz music. Some "traditional" fiddlers dislike bluegrass because "it sounds too modern," yet now that bluegrass has been around for forty-five years or so, some people who prefer bluegrass are complaining that bluegrass itself is becoming too modern, as it evolves into jazz-like music. So now we hear about people who would like to preserve "traditional" bluegrass.

It seems that as fiddling traditions evolve, each new style attracts followers who strive to keep that particular tradition alive. This helps keep the music going in many directions and gives us (the fiddlers and the listeners) a wide choice of styles to choose from and enjoy. Personally, I like many different styles of fiddling, but like every fiddler, I find that some kinds are more interesting and fun to play than others.

Fiddle contests tend to reflect the fiddling preferences of the folks who organize them, and so the criteria for winning varies widely around the country. Many contest officials, however, recognize that there are diverse styles of fiddling, and so they require that the contestant play a variety of styles. Typically, a waltz (3/4 time), a hoedown (2/4 time), and a tune of choice (neither a waltz nor a hoedown) is required. Fiddlers often play jigs, rags or schottisches as tunes of choice. Each of the three tunes for the contest demand different skills and abilities from the fiddler. (See the contest rules included in this book.)

Some of the larger contests place the judges behind a screen so that they can't see the players. Others even interrupt the sound to the judges when the fiddler's name is called, so that all the judge hears is the music. Audience applause is also blocked out.

I've judged a number of contests myself and find it very difficult to be completely objective. It's harder than grading term papers for the college courses that

I've taught. Sometimes a judge is confronted with several or more fiddlers, all excellent, and all playing very different styles, for example: Southern Appalachian, French Canadian, and Texas style. Three equally good term papers can each get an A. In a fiddle contest, somebody has to get 1st, 2nd, and 3rd. Fortunately, there are usually several judges, so that the various preferences are averaged out somewhat.

In some contests there is an interesting stigma attached to the playing of fiddle tunes which are not "old enough," or "traditional." Many judges will disallow tunes which do not meet these somewhat ambiguous criteria. I am reminded of an "old time" fiddle contest for which I served as a judge in 1979. One of the entrants, Mr. Clem Meyers, an exceptionally fine Northeast fiddler, asked me prior to the contest whether of not he could play one of his own compositions. After I replied in the affirmative, he proceeded to play a tune which he announced to the audience as being an original tune composed in 1939. Isn't forty years "old enough"? Apparently not to some, as Delores "Fiddling De" De Ryke writes:

> "Orange Blossom Special" cannot be played by a true old time fiddler until at least 1988—and most will never accept it as old time fiddling material. As a novelty tune after 1988—perhaps—but we adhere strictly to a 50 year rule. A tune must be 50 years old before we consider playing it — and the stricter fiddlers play nothing developed since 1911.

FIDDLE CONTEST - No Entry Fee

A DAY OF
TRADITIONAL
MUSIC

SATURDAY
SEPTEMBER 10
1983

✴✴✴✴ fourth annual ✴✴✴✴

Banjo & Fiddle Contests

12 Noon, Market Mills Summer Stage, Lowell, MA.

"Among bluegrass fiddlers a bizarre evolutionary trend has been noted wherein, through a process of natural selection a brand new species is emerging. On stage the typical specimen becomes totally absorbed in the production of endless variations, contusions, and abrasions of a monumental banality called the 'Orange Blossom Special,' a tune which has been so overplayed that no one even refers to it by name anymore, but simply by its initials."
— **John Burke,**
The Old Hat Band, California
(9th Annual San Diego State Folk Festival Program)

In recent years, many large contests have discontinued the "1911 rule," but as late as 1977 I was prohibited from playing a "rag" at a large Northeast contest even though none of the designated "fiddle tune experts" could document the age of the particular tune that I wished to play. Of course many experienced fiddlers including myself compose their own tunes, and some even publish collections of original material. Many fiddlers who compose tunes tend to keep them close to traditional styles, though.

Part of the reason that some traditionalists complain about the tune "The Orange Blossom Special" is that it has more fiddle pyrotechnics and "flash" than most traditional tunes. The bowing patterns involved, which some label as a "double shuffle," are outlawed in most fiddle contests no matter what the tune is that uses them. Aside from contests, of course, the tune is very popular with the general public. I played it every night, six days a week, for months when I was on tour with a country rock band. Audiences always wanted to hear it. I'll admit that it was fun to play, as we went faster and faster to the drummer's top speed.

The Folk Arts Center of New England, Inc., presents the

6th Annual
NEW ENGLAND

Dance
Fiddlers'
Contest

Saturday
October 31, 1981
Concord, Mass.
Produced by Donna Hinds

"The Orange Blossom Special" was first recorded on June 16, 1939 (Bluebird B-8218) with musicians Ervin Rouse (vocal and fiddle) and Gordie Rouse (vocal and guitar). Ervin Rouse wrote the words, but Chubby Wise also claims authorship of the tune. The name itself referred to a train which ran from Miami to New York. Many contests now have a separate category for "bluegrass" in which the "OBS" can be played, although at some contests I've attended, it had to be played in the "Trick and Fancy" category.

Fiddle contests can be a lot of fun, especially if you go with the attitude that it doesn't matter if you win or not. Most people who attend fiddle contests love fiddling and are very supportive of the fiddlers who play, even of the beginners.

If you are interested in winning a prize, it helps to know who the judges are, and their likes and dislikes in fiddling. Fiddling contests are evolving and changing as fiddling styles evolve. The National Old-time Fiddle Contest in Weiser, Idaho has recently added a "Men's" category in addition to the "Grand Champion" division, partly in response to the trend among some of the younger virtuoso fiddlers to play jazzier, flashier versions of traditional tunes.

By adding another category there are more chances for fiddlers who excel at either the newer or older "Weiser winning" styles to win a prize. This is significant when you realize that the total prize money for the 1984 contest was over $11,000.

The type of fiddling that wins at Weiser, however, is different than that which would win at the "National Traditional Old Time Fiddler's Contest" in Barre, Vermont. Still different is the style of fiddling that one might hear at the large Union Grove Old Time Fiddler's Contest in North Carolina. I've had the experience many times of hearing exceptionally fine fiddlers who failed to win anything because they were playing the "wrong style" for a particular set of judges.

The late Benny Thomasson, who was 1st place winner at Weiser in 1974 and at the Crockett, Texas "World Championships" in 1955, 1956, and 1957, never played professionally, although he could play along with the best. In his many years of fiddling he noticed how contest rules changed over time. When Stacy Phillips asked him about tricks that fiddlers used to impress judges, he replied,

> Old Eck Robertson, he'd play a tune, he'd sing along with it. That was his deal. There were more fiddlers that came around later that did "(Listen to) The Mockingbird" and they'd put birds and all that stuff into it. Made it real nice, I liked it. Of course the judges didn't like it 'cause it was getting so far ahead of the guys that never did it. Before cross tuning went out, now they retuned fiddles. When I was a young fellow most everybody crosstuned.
>
> But when it got to later years the younger ones came up that didn't cross-tune, they were raising cane about it, you know, and stopped all cross-tuning. There were certain pretty powerful fiddlers who didn't cross-tune. They didn't want no one else to, because it sounds so much better, you see.
>
> I can play either way as far as it goes. Major Franklin was one that would stomp you to death if you would. (laughs) They'd come around and thump (pluck) your fiddle to see if you had it cross-tuned. "Black Mountain Rag" and stuff like that, show tunes, they finally cut that out.
>
> (*Contest Fiddling*, by Stacy Phillips)

"Susanna Gal"

"I'd rather my son be a happy fiddler than an unhappy engineer."
— **Tex Logan, PhD mathematician and fiddler with Lilly Brothers and many other bands (Frets)**

Fiddling Do's and Don'ts

There will be four divisions. Fiddlers will enter the Senior, Junior or Open Division according to their age. (Junior--16 and under; Senior--60 and over; Open--everyone else) In these divisions, each fiddler will play a waltz, a hoedown, and a tune of choice in that order. The Trick and Fancy Division is open to all fiddlers, regardless of age. Any tunes may be played in the Trick and Fancy Division.

The judges will listen to the contestants through a separate sound system in a remote area. They will not know the names of the fiddlers. They will judge each tune separately, using the following criteria and point system.

1. RHYTHM & TIMING--25 points--The ability to set and maintain a steady, danceable tempo, with no unevenness, breaks in rhythm or dropped beats. Extra beats or measures are allowed if they are part of the tune as traditionally played. Dotted notes or syncopation, when appropriate to the tune, are also allowed.

2. CLARITY & TONE--25 points--Notes should be played clearly, on pitch, with good tone. Avoid running notes together in a fuzzy or in- distinct manner. Good tone does not mean soun- ding like a concert violinist, but at the same time, tone should not be harsh or unpleasant.

3. OLD TIME ABILITY--25 points--The ability to play danceable music in a traditional manner in good taste. The fiddler must have a basic res- pect for the structure of the tune and for the tradition or style of the tune's source. Any variations should enhance the distinctive flavor of the tune, not obscure or detract from it. REMEMBER! The tune must be danceable. The diffi- culty of the tune will also be considered.

4. EXPRESSION--25 points-- The ability to move the listener or dancer by putting something of one's own personality into the music. The tasteful use of ornamentation, phrasing and dynamics. "What- ever it is in a beautifully played, slow waltz that makes people want to cry; whatever it is in a lively tune that makes them feel happy." (Vivian Williams, Seattle, former Women's Na- tional Champion)

Over, Please......

We of the Northeast Fiddlers' Association, cordially invite you to attend our Seventeenth Annual Traditional Old-Time Fiddlers' Contest.

Open to all fiddlers in the United States and Canada. The winner of this contest becomes the 1984 National Champion of Traditional old time fiddling.

The ultimate goal of the Association is the preservation and promotion of all arts and skills pertaining strictly to *"Old Time Fiddling."*

Being one of the largest organizations in the U.S. today dedicated solely to *"Old Time Fiddling,"* we feel it is our responsibility, duty and privilege to provide the public with an opportunity to share and enjoy the type of music handed down generation after generation, in its original form.

Attending the contest is without a doubt the best opportunity ever devised by the organization for you to hear and enjoy *"Old Time Fiddling"* at its best, and to become involved with the true meaning of music that played so important a role in our American heritage.

Recognized as the "Granite Center of the World," Barre is located in north central Vermont on U.S. 302, (or Exit 7) of I-89, six miles from the state capitol in Montpelier. At contest time, the center of attraction becomes the Barre Auditorium, a spacious building, situated on Seminary Hill. It provides a seating capacity of 3,000 persons. A well lighted and tastefully decorated stage induces a relaxed atmosphere, adding to your enjoyment of the well balanced and skillfully controlled sound system.

A stepdancing contest was introduced as an added attraction for your enjoyment in 1982, and will be featured again this year. Dancing has always been a part of fiddling and should attract many performers. This is an art that will provide much excitment with their footwork to try to win this division.

GENERAL REQUIREMENTS

FOR CONTESTANTS

This is an old time fiddle contest and old time rules will prevail.

Contestants must play — 1. Waltz; 2. A tune of choice; and 3. A hoe down IN THAT ORDER in each round. A hoe down will be considered any tune used for square dancing — other than a jig, schottische, rag or polka. A tune of choice can be any fiddle tune other than a hoe down or a tune played in ¾ time.

Contestants will be judged on old time ability, rhythm, timing, expression and clarity.

A total of four minutes will be allowed for each appearance. Due to the growing number of contestants each year this rule will be strictly enforced.

Upon receipt of entry fee, contestants will be mailed a complete set of contest rules.

Professional fiddlers will not be allowed in the Old Time part of the contest. For the purposes of this contest, a professional is one who earns more than 50% of his annual income by fiddling.

No contact microphones or amplified instruments allowed during contest play.

Contestants may play with an accompanist or with no more than two, as he chooses.

Contestant must stand well in front of the accompanist while performing.

Fiddler must lead at all times. Accompanying instrument shall pick or play only rhythm.

At registration, all contestants shall draw for initial order of appearance for the first preliminary round of each contest being entered. Contestants in future rounds will draw before each round for new order of appearance. CONTESTANTS MUST BE READY TO PLAY WHEN CALLED.

Judges will be Certified members of "The North American Old-Time Fiddling Judges, Inc." They are authorized and qualified adjudicators of traditional fiddle music.

NATIONAL OLDTIME FIDDLERS' CONTEST

Weiser, Idaho 83672

Third Full Week in June

GENERAL INFORMATION

PURPOSE—The original and continuing purpose of the National Oldtime Fiddlers' Contest is to help perpetuate the oldtime fiddling of pioneer America; to help develop a more genuine audience appreciation, understanding and participation; to preserve the oldtime fiddling tunes; to develop and encourage oldtime fiddlers' jam sessions and contest; to permanently record and display the history, relics and mementos of past oldtime fiddlers' art; and to acknowledge the present-day oldtime fiddlers who are helping to preserve the traditional expressions.

CONTESTS—Seven Contests--GRAND CHAMPION, SENIOR, MEN, LADIES, JUNIOR, JUNIOR-JUNIOR, and SMALL FRY Contest conducted annually. Contestants must be a resident of North America. (Rules available for specific information regarding each Contest.)

JUDGING—Judging will be done by five (5) qualified judges and the high and low scores for each contestant at each appearance will not be used in calculating total points. Judging will be done by remote and no judge can see any contestant or hear an introduction or commentary. Contestant is identified only by number.

STOP WATCH—Stop watch will be used in the judging room to enable strict enforcement of the four minute rule.

CERTIFIED CONTESTS—The National Fiddlers' Certification and Advisory Council, with members from states throughout the nation, certifies local, regional and state contests that qualify. There are many advantages to being certified. Complete information available from the above Council, c/o Chamber of Commerce, Weiser, Idaho 83672. Please notify us of any contests in your area that would like to be certified and complete information will be sent.

NATIONAL FIDDLERS' HALL OF FAME—It pays tribute and honors oldtime fiddlers of renown and Certified Contest winners throughout the nation. It has established an archives of oldtime fiddling tunes, fiddling papers, notes, and books; to be preserved for future generations. Old fiddles, fiddle mementos and pictures of honored fiddlers are on display. If you have any fiddling relics, mementos, recorded tunes, or information you wish to donate, please contact our committee, c/o Chamber of Commerce, Weiser, Idaho 83672.

PARADE—This is strictly an "oldtime parade" held on Saturday each year. In keeping with the general aims of our Contest, which is to perpetuate and promote oldtime fiddling, to collect and preserve authentic relics and mementos of the past; we are urging individuals and groups to restore and preserve antique items in the area as a continuing program. Fiddlers and other participants are invited to enter "oldtime" floats. Prizes are awarded in different categories.

DRESS—In keeping with the theme and purpose of the Contest, everyone is urged to wear "oldtime" dress of pioneer America. Prizes are awarded on this basis. However, since western dress is customary in this community, it will be acceptable if "oldtime" dress is not possible. Persons wearing beach wear, shorts, or sun wear will feel "out of place." Dressy clothing is urged for all evening performances.

TICKETS—A registered fiddler will receive one pass for personal use plus one guest pass. These passes will allow them entrance into all the shows, except Saturday, when tickets must be purchased. A registered Junior-Junior and Small Fry fiddler will receive one pass for personal use. A Junior-Junior and Small Fry may purchase one Parent Pass if they so desire.

NOTE—All questions, decisions and plans will be governed by the over-all committee on the basis of our Purpose.

NATIONAL OLDTIME FIDDLERS' CONTEST

GENERAL CONTEST RULES
Amended 1983

(Apply to National Grand Champion, Senior, Men, Ladies, Junior, Junior-Junior, Small Fry Contests)

1. Entry blank must be completed and entry fee paid before June 1 to avoid late fee. Exception may be granted for due cause upon request to the Contest Chairman. We need pre-registrations to more effectively run the program. Money will be refunded to anyone who paid entry fee and cannot attend, if they inform the committee of withdrawal prior to the contest's beginning.

2. All commercial recording rights are reserved and shall become the property of the Weiser Chamber of Commerce, the non-profit and legal entity for the National Oldtime Fiddlers' Contest Committee. Signing of registration for the Contest shall waive such rights.

3. The fiddle committee officials will randomly select the initial order of appearance for the first preliminary round. Judging Chairman in future rounds will draw before each round for new order of appearance. Announcements will be made of the drawings, and contestants must be ready to play when called. Any contestant registered and not playing will be eliminated from next year's Contest. Contestant's badge and guest badge will be revoked for remainder of this year's Contest.

4. Any accompanist registered and not accompanying a contesting fiddler on stage during at least one of the fiddlers rounds during the Contest will not be allowed to register as an accompanist for next year's Contest. Accompanist's badge will be revoked for remainder of this year's Contest.

5. Contestants at each appearance must first play a hoedown; second, a waltz, and third, a tune of their choice **other than** a hoedown or waltz. No tune shall be played more than once during all appearances of a contestant. Four minute playing time will be strictly adhered to. Ten points will be deducted from total score for each 30 second interval or portion thereof.

6. If string breaks, the FIDDLER will have the option to continue or stop at that point. If the tune is completed it will be judged as played. If the fiddler stops play he will be allowed to begin with that tune and complete his program.

7. Contestants may play without accompanist or with not more than two, but may register only one.

8. Any danceable folk tunes played in oldtime fiddle fashion are acceptable.

9. Contact microphones and amplified instruments will not be permitted.

10. No trick or fancy fiddling allowed during the contesting appearances. No cross tuning on stage.

11. No sheet music shall be displayed in the contesting area.

12. Judging will be scored for oldtime fiddling style, danceability, rhythm or timing, and tone quality. Scores will be accumulative commencing with round one. Points will be deducted for any violation of the above rules, No. 5 through 10 (inclusive).

13. Any contestant winning three consecutive years in the Grand National Division must either judge next year's Contest or sit out the next year's Contest.

14. Any contestant winning three consecutive years in the Senior, Men, Ladies and Junior divisions automatically move into the Grand National Division. Any Junior-Junior winning three consecutive times will automatically move into the Junior Division. Any Small Fry winning three consecutive times will automatically move into the Junior-Junior Division.

15. Any protest must be submitted in writing to the Contest Chairman, and signed by not less that three contestants of the Contest involved, within three hours of protest occurrence.

16. All decisions of the Judges and of the Contest Committee will be final.

SPECIAL CONTEST RULES
Contestants may enter only one of the following contests:

NATIONAL: 1. Contestants, open to all regardless of age. **6 Rounds**
2. Contestants may be of either sex.

SENIOR: 1. Contestants must be at least 65 years of age. **4 Rounds**
2. Contestants may be of either sex.

MEN: 1. Contestants must be at least 18 years of age. **4 Rounds**
2. Contestants — Men only.

LADIES: 1. Contestants must be at least 18 years of age. **4 Rounds**
2. Contestants — Ladies only.

JUNIOR: 1. Contestants must be less than 18 years of age. **4 Rounds**
2. Contestants may be of either sex.

JUNIOR-JUNIOR: 1. Contestants must be less than 13 years of age. **3 Rounds**
2. Contestants may be of either sex.

SMALL FRY: 1. Contestants must be less than 9 years of age. **2 Rounds**
2. Contestants may be of either sex.

A General Listing of Sources
for Records, Books, Supplies, Instruments, Repairs, etc.

Editor's notes:

An independent record label company produces its own records. Some of these companies only sell the records that they produce, others sell their own records plus those of other companies. Some firms produce their own records and also sell records, books, instruments and musical supplies from other companies. Some outfits sell all of the above yet don't produce their own records. Some firms also offer instrument repair and retail outlets. Some companies offer mail order services, some don't.

I've lumped all of the above into two categories: "Folk-Oriented Record Labels with Fiddling," and "A General Listing of Sources for Records, Books, Supplies, Instruments, Repairs, etc." The listing of record labels is only a sample of the many small labels that offer fiddle music. The general sources listing is also only a partial listing, yet includes most of the best known distributors of folk music supplies in the U.S., and a few of the violin shops and dealers that are known to me.

These listings are intended to be informational only, and not an endorsement of any of the firms listed.

Kenway Records - Rt. 1, Box 395, Milner, GA 30257, c/o K.W. Jones. "Hard to find country and bluegrass records." (404) 227-8981.

Record Revival - 7121 W. Vickery #118, Fort Worth, TX 76121. Records for collectors, books, reviews.

Records by Mail - PO Box 120478, Nashville, TN 37212. Dealer in 45s, albums, tapes.

Dave Cook - 303 Elm Street, Crawford, NE 69339. Records for collectors. Send for current auction list containing many bluegrass records from the 1950s, mention if you collect 78s, 45s, or LPs.

Bob Fuller, Old Time Country Music Club of Canada - 1421 Gohier Street, St. Saurent, Quebec, Canada H4L 3K2. Records, books, magazines. (514) 748-7251.

Elderly Instruments - PO Box 14210 BR, Lansing, MI 48901. Free catalogues. Fiddle records, supplies in the folk music vein. They carry many of the books I've listed. (517) 372-7890.

Alcazar - Box 429, Dept. BSR, Waterbury, VT 05676. $1.00 refundable with 1st order catalogue of independent label records and books, over 5,000 titles, fiddle records, and many of the books I've listed. (800) 244-5178.

Fiddler's Choice Music Store, The Humiston House - 41 E. Main Street, Jaffrey, NH 03452. Fiddles, other folk instruments, lessons, repair, free mailing list. "Bluegrass our specialty."

Fiddler's Fix - 79 Daniel Street, Portsmouth, NH 03801. Fiddles, other folk instruments, lessons, repairs. (603) 436-4478.

The Music Emporium - 2018 Massachusetts Avenue, Cambridge, MA 02140. Folk instruments, some fiddles and supplies, music instruction. (617) 661-2099.

Hambone Music and Folk Arts - 7 Phila Street, Saratoga Springs, NY 12866. Books, accessories, and records. (518) 584-5670.

House of Musical Tradition - 7040 Carroll Avenue, Takoma Park, MD 20912. Books, records, dances, accessories, concerts, repairs, workshops. (301) 270-0222, (301) 270-9800.

Andy's Front Hall - Drawer A, Voorheesville, NY 12186. Free folk catalogue. Books, records, also home of "Front Hall Records."

Shar Products Company - 2465 S. Industrial, PO Box 1411, Ann Arbor, MI 48106. Instruments (violins, violas, cellos, bows) focus on needs of the classical musician. Strings, cases, supplies, sheet music, metronomes, etc. Toll free (800) 521-0791.

Kicking Mule - PO Box 158, Alderpoint, CA 95411. Records, books, record and book recycling service. Focus on folk. (707) 926-5312.

Lark in the Morning - Box 1176, Mendocino, CA 95460. Folk music supplies, instruments, violins, viola da gamba, etc. (707) 964-5569.

Country Music Store - PO Box 621, Brighton, CO 80601. They specialize in bluegrass, old country, and accoustic records. (303) 659-5022.

Fiddlepicker - Box 1033, Mountainside, NJ 07092. Free price list. Fiddles, Barcus Berry 4 & 5-string fiddles, pickups, preamps, strings. Jules Terry (201) 379-9034, Jack Skerratt (201) 233-0751.

Roundup Records - PO Box 154 (Dept. BSR9), N. Cambridge, MA 02140. Good source for fiddle records, hundreds of labels, catalogues and monthly update, record reviews. (617) 354-0700.

Folk Arts Rare Records - 3611 Adams Avenue, San Diego, CA 92116. Lou Curtis can locate almost anything that was ever recorded. He also has 15,000 hours of field recordings of fiddle, folk, blues, etc. on tape, sponsors concerts, and the 18th annual San Diego Folk Festival in Oct. 1984. Write for prices for records and tape copies or call (619) 282-7833.

Susan Norris and Fred Carlson - Box 147, Plainfield, VT 05667. "Unusual handmade stringed instruments," fiddles, etc., repairs, records. (802) 479-0862.

Jolly Swagman Music Shop - Box 15, 17 Central Square, Chatham, NY 12037. Fiddles, other folk instruments, repairs, "specializing in quality bizarre instruments." (518) 392-4420.

Vintage Fret Shop - 20 Riverside Drive, Ashland, NH 03217. Fiddles, other folk instruments, repairs, records, books, newsletter. (603) 968-3346

Sandy's Music - 896A Mass. Ave., Cambridge, MA. Records, fiddles, other folk instruments, accessories, repairs. (617) 491-2812.

Down Home Music - 10341 San Pablo Avenue, El Cerrito, CA 94530. Folk, traditional, ethnic, old timey, bluegrass records, books, newsletter. (415) 525-1494.

Rose's Collectors Records - 300 Chelsea Road, Louisville, KY 40207. Old country western records, etc. Free price list. (502) 896-6233.

Norsk Ltd. - 800 Linden Avenue, Boulder, CO 80302. Mail order selection of Swedish and Norwegian records with fiddling.

Shanachie Records - Dalebrook Park, Ho-Ho-Kus, NJ 07423. Mail order records from various labels. Focus on Irish and British Isles, but also records of jazz, country, blues, early rock, etc. Regular newsletter with reviews of traditional Irish music.

Arhoolie Records - 10341 San Pablo Avenue, El Cerrito, CA 94530. Folk and ethnic fiddle records of jazz, Cajun, old time, bluegrass, Mexican, Ukrainian, Polish, and western swing. Catalogues, newsletter.

County Sales - PO Box 191, Floyd, VA 24091, c/o Dave Freeman. Record sales, mail order only. 3,000 bluegrass records in stock.

Sonyatone Records - PO Box 567, Dept. DR, Santa Barbara, CA 93102, c/o Peter Feldman. Old timey, bluegrass, and instruction LPs with music and tab books. (805) 682-8624.

Kicking Mule Records, Inc. - Box 158, Alderpoint, CA 95411. Records, books, supplies, etc. (707) 926-5312.

Copper Creek Records - PO Box 1482, Sandy Spring, MD 20860. Bluegrass. (301) 253-6850.

Bill Dodge - 124 Honeoye Street, S.W., Grand Rapids, MI 49508. D-64 record sales. Bluegrass.

George Chestnut - 2305 Deerwood Road, Nashville, TN 37214. Custom violins, bow rehairing, restoration. (615) 889-6454.

The Fiddle Doctor - PO Box 1012 Nolan Boulevard, Madison, AL 35758, c/o 'Doc' Lyles. Custom violins and restoration. (205) 772-3647.

David H. Forbes - 4031 N.W. 36th Street, Gainesville, FL 32605. Violin and bow maker, custom built violins, bows, repairs and restoration. (904) 375-2609.

Fret 'N Fiddle - #1 Heritage Village, Huntington, WV 25704, c/o Dianne Dobbs; and 807 Pennsylvania Avenue, St. Altans, WV 25177, c/o Joe Dobbs. Instruments, books, records, repair, restoration. (304) 522-7122; (304) 722-5212.

Hill Music - Rt. 7, Box 110, Durham, NC 27707, c/o Dave Kielar, Nowell Creadick. Violins, bows, restoration, appraisals. (919) 968-4334.

La Gitana Instruments - 83 Riverside Avenue, West Concord, MA 07142. Handcrafted violins, other instruments, classes in instrument making.

Stringed Instrument Workshop - 15 Arnold Place, New Bedford, MA 02740. Repair and restoration of vintage stringed instruments, private lessons in fiddle, other instruments. (617) 993-0156.

Wallo Violin Shop - 5127 Lee Highway, Arlington, VA 22207. Full scale plans and parts for violins, other stringed instruments. Catalogue, 75¢.

White Brothers String Shop - 4245 Okemos Road, Okemos, MI 48864, c/o William White. Violins, hammered dulcimers, repair, books, etc. (517) 349-3806.

David Wiebe, Violin Maker - 715 Fourth Street, David City, NE 68632. Information on request. (402) 367-4415.

Antanas Raczus - Violins and Bows - 9 Stevens Way, Durham, NH 03824, c/o Jonathan Chorlian. Bow making, violin repair, restoration, appraisal. (603) 868-5399.

Bein & Fushi, Inc., Dealers in Rare Violins - The Fine Arts Building, 410 South Michigan Avenue, Chicago, IL 60605. Top quality bows and violins, appraisal, insurance, etc. (312) 663-0150.

Thomas Dignan, Bowmaker - 295 Huntington Avenue, Boston, MA 02115. Bow repair, etc. (617) 262-5511.

Royal Exchange Violins, Violas, Cellos - 11 Mt. Auburn Street, Cambridge, MA 02138. Instruments, repairs, supplies. (617) 864-0567.

Kschier Brothers, Inc. - 634 Washington Road, Pittsburgh, PA 15228. Mail order and retail shop, instruments, supplies, tuners, books, music, rentals. Catalogue $1. (412) 561-2130.

Mel Bay Publications, Inc. - P.O. Box 66, #4 Industrial Drive, Pacific, MO 63069-0066. Music and instruction books on fiddling and other instruments.

Oak Publications - Dept. BA, 33 West 60th Street, New York, NY 10023. Books on fiddling and many other topics for all aspects of music. Books may be mail ordered. Send for catalogue.

Quinlin Campbell Publishers - Box 651, Boston, MA 02134. Books about traditional Irish music, tune books. Free brochure.

T. F. Barrett Company - Box 187, Putney, VT 05346. 4 and 5 string solid body electric violins. (802) 387-4519.

"Before long, I was sittin' in on a few things, and then I got into performing with them. At first, all the volume on stage nearly blew my brains out. But after a while, I found me a dead spot, and then I got my own amp and blew those cats away."

**— Papa John Creach
Blues, jazz, rock fiddler
with Jefferson Starship,
Hot Tuna, etc.,
when playing with
Jefferson Airplane (*Frets*)**

Folk-Oriented Record Labels with Fiddle Music

Arhoolie Records - 10341 San Pablo Avenue, El Cerrito, CA 94530. "Old Timey," vintage swing fiddle, Cajun, new country swing, etc.

Bay Records - 1516 Oak Street, Suite 320, Alameda, CA 94501. Recording studio and record publisher, specializing in folk, country and bluegrass. (415) 865-2040.

Biograph Records, Inc. - 16 River Street, Chatham, NY 12037, c/o Arnold S. Caplin. Records by Stanley Brothers, Bottle Hill, Red Allen's Kentuckians, etc. Other folk, jazz, blues, etc. Catalogue, $1.00. (518) 392-3400.

Boot Records - 1343 Matieson Boulevard, East Mississauga, Ontario, Canada L4W 1R1. Free catalogue.

Flying Fish Records - 1304 W. Schubert, Chicago, IL 60614. Bluegrass, Irish traditional, etc. Examples: Boys of the Lough, New Grass Revival, Hot Rize, etc. c/o Jim Netter. (312) 528-5455.

Folk-Legacy Records - Sharon Mountain Road, Sharon, CT 06069. Traditional balladeers, fiddling, other folk music.

Folkways - 43 W. 61st Street, New York, NY 10023. Bluegrass, folk, jazz, etc. Free lists of records and cassettes.

Front Hall Records - Drawer A, Voorheesville, NY 12186. Contra dance music, Fennig's All-Star String Band, etc. Also mail order folk music supplies and items.

Grass Mountain Records - PO Box 12937, Fort Worth, TX 76116. Record label.

Green Linnet Records - 70 Turner Hill Road, New Canaan, CT 06840. Known for traditional Irish music, but other styles available.

Green Mountain Records - Garvey Hill, Northfield, VT 05663, c/o Richard Longfellow. Record sales, album production.

Heritage Records - Rt. 3, Box 278, Dept. D, Galax, VA 24333. Albums of Galax Old Fiddler's Convention, recording studio. Free list of records.

June Appal Records - Box 743, Whitesburg, KY 41858. Appalachian, "Old Timey," bluegrass, folk, etc. Example: John McCutcheon, Larry Sparks, etc. Free catalogue.

Kicking Mule Records - Box 158, Alderpoint, CA 95411. "Old Timey," Celtic music, other folk, etc.

Leather Records - PO Box 44, Fincastle, VA 24090, c/o M.G. Haynie. Record label. Free catalogue. (703) 473-3111.

Old Homestead Records - Box 100, Brighton, MI 48116. Record sales, Old Homestead label. Catalogue available.

Philo Records - 70 Court Street, Middlebury, VT 05753. Fiddle, many styles of folk music.

Rebel Records - Box 3057, Roanoke, VA 24015, mostly bluegrass such as Seldom Scene, The Country Gentlemen, Ralph Stanley, etc.

Revonah Records - PO Box 217, Ferndale, NY 12734, c/o Paul Gerry. Bluegrass, country, gospel. (917) 292-5965.

Ridge Runner - c/o Richey Records, Box 12973, Fort Worth, TX 76116. Mostly bluegrass such as Alan Munde, Country Gazette, Dan Huckabee, Bob Black, etc.

Rooster Records - RFD 2, Bethel, VT 05032. Fiddle, other folk records, "Old Timey," etc. Free catalogue.

Rosebud Records - 611 Empire Mill Road, Bloomington, IN 47401. "Old Timey," jazz, etc.

Rounder Records - 1 Camp Street, Cambridge, MA 02140. Many fiddle records, other folk.

Sierra Records and Video - PO Box 5853, Pasadena, CA 91107. Record company. (213) 388-0181.

Sugar Hill Records - Box 4040, Duke Station, Durham, NC 27706. Much bluegrass such as Ricky Skaggs, Doyle Lawson and Quicksilver, The Country Gentlemen, Berline, Crary and Hickman, country also. (919) 489-4349.

Windham Hill Records - Box 9388, Stanford, CA 94303. Guitar and fiddler/violinists such as Darol Anger, etc.

Voyager Recordings - 324 35th Avenue, Seattle, WA 98122. Many records of fiddle and old time music. Free catalogue.

THE HUNGARIAN BAND.

A List of Jazz Fiddle Recordings

Jean-Luc Ponty
Violin Summit, (with Asmussen, Grappelli, Smith) - EMI MPS 5C 064 61227 (import).
Les Grandes Violinistes de Jazz, (with Grappelli) - Philips 6612 039.
Sunday Walk - PA USA 7033 (MPS).
More Than Meets the Ear - World Pacific Jazz St 20134.
Electric Connection - World Pacific Jazz St 20156.
Canteloupe Island - Blue Note LA632 H2.
Upon the Wings of Music - Atlantic SD 18138.
Aurora - Atlantic SD 18163.
Imaginary Voyage - Atlantic SD 18195.
Jean-Luc Ponty and Stephane Grappelli - Inner City 1005.

Stephane Grappelli
Djangologie #1 - 20/Stephane Grappelli with Django Reinhardt - EMI Pathé CO54 16001 through 16020. Also on GNP Crescendo 9001, 9002, 9018, 9019.
Stephane Grappelli - Everest FS 311, 306.
Stephane Grappelli/Homage to Django - Classic Jazz 23.
Django Reinhardt/Stephane Grappelli - Angel S-36985.
Stephane Grappelli/Afternoon in Paris - MPS 20876.
Stephane Grappelli - Pye 12115.
Stephane Grappelli/I Hear Music - RCA Victor 730107.
Stephane Grappelli/Steff and Slam - Black and Blue 33.076.
Stephane Grappelli/The Talk of the Town - Black Lion 313 stereo.
Stephane Grappelli/Recorded Live at the Queen Elizabeth Hall, London - Pye 12123.
Stephane Grappelli - Pye 12135.
Stephane Grappelli/Satin Doll - Vangard VSD - 81/82
Stephane Grappelli Plays Cole Porter - Festival 240.
Stephane Grappelli Plays George Gershwin - Festival 205.
Stephane Grappelli/I Got Rhythm - Black Lion 047 (stereo).
Stephane Grappelli/Le Toit de Paris - RCA Victor 740.038.
Stephane Grappelli/Violinspiration - MPS MC 22545.
Stephane Grappelli: 1973 - Pye NSPL 18403.
Stephane Grappelli/Just One of Those Things - Black Lion BL-211.
Feeling + Finesse = Jazz/Stephane Grappelly (sic) - Atlantic 1391.
Stephane Grappelli and Barney Kessel/I Remember Django - Black Lion 105.
Stephane Grappelli and Barney Kessel/Limehouse Blues - Black Lion 173.
Stephane Grapelli—Bill Coleman - Classic Jazz 24.
Stephane Grappelli/Grand Gala Special - Exclusive Ste 6201.
Stephane Grappelli and The George Shearing Trio/The Reunion - MPS 5D0642 99457.
Stephane Grappelli and Oscar Peterson - Prestige 24041.
Stephane Grappelli and Yehudi Menuhin/Jalousie — Music of the Thirties - Angel SFO 36968.
Stephane Grappelli and Yehudi Menuhin/Tea for Two - Angel S 37533.
Stephane Grappelli/Uptown Dance - Columbia 35415.
Stephane Grappelli/I Remember Django - Black Lion Records AFE BL 105.
Stephane Grappelli/Parisian Swing - GNP Crescendo 9002.
Stephane Grappelli/Homage to Django - Classic Jazz CJ 23.

Joe Venuti
Stringing the Blues - Columbia CL 1926.
Hot Strings - RCA Black and White Vol. 118 FPMI 7016.
Venuti—Lang/1927 – 1928 - The Old Masters TOM 8.
Venuti—Lang/1929 – 1930 - The Old Masters TOM 7.
Benny Goodman and the Giants of Swing - Prestige 7644.
The Radio Years - London HMG 5023.
Louis Armstrong/All Star Dates 1947 – 1950 - Alamac QSR 2436.
Welcome Joe - Durium msA77356.
Joe Venuit in Milan - Durium msA77277.
Joe Venuti/Jazz Violin - Vangard VSD 79405.
Sliding By, Sonet SNTF 734.
Joe Venuti and George Barnes/Gems - Concord Jazz 14.
Joe Venuti and George Barnes/Live at the Concord Summer Festival - Concord Jazz 30.
The Maestro and Friend/with Marian McPartland - Halcyon 112.
Nightwings/with Bucky Pizzarelli - Flying Dutchman BDL1 1120.
S'Wonderful - Flying Fish 035.
In Chicago, 1978 - Flying Fish 077.
Joe and Zoot - Chiaroscuro 128.
Joe Venuti Blue Four - Chiaroscuro 134.
Hot Sonatas with Earl Hines - Chiaroscuro 145.
Hooray for Joe - Chiaroscuro 153.
Alone at the Palace with Dave McKenna - Chiaroscuro 160.
Joe Venuti and his Big Band - Golden Era Records LP 1506(1).

Stuff Smith
Black Violin - MPS 20650.
Stuff Smith - Everest FS 238.
Hot Swing Fiddle Classics - Folklyric 9025.
Swinging Stuff/Stuff Smith Quartet - Storyville SLP 4087.
Have Violin, Will Swing - Verve MGV 8282.
Stuff Smith - Verve MGV 8206.
Dizzy Gillespie/Stuff Smith - Verve MGV 8214.
Also appears on *The Changing Face of Harlem, Vol. 2* - Arista Savoy 2224 (3 cuts).

Svend Asmussen
Hot Swing Fiddle Classics - Folklyric Records 9025.
Toots and Svend/Yesterday and Today - A & M Sp 3613.
Svend Asmussen/Amazing Strings - MPS 20 22373 6 (import).
Svend Asmussen Spielt Welterfolge - Telefunken Musik für alle NT 421 (import).
Duke Ellington's Jazz Violin Session, with Svend Asmussen, Grappelli, Ray Nance - Atlantic SD 1688.

Elek Bacsik
Bird and Dizzy/A Musical Tribute - Flying Dutchman BDLI 1082.

Itzhak Perlman
Itzhak Perlman/A Different Kind of Blues - Angel D5-37780.

Eddie South
Djanglogie #5 and #6 - EMI Pathé C054 16005 and C054 16006.
The Dark Angel of the Fiddle - Trip TLP 5803.

Piano-Playing Fiddler Makes Music on Both —At the Same Time

CHELSEA, Vt. (AP) — Harold Luce's fiddle playing may get people dancing, but it's what he does with his own feet that sets him apart from other old-time Vermont musicians.

For more than 40 years, he has entertained rural fairgoers and dance hall crowds by playing the fiddle with his hands and the piano with his feet—both at the same time.

"Does sort of make folks stop and take a notice," he observes, a grin threatening to break through the traditional Yankee reserve.

Mr. Luce accomplishes this feat with a collection of bedboard slats, pieces of an old wooden table and a healthy supply of rubber bands to hold everthing in place.

The end result is a foot-powered, piano-playing machine, the product of a farm boy's brainstorm and a mother's willingness to look the other way as her son sawed up the kitchen table for parts.

Aping a Bob-tailed Cat

"I was about 17, I guess, when I was playing fiddle with our bob-tailed cat sittin' on my lap," recalls Mr. Luce, now in his 60's.

"And I noticed that old cat was just a pawing away on my knee in time with the music. So I figured if he could do it, I could too."

Before long the young inventor was pumping on foot pedals connected to dowels that led to cross bars that pressed down the chords.

"And they still do all that, if I can get everything strung up here right," Mr. Luce mutters, as he hauls the unwieldy contraption out of a closet.

Soon the strains of "Let Me Call You Sweetheart" waft through a spirited rendition of "In the Good Old Summertime."

"Some people just play, you know, but Harold's music makes people want to dance," says Edith, his wife of 40 years. "Kinda tickles their feet, if you know what I mean."

A row of trophies from old-time fiddling contests across New England bears witness to her description.

"For it to be authentic old-time style, you've got to play just the melody, one note at a time," Mr. Luce says. "None of this fancy stuff that the younger fellows go in for."

Duets Now a Rarity

A former dairy farmer who now works for a Springfield tool company, Mr. Luce also numbers among his inventions a foot-powered device that strums chords on a guitar.

Nowadays, the fiddler says, his one-man duets are a rarity.

"I mostly play the violin now. I go to a few of the contests every year, and when we get going, we can play for hours," he says.

He still mourns the passing of Vermont's country dancehalls, wooden-floored meeting houses that were given names like "Dreamland" one night a week.

"They're all gone now. And I don't know anything but these old songs," he says. "But they're still good enough for me."

A List of Blues Fiddle Recordings

Howard Armstrong - Rounder 2003.

Will Batts - Mamlish S-3803.

Andrew Baxter - Folkways FP-2521, FA-2952, 47181-3.

Clarence "Gatemouth" Brown - (First American Records/Blackjack) Folkways 2952.

Jimmy Brown - Testament T-2205, Storyville SLP 180.

Butch Cage - Folk Lyric FL-111, Storyville ST 21014, SLP 129, 135, Folkways Fa 2431, Arhoolie F1005, 1006.

Lonnie Chatmon - Mamlish S3804, Biograph BLP 12041.

Morris "Big" Chenier - Zydeco Blues, Arhoolie F1031, Bayou 704, 705.

Beauford Clay - Arhoolie F1012, F1015.

Chasey Collins - Arhoolie BC2.

Conray Fontenot - Melodeon MLP-7330.

Don Sugarcane Harris - Rush 1002, BASF MB-21792.

Nap Hayes - Historical Records HR HLP-8002.

Leroy Jenkins - India Navigation Co. 1028, JCOA Records 1010, Re Records 3117, Horizon SP 0708.

Carl Martin - Testament 2220.

Charlie Pierce - Arhoolie BC2.

Henry "Son" Sims - Belzona L1001.

Eddie South - Trip Records TLP-5803.

Claude Williams - Sackville 3005.

For more information on blues fiddlers, see *Blues Fiddle*, by Julie Lieberman (Mel Bay Publications).

Research Organizations

John Edwards Memorial Foundation - Greenlaw Hall, University of North Carolina, Chapel Hill, NC 27514. Largest resource of country, old time, bluegrass, Cajun, blues, western swing, folk, and gospel. 14,000 78 rpm discs, 10,000 45 rpm discs, 1,000 long playing albums, 2,000 tapes, reference library, photographs, correspondence, etc. Visitors welcome.

Archive of Folk Culture - Library of Congress, Washington, DC 20540, c/o Joseph C. Hickerson. Historic recordings, LPs, bibliographies, directories and finding aids, intern program, referral service. (202) 287-5510.

The Country Dance and Song Society of America - 505 Eighth Avenue, New York, NY 10018

Books of Fiddle Music

This book list, athough fairly extensive, is not a complete listing of all published books of fiddle music. I have, however, included most of the books which are presently available through book sellers and folk products distributors. I have also included a number of books that are out of print, but which can be found in used bookstores.

I have purposely left out a number of books which were published prior to 1940, since they are difficult to locate, although I've included a few of the more important ones.

I've included as much information about each book as I've been able to dig up from my sources, and so there is a lot for many books, and only a bit for others. The prices listed are the latest that I have available. The interested reader should note that these prices vary between different booksellers and distributors, and by mail order, and may change at any time.

Mel Bay Anthology of Fiddle Styles by Dave Reiner. 86 pages. Separately available - Tape, Anthology of Fiddle Styles. $5.05.

Appalachian Fiddle by Miles Krassen. 88 pages, 58 transcriptions of breakdowns, jigs, hornpipes and modal tunes based on the playing styles of traditional Appalachian fiddlers. Includes fingering positions in the four principal keys, bowing techniques, double stops chart and discography. Oak Publications, 1973. $5.90.

Kenny Baker — Fiddle by David Brody. 72 pages, 22 tunes, hoedowns, waltzes, twin fiddling piece, Bill Monroe tunes, originals, discography, bibliography of Baker, techniques. $5.90.

Beginning Old Time Fiddle by Alan Kaufman. Instruction guide with 38 tunes in the styles of J.P. Fraley, Gaither Carlton, Lowe Stokes, Frank George, Gid Tanner, etc., in standard notation and fiddle tablature, discography, illustrated, 112 pages. Oak Publications, 1977. $6.75.

Bluegrass Fiddle by Gene Lowinger. 64 pages, 29 tunes. Tunes by Bill Monroe, Bradford Keith, Gladys Stacey, Ellen Martin, Tom James, Vaughn Horton, Ervin Rouse. Oak Publications, 1974.

Bluegrass Fiddle for Beginners by Warren Kennison. 48 pages, 18 tunes. "One of a series of beginning bluegrass books for guitar, banjo, mandolin and fiddle. All books use the same tunes so that any combination of instruments can play together." Alfred Publishing Co., 1980. $4.95.

The Bluegrass Fiddle Songbook by Cathye Smithwick. 32 pages. Charles Anderson Music Publishing and Sales. $4.20.

Mel Bay Bluegrass Fiddler by Burton Isaac. 48 pages, 35 tunes, jigs, hornpipes, hoedowns, reels. Mel Bay Publishing Co., 1974. $2.50.

Cowboy Dance Tunes by Frederick Knorr and Lloyd Shaw. Caldwell, Idaho: Caxton Printers, Ltd., 1939.

100 WLS Barn Dance Favorites compiled by John Lair. Chicago: M.M. Cole Publishing Co., 1935.

Good Morning: Music, Calls, and Directions for Old-Time Dancing as Revived by Mr. and Mrs. Henry Ford. Fourth edition, Dearborn, Michigan: Henry Ford, 1941.

The Twin & Triple Fiddle Tune Book by Deborah Greenblatt. 22 twin and 11 triple fiddle tunes, some original, associations and fiddle clubs. $7.95 plus $2.00 for shipping to Deborah Greenblatt, PO Box 11253, Omaha, Nebraska 68111.

Beginners Country Fiddle and Guitar. Each volume comes with tablature and a 90 minute cassette tape. Free brochure. Glenn Waters Music, Box 10662, Odessa, Texas 79767.

Fiddle Tunes. Cassette tape, 22 tunes at moderate speed, jigs, reels, Irish, bluegrass, hornpipes. East Hill Co., 2753 Gulf Road, Varysburg, NY 14167.

Hot Licks for Bluegrass Fiddle by Stacy Phillips. 450 written bluegrass licks. $12.20 postpaid. 152 Quaker Hill Road, Monroe, NY 10950.

Folk Fiddle by Isaac Burton. 32 pages, Mel Bay, 1964.

Folk Songs and Fiddle Tunes of the USA by Hazel Kinscella. 42 songs and 7 fiddle tunes, piano arrangements and chord symbols, 48 pages. Carl Fischer Publisher, 1959.

How to Play Bluegrass Fiddle, Vol. 1 by Peter Feldmann. A record with a 16 page booklet.

What is Old Time Fiddling? A two-track reel-to-reel tape at 3¾ ips, put out by "American Fiddler News," (no address available).

Bluegrass Fiddling: Fiddlers and Styles by Gene Lowinger. 67 pages, 72 tunes, hoedowns, blues, tunes by E. Rouse, Jimmy Driftwood, Martin and Williams, Martin and Humphrey, Martin and White, Critchfield and Maxwell, Raye and DePaul, Bill Monroe, discography. Published by G. Shirmer.

The Country Fiddle Songbook by Cathye Smithwick. 32 pages. Pacific Coast Music, P.O. box 42069, San Francisco, California 94142.

Merle Haggard Presents Swinging Texas Fiddling by Tiny Moore, Warren Helton and Vernon Soloman. 60 pages.

Basic Chords for the Fiddler by Emerson P. Smith. 35 pages.

Masters of Old Time Fiddling by Miles Krassen. With sound sheet. Focus on southern style tunes, notes on the musicians, 49 transcriptions from 14 musicians, 139 pages.

Mel Bay—Contest Fiddling by Stacy Phillips. 33 hoedowns, waltzes, and "tunes of choice," in Texas style with ornaments, variations, chords, some fingerings, interviews, fiddle association lists, bibliography, discography, 174 pages. 152 Quaker Hill Road, Monroe, New York 10950. $10.95 book postpaid. $11.00 tape postpaid.

FiddleTunes

151 Brand New Old Time Fiddle Tunes by Pacific Northwest Champions, Vol. 1 by Vivian Williams. 46 pages. Waltzes, jigs, hornpipes. Voyager Publications, 424 35th Avenue, Seattle, Washington 98122.

Advanced Fiddling: Solos, instruction, and technique by Craig Duncan. 117 pages. Tape also available.

Byron Berline's Fiddle Lessons. Tapes 1–6: 1-starter tape, 2-basic tunes, 3-Texas flavored tunes, 4-fancy tunes, 5-advanced tunes, 6-licks and tricks. All tapes have tablature. Ridge Runner, Dept. FR-506, P.O. Box 12937, Fort Worth, Texas 76121.

Bluegrass and Country Fiddle by Kenny Kosek. Tapes 1–6, 35 tunes, old-timey, blues, Cajun styles, bluegrass. Homespun Tapes, Box 694F, Woodstock, New York 12498.

Western Swing Fiddle by Matt Glaser. Tapes 1-6, 25 tunes and variations on styles of Benny Thomasson, Bob Wills, Mark O'Connor, Johnny Gimble, etc. Homespun Tapes, Box 694F, Woodstock, New York 12498.

Jazz Violin by Matt Glaser and Stephane Grappelli. 25 solos transcribed from the playing of Grappelli, Eddie South, Joe Venuti, Stuff Smith, Svend Asmussen, Jean-Luc Ponty. Photos, interviews, discography, 144 pages. Oak Publications, 1981. $8.45.

Solo Jazz Violin: A collection of melodic jazz solos designed to instruct the aspiring Jazz Violinist by Warren Nunes & Cathye Smithwick. 32 pages. Shattinger Int. Music Corp., New York, New York. $3.35.

Mel Bay Deluxe Anthology of Jazz Violin Styles by Dave Reiner & Glenn Asch. 135 pages, tape also available.

The Musical Styles of Jean Luc-Ponty. 104 pages.

Jazz Improvisation Method for Strings - Book I: Violin & Viola by David Baker. 160 pages.

A Basic Chord Improvisation Method for Violin or Fiddle by Judith Zoss. 50 fiddling solos, chord patterns. Mel Bay. $6.95.

Jazz Violin: Roots and Branches by Gene Lowinger. 93 pages, transcriptions and comparisons of jazz styles by Joe Venuti, Stephane Grappelli, Eddie South, Stuff Smith, blues styles by "Papa" John Creach, Don "Sugarcane" Harris, Jean-Luc Ponty, Michal Urbaniak, discography. G. Shirmer, 1981. $7.95.

Jazz Fiddle by Anthony le Fleming. 60 pages, violin and piano arrangements of jazz standards, 21 tunes. Chappel International Music Publishers, 1979.

Mel Bay - Blues Fiddle by Julie Lieberman. 80 pages, history, lore, transcriptions, discography, 1982. $5.05. Tape available, $6.75.

Fiddlescapes by Deborah Greenblatt. Care of the fiddle, performing tips, backup techniques, scales, hoedowns, polkas, waltzes, rags, etc. 1980. Deborah Greenblatt, P.O. Box 11253, Omaha, Nebraska 68111. Tape available for $6.50 postpaid. Rhythm on one track, fiddle on the other.

Vassar Clements — Fiddle by Matt Glaser. 63 pages, hoedowns, blues, rags, tunes by Vassar, Millie Clements, Arthur Smith, Bill Monroe, Bradford Kieth, Leon McAuliffe, discography, biographical notes on Clements, photos, etc.

Teach Yourself Bluegrass Fiddle by Matt Glaser. 61 pages, left hand bowing techniques, solos, backup, selection of tunes. Armsco Music Publishing Company, number 020183. $5.05.

Bluegrass Fiddle Styles by Stacy Phillips and Kenny Kosek. 57 tunes, 112 pages, hoedowns, blues, rags, 3 twin fiddling tunes, 1 triple fiddling tune, tunes by Arthur Smith, Jimmie Rodgers, Roy Carter, Bill Monroe, Lester Flatt, Earl Scruggs, James Smith, Certain and Stacy, Austin Allen, Jim and Jesse McReynolds, A. P. Carter, Kenny Baker, Kirk McGee, Leroy Mack, Buck Graves, Cy Cobin, Johnny Gimble, Gene Sullivan, etc.

Bluegrass Fiddle Jamboree by Cathye Lynne Smithwick, Charles Hanson II Music Books of California. 17 tunes, hoedowns, twin fiddling, 31 pages. Pacific Coast Music, P.O. Box 42069, San Francisco, California 94142. $2.50.

How to Play Hoedown Fiddle in America by Bill Cunningham. 67 pages, 29 tunes, techniques. Ryckman and Beck Music Publishing.

Mel Bay's Deluxe Anthology of Fiddle Styles by David Reiner. 43 tunes, hoedowns, reels, waltzes, polkas, schottisches, hornpipes, jigs, blues, ragtime, twin fiddling, triple fiddling, kickoffs, endings, chords, techniques, discography.

Irish Bluegrass Roots by Jerry Scordan and Jeff Yates. Charles Hanson II Music Books of California, Inc. 193 tunes from O'Neil, 37 pages. Pacific Coast Music, P.O. Box 42069, San Francisco, California 94142.

Country Fiddling for Four Violins by Burton Isaac. 34 pages.

Deluxe Fiddling Method by Craig Duncan. 104 pages. Also available is a tape with the same title.

Mel Bay Learn to Play Country Fiddle by Frank Zucco. 48 pages. $2.50.

Great Country Fiddle Solos (Learn to Play, Vol 2) by Frank Zucco. 42 pages. $2.50.

Mel Bay 100 Fiddle Tunes by Bill Guest. 66 pages. $5.05.

How to Play Old Time Country Fiddle by Jerry Silverman. 174 pages, 75 hoedowns, jigs, rags, square dance calls. Chilton Book Co. $8.50.

Easy Fiddle Tunes Book One by Jerry Silverman. 40 tunes, hoedowns, waltzes, piano accompaniment. G. Shirmer.

Easy Fiddle Tunes Book Two by Jerry Silverman. 36 tunes, jigs, hoedowns, rags, reels, piano accompaniment. G. Shirmer.

Mel Bay Easy Way Fiddle Solos by Frank Zucco. 24 pages, 39 tunes, hoedowns, waltzes, reels, hornpipes, originals.

Mel Bay Old Time Fiddle Solos. 24 pages, 68 tunes, hoedowns, jigs, schottisches, hornpipes, waltzes, cross tuning pieces. $2.50.

Violin Pieces Country Style by Betty Barlow. 71 pages.

One Thousand Fiddle Tunes. Jigs, hornpipes, strathspeys, reels. Includes calls for country dances. 128 pages. Cole Publishing, first copyright 1940. $9.30.

The Fiddle Book by Marion Thede. 160 pages, 150 tunes including cross tunings, southern style. Oak Publications.

Mel Bay Folk Fiddle Styles by Burton Isaac. 32 pages. $1.70.

If Stradivarius, the famous violin maker, had been as popular as Henry Ford.

From the collection of Linn S. Schulz

The Old Time Fiddler's Repertory by R. P. Christeson. 224 pages, 245 tunes, breakdowns, hornpipes, waltzes, quadrilles, pieces, some piano accompaniment. Focus on Missouri styles, tunes collected from fiddlers between 1948 and 1960. $15.95 paperback.

The Old Time Fiddler's Repertory, Volume 2. 208 pages. over 200 tunes, background information. $24.95.

Old Time Fiddler's Repertory Historic Field Recordings of Forty-One Traditional Tunes. Two records, monaural. University of Missouri Press, P.O. Box 7088, Columbia, MO 65205-7088.

Old Time Fiddlers Favorite Barn Dance Tunes by E. F. Adam, 1931.

Hartford Tune Book by Will Welling. 55 tunes from the U.S. and Canada. 26 pages, 1974. $2.50.

Belknaps March by Bill Wellington. 13 original tunes notated for melody, piano right and left hands, guitar chords. Tape also available with 4 traditional tunes in addition to the tunes from the book. Contact Bill Wellington, Upper Tract, West Virginia 26866. Book, $5.00; Cassette, $6.00. Both $10.00. Postage $1.00.

Square Dance Chord Book (second edition) by Jack Slonacker and Tony Parkes. Chords to accompany 500 of the tunes commonly played in New England, cross indexed to books and records containing the melodies. $8.50.

The Fiddle Tree Manuscript by John Turner. 17 pages, $3.50.

The Fiddlers Tune Book by Peter Kennedy. 46 pages, 100 tunes, hornpipes, reels, polkas, jigs, waltzes, schottisches. The English Folk Dance and Song Society. $2.50.

The Second Fiddlers Tune Book by Peter Kennedy. 43 pages, 100 tunes. $2.50.

Hall's Fiddle Book by Charles Hall. 72 pages, 65 tunes from the U.S. $9.30.

The Nelson Music Collection by Newton F. Tolman and Kay Gilbert. 63 tunes collected over 50 years in Nelson, New Hampshire and used for contra and square dances. Introduction, jigs, reels, hornpipes, strathspeys, planxtys, rants, degenerate period hornpipes, original hornpipes by N. F. Tolman. 1969.

Harding's Collection of 200 Jigs and Reels. New York: Paul Pioneer Music Co., 1928.

Fiddlecase Book of 101 Polkas by J. Perron and R. Miller. Fits in your fiddle case. $3.40.

New England Fiddler's Repertoire by J. Perron and R. Miller. 168 tunes. Fiddlecase Books. $8.00.

The Robbins Collection of 200 Jigs, Reels, and Country Dances. 64 pages, for piano also. New York: Robbins Music Corp., 1933, 1961. $3.35.

Allan's Irish Fiddler by Hugh McDermott. 120 reels, jigs, hornpipes, piano accompaniment available. Glasgow: Mozart Allan. $3.00.

Reels and Strathspeys by Mozart Allan. $3.00.

The Grumbling Old Woman by Donna Hinds. 40 pages, 61 square and contra dance tunes, chords, introduction. Published 1981 by Hand to Mouth Music, P.O. Box A, Bedford, MA 01730. Tape also available. Book, $8.00; tape, $7.00. Both, $12.00.

50 Fiddlin' Dance Tunes by Mellie Dunham. Waltzes, schottisches, hornpipes, jigs, reels, polkas, hoedowns, from the champion fiddler of Maine in the 1920s. Carl Fischer Publisher, 1926. $2.50.

American Tunes. 18 reels and jigs for square and country dance collected from the Benacre Notebooks by K. Bliss. English Folk Dance and Song Society, 1959.

The Athole Collection of the Dance Music of Scotland, composed and arranged by James Stewart Robertson. Edinburgh and London: Oliver and boyd, 1961. Reprinted from the 1884 edition.

Country Dance Tunes collected from *The English Dancing Master* by John Playford, arranged by A. W. Foster. London: Novello & Co., 1929. Reprinted by the English Folk Dance and Song Society.

Country Dance Tunes collected by Cecil Sharp. London: Novello & Co., 1924.

Nathaniel Gow's Complete Repository, Part 1, 2, 3. 1799, 1806, 1809. Strathspeys, reels, etc.

Okay, Let's Try a Contra by Dudley Laufman. Original and traditional tunes. New York: Country Dance and Song Society, 1973.

The Ralph Page Book of Contras by Ralph Page. Original and traditional tunes to go along with the dances. London: English folk Dance and Song Society, 1969.

Master Collection of Dance Music for Violin by Richard Carlin. 299 tunes of British Isles, French Canada. Includes guitar chords. Mel Bay. $9.95.

Traditional Music of America. Fiddle tunes. Hatboro, Pennsylvania: The Folklore Association, 1965. Reprint from the 1940 edition.

Favorite Old Time Tunes for Violin and Piano. Theodore Presser Co., 1920.

William Litten's Fiddle Tunes 1800–1802 by Gale Huntington. 129 tunes, reels, strathspeys, jigs, waltzes, hornpipes, minuets, marches. Transcriptions of the official fiddle player aboard the HMS *Gorgon.* Hines Point Publishers. $4.50.

Messer's Anthology of Fiddle Tunes by Don Messer. Nearly 200 tunes from Canada and New England, 128 pages. $5.90.

Bob's Notebooks 1, 2, 3, 4, 5, 6. Original tunes by Bob McQuillen, accordianist and pianist for many New England contra dance bands. Books 1 and 2, $8.00 for both. Others $6.00 each.

Kerr's Merry Melodies for the Violin, Vols. 1, 2, 3, 4. Scotch and Irish reels and jigs, highland schottisches, country dances, hornpipes, clog dances, waltzes, polkas. $4.00 each.

Kerr's Caledonian Collection. 109 airs, hornpipes, reels, jigs, strathspeys, and country dances. Glasgow. $1.50.

Kerr's Collection of Reels and Strathspeys. $2.50.

Kerr's Thistle Collection. $5.50.

24 Scottish Airs by Cutler. $2.50.

Reels and Strathspeys by Cutler. $3.00.

Airs and Melodies Peculiar to Highlands of Scotland and the Isles by Captain S. Fraser. $12.95.

100 English Folk Dance Airs edited by Maud Karpeles and Kenworthy Schofield. Jigs, reels, country dance tunes. Originally published by The English Folk Dance and Song Society, London, 1951, now by Hargail Music Press, 51 East 12th Street, New York, New York 10003. $4.00.

A Collection of the Ancient Music of Ireland. 1840, reprint edition bound with two other Bunting collections under the title *The Ancient Music of Ireland.* Dublin: Walton's Piano and Musical Instrument Galleries, 1969.

The Strathspey, Reel, and Hornpipe Tuter by William C. Honeyman. Newport, Dundee, Scotland: Honeyman Music Publishing Co., (c. 1900).

Old Time Dance Tunes by Harry Jarman. New York: Broadcast Music, Inc., 1951.

Lowe's Collection of Reels, Strathspeys and Jigs by Joseph Lowe. Edinburgh or Glasgow: Paterson and Sons, (1844).

Collection of Irish Airs, Marches, and Dance Tunes. Dublin: Pigott & Co., Ltd., 1911.

Favorite Reels, Jigs and Hornpipes for the Violin. From the "Half Dollar Music Series." Boston: Oliver Ditson Company, 1907.

Quick Tunes and Good Times by Newton F. Tolman. "Stories of the early days of the traditional music revival by one of its pioneers, an 8th generation New Hampshireman." Dublin, New Hampshire: William L. Bauhan, Inc., 1972.

The Treasure Chest of Irish Songs, Jigs and Reels. New York: Treasure Chest Publications, 1943.

Arthur Scott Robertson Scottish Tune Books in 3 Vols. Fiddlecase Books, P.O. Box 540-A, Peterborough, New Hampshire 03458.

Way Down East by Don Messer, Gordon Thompson. 1948. Out of print.

Don Messer's Square Dance Tunes. Canadian Music Sales, 1952. Out of print.

Don Messer's Favorite Melodies. Canadian Music Sales, 1950. Out of print.

Ward Allen's Fiddle Tunes by Ward Allen. 1956.

The Skye Collection compiled by K. N. Macdonald. Originally appeared in 1887. Over 400 tunes of Scotland, reels and strathspeys, arranged for violin and piano. $12.70.

Marshall's Scottish Melodies assembled from four volumes published from 1781 to 1845, 120 pages. Published by Fiddlecase Books, Harrisville, New Hampshire 03450. $5.10.

The Scottish Violinist by J. Scott Skinner. 150 tunes. Skinner composed in the traditional idiom during the beginning of the 20th century. Glasgow: Bayley and Ferguson, Ltd. $4.00.

Cape Breton Collection of Scottish Melodies for the Violin by Gordon F. MacQuarrie. Marches, slow airs, strathspeys, reels, jigs, hornpipes, mostly original.

The Caledonian Companion by Alastair J. Hardie. 143 pages, history of the Hardie family, collection of traditional Scottish fiddle music. Over 110 tunes and tune variations. EMI Publishing Ltd., London, 1981.

English, Welsh, Scottish and Irish Fiddle Tunes selected by Robin Williamson. 100 tunes, 96 pages, introduction, lore, discography. Oak Publications, 1976.

Irish Traditional Fiddle Music, Vols. 1, 2, 3 selected by Randy Miller and Jack Perron. Over 200 tunes, jigs, reels, hornpipes, airs, discography. First published 1973.

The Dance Music of Ireland, Vols. 1, 2 compiled by Breandan Breathnach from players residing in or passing through Dublin, Ireland. 214 tunes, introduction in Gaelic, French, and English, chart explaining traditional embellishments in musical notation. $6.95.

Dance Music of William Clancy by Pat Mitchel. $10.95.

The B Flat Book, Vol. 1 by Sylvia Miskoe and J. M. Graetz. $5.00.

Waifs and Strays of Gaelic Melody by Francis O'Neill. 186 pages. $13.55.

O'Neil's Music of Ireland. 1850 fiddle tunes. $11.00.

1,001 Gems, The Dance Music of Ireland by Francis O'Neil. The original book of tunes containing an additional 150–200 tunes not found in the O'Neil 1850 collection. Chicago: Lyon and Healy, 1907.

O'Neil's Music of Ireland New and Revised by Miles Krassen. With introduction defending revision, over 1,000 tunes, jigs, reels, hornpipes, marches, long dances, Irish ornamentation, compositions by O'Carolan. Oak Publications, 1976. $11.00.

Peacock Tune Book by John Peacock. Actually written primarily for Northumberland small pipes. 26 pages. $5.95.

Sully's Irish Music Book by Anthony Sullivan. 34 pages. $5.90.

A Trip to Sligo by Tony Demarco and Miles Krassen. Irish fiddling Sligo style, photos, examples, techniques, bowed triplets, 3 versions of each tune, slurs, etc., discography. 70 pages. 90 minute cassette tape available. Book, $5.05. Tape, $5.05.

Bowing Styles in Irish Fiddle Playing, Volume 1 by David Lyth. 89 pages, a collection of 93 reels and hornpipes of the "Sligo" style, transcribed from 1920s and 1930s recordings of Michael Coleman, Paddy Killoran, and James Morrison, discography. Comhaltas Ceoltóirí Éireann, 1981.

Music and Songs of the Boys of the Lough. 40 tunes, 15 songs of Ireland, Scotland, and Shetland Islands.

Hand Me Doon Da Fiddle by Tom Anderson and Pam Swing. 55 Shetland tunes with notes in dialect.

"And Out of His Knapsack He Drew a Fine Fiddle": An Introduction to the Technique of English Fiddle by John Timpany. 43 pages. $3.85.

Charleton Memorial Tunebook by Hall and Stafford. 64 pages. $5.95.

Northumbrian Piper's Tune Book by the Northumbrian Pipers Society. 49 pages, more piper's tunes which could be played on fiddle. Second tune book, 78 pages.

The Fifer's Delight: A Fife Method and Collection of Traditional Tunes for Marches and Dances (for fife, flute, fiddle) by Ralph Sweet. 81 pages. $6.40.

More Than 1000 Songs and Dances of the Irish People by James McPheeley. 356 pages.

Mel Bay's 14 Fancy Fiddle Tunes by Joseph Castle. 68 pages.

The Music of Corktown: The Reavy Collection of Irish-American Traditional Tunes, Vol. 1 by Joseph Reavy. 56 pages.

The Roche Collection of Traditional Irish Music: 566 Airs, Dance Tunes and Marches, Vols. 1–3 by Frank Roche. 223 pages.

The Fiddler's Fake Book (American and British Isles Tunes). Nearly 500 tunes, introductions to regional styles, bowing and ornamentation, discography for each tune, list of alternate titles. Spiral bound, 301 pages, 1983.

Irish Fiddle by Kevin Burke. 6 one-hour tapes. Jigs, reels, slides, hornpipes, airs, ornaments. Homespun tapes, Box 694F, Woodstock, New York 12498.

The Northern Fiddler: Music of Musicians of Donegal & Tyrone by Alan Feldman and Eamonn O'Doherty. 251 pages, history, lore, interviews, illustrations, 192 tunes. Blackstaff Press Limited, Belfast, 1980.

Charlton Tune Book. Northumberland pipe tunes which can be played on fiddle.

Learn to Play the Fiddle with Armagh Piper's Club (from Ireland) by Eithne and Brian Vallely. 48 pages.

The Celtic Society Tunebook. Put out by the organization of the same name in Urbana, Illinois. 42 pages, 123 tunes, Irish, Scottish, Cornish, jigs, reels, slides, hornpipes.

Fiddle Tunes of Omer Marcoux by Omer Marcoux and Sylvia Miskoe. This book was made when Omer was 82 and includes tunes learned from his father and grandfather. Omer had spent the last portion of his life in New Hampshire and the tunes reflect a French Canadian/New England style. $5.00.

Dance to the Fiddle, March to the Fife: Instrumental Folk Tunes in Pennsylvania by Samuel P. Bayard. 628 pages.

Across the Fields: Traditional Norwegian-American Music from Wisconsin (fiddle and button accordion tunes) by Phil Martin and Bob Wernerehl. 48 pages.

Scandinavian Folk Dances and Tunes published by Folklore Village Farm. 13 dances and 45 tunes with melodies, some harmony parts, and chords, collected from visiting Scandinavian musicians. 36 pages.

Leaves of Cabbage—Music for Scottish Country Dancing by Barbara Bounsina and Robert McOwen. 360 reels, jigs, strathspeys. 2nd edition, 1979.

Band Call: 76 Tunes for Folk Dance Musicians and Bands by Dennis Darke. 21 pages.

New England Traditional Fiddling: An Anthology of Recordings, 1926-1975. Over 22 tunes, jigs, reels, hornpipes, a waltz, from the playing of Ron West, Uncle Joe Shippee, The Plymouth, Vermont Old Time Barn Dance Orchestra, Mellie Dunham's Orchestra, Ben Guillemette, etc. Includes 32 page book with social history of fiddling in New England. Written tunes, bibliography, discography. The John Edwards Memorial Foundation, Inc., 1978.

Scandinavian Songbook. Songs and tunes, 80 pages.

Fiddle Tunes for the Violinist by Betty M. Barlow. 71 pages with pullout sections. $5.05.

Scandiavian Folk Dance and Tunes by Werner.

Traditional Cajun Fiddle by Dewey Balfa and Tracy Schwarz. 7 tunes, second fiddle parts, diagrams and text in a 16 page booklet which accompanies the record. Folkways Records and Service Corporation, 43 West 61st St., New York, New York 10023.

Sylvia Miskoe
102 Little Pond Road
Concord, N. H. 03301
May 2, 1982

Dear Mr Thomson,

While perusing the UNH spring course catalogue I found your traditional styles of fiddling course.

I have just co-authored a book of fiddle tunes by Omer Marcoux. Omer is now 82, a remarkable fiddler of the French Canadian tradition. Many of the tunes he plays are only rarely played by others and include tunes learned from his father and grandfather.

We have written these tunes exactly as they are played, complete with double stops (Omer never plays one note where 2 are possible) and all the irregularities of beat which are so unique to French Canadian fiddling. We have also edited many of the tunes and put them into a 32 measure form so they may be used for contra dancing.

You, and your class, are cordially invited to a celebration of this book at the NH Historical Society, Park St, Concord on Friday, May 16th from 4:30 & 6:30 pm.

Omer, and all his friends, will be making joyous music in the best of French Canadian and New England traditions

Sincerely,
Sylvia Miskoe

Books Relating to Fiddle Music

Bluegrass by Bob Artis. 182 pages. History of bluegrass. Hawthorne Books Inc., New York, 1975.

The Big Book of Bluegrass edited by Marilyn Rochman. Interviews and articles with bluegrass greats such as Bill Monroe, Earl Scruggs, Kenny Baker, Byron Berline, Mark O'Connor and others. Instructional tips, some tablature and music for fiddle, guitar, banjo, mandolin, dobro. Book is mostly text with photos, 278 pages. GPI Publications, 1984. $12.95.

Musical Instruments of the Southern Appalachian Mountains. 2nd edition by John Rice Irvin. 104 pages, photos and text of homemade fiddles, banjos, dulcimers, etc. Schiffer Pub. Co., Ltd., 1983.

Rantin' Pipe and Tremblin' String: A History of Scottish Dance Music by George S. Emmerson. 278 pages, 104 tunes, but mostly text. Chapters on dance, composers, fiddlers, bagpipes, etc. J. M. Dent and Sons, Publisher, 1971.

A Time to Dance by Richard Nevell. 272 pages, history of New England contra dancing, contras, fiddlers, lore, dances, a few tunes, photos, sources. St. Martin's Press, New York, 1977.

Learning the Fiddler's Ways by Matthew Guntharp. A book about collecting fiddle tunes in central Pennsylvania. Interviews, lore, photos, fingering diagrams, discussion of styles. 31 tunes, hoedowns, waltzes, etc. 159 pages. The Pennsylvania State University Press, 1980. $7.50.

The Bluegrass Band by Roger Holtman. 73 pages.

Country Music Recorded Prior to 1943: A Discography of LP Reissues compiled by Willie Smyth with a preface by Norm Cohen. 83 pages, 50 pages of just albums and titles. Also informative preface, artist and title index. $7.50 from The John Edwards Memorial Foundation, Inc.

A Social History of Scottish Dance by George S. Emmerson. 352 pages, chapters on all aspects of Scottish dancing, jigs, reels, hornpipes, bibliography, etc. Montreal: McGill-Queen's University Press, 1972.

Publications Relating to Fiddle and Folk Music

Frets: The magazine of accoustic stringed instruments - Frets Subscription Dept., Box 2120, Cupertino, CA 95015. Features regular column on fiddle, articles on professional fiddlers, and many other articles on all aspects of accoustic stringed instruments.

Quinlin Campbell Publishers - Box 651, Boston, MA 02134. Free brochure. Books and tune books on traditional music and musicians: Sean O Riada, Paddy Tunny, Willie Clancy, etc.

The New England Folk Directory - by Wayne Licwov, 8 North Street, Brattleboro, VT 05301. Lists musicians, bands, dance callers, organizations, clubs and concerts, festivals, other directories.

Bluegrass Directory - Box 412-E, Murphys, CA 95247. 192 pages, instruments, records, books, supplies, published bi-annually. $6.13 postpaid.

Down East Friends of the Folk Arts - c/o M. Halley, RFD #1, Box 1760, Freedom, ME 04941. Promotes folk arts in Maine and vicinity, lists radio programs, classes, concerts, dances, festivals, etc. $6/year for newsletter. (207) 589-4503.

Cuzin' Isaac's Bluegrass Gazette - P.O. Box 252, Alstead, NH 03602. Lists bluegrass festivals, radio shows, listings by performers, etc. Mostly northeast USA. $4/year, published monthly.

New England Folk Festival News - Listings of festivals, square and contra dances to live music, and related events in the New England area, annual large folk dancing festival in Natick, MA with fiddle workshops. 309 Washington Street, Wellesley Hills, MA 02181, (607) 235-6181.

Folk Arts Network Resource Guide - P.O. Box 867, Cambridge, MA 02238. Folk arts teachers, radio programs, stores, meetings, etc. Listings $1.00. (617) 864-2970.

The Devil's Box - published by the Tennessee Folklore Society, 305 Stella Drive, Madison, AL 35758, (205) 837-4235. Quarterly publication on fiddling lore, history, interviews, instrument repair, music, record reviews, etc. 1 year subscription $7.00. Back issues available. Highly recommended.

Old Time Music - 33 Brunswick Gardens, London W8 4AW, England. Also available from Rounder Records. Mostly articles on fiddlers and oldtime string bands in the U.S., illustrated.

Mel Bay Publications - 4 Industrial Drive, Pacific, MO 63039. Instruction books and music for fiddling, other instruments.

Black Sheep Review - 27 Dana Street, Cambridge, MA 02138, c/o Kari Estrin. Bi-monthly folk and accoustic music magazine for New England and northeast states. $8/year, 5 issues.

Bluegrass Alternative and National Fiddler - 3435 Polley Drive, Vista, CA 92083. Monthly magazine combining bluegrass and old time fiddling. Nationwide events, tabs, ads, stories, reviews. $10/year includes membership in the National Old Time Fiddler's Association.

Bluegrass Music News - P.O. Box 16, Elm Springs, AR 72728. Local and regional news. c/o Chuck Stearman. (816) 665-7172.

Bluegrass Newsletter - P.O. Box 4600, Austin, TX 78765, c/o Jamie Maclaggan. Bi-monthly newsletter, record reviews, points of view, interviews, event calendar. Free sample copy with SASE business sized envelope. Subscription $8/year, $12/two years.

Bluegrass Unlimited - P.O. Box 111, Broad Run, VA 22014, c/o Peter V. Kuykendall. Monthly bluegrass magazine. Subscription $12/year. (703) 361-8992.

Publications Relating to Fiddle and Folk Music

Oak Publications - 33 West 60th Street, New York, NY 10023. Books on fiddling and other topics in folklore and music. Toll-free number for catalogue (800) 431-7187.

Canadian Bluegrass Review - P.O. Box 143, Waterdown, Ontario, Canada LOR 2HO, c/o Pat Buttenham. Bi-monthly magazine, subscription $10/year Canada, $11/year U.S. (416) 689-5861.

Country Heritage - R.R. 1, Box 320, Madill, OK 73446, c/o Beverly King. Monthly publication, traditional country music, songs, interviews, news, reviews. Sample copy 60¢.

Country Music Foundation - 4 Music Square East, Nashville, TN 37203. Journal of country music, historical reprints, book-length studies. Free printout of books available.

Country Music Illustrated - 299 Chelsea Street, Buffalo, NY 14223. 8 page western New York country music guide, monthly. $12/year.

Legacy Books - P.O. Box 494, Hatboro, PA 19040. Domestic and imported books on folk music and dance.

MIH Publications - 15 Arnold Place, New Bedford, MA 02740. Magazines, catalogue reprints, and books dealing with old musical instruments. (617) 993-0156.

Mugwumps - 15 Arnold Place, New Bedford, MA 02740. Magazine specializing in old instruments, collection, repair, value, classified section. (617) 993-0156. Mugwumps Bookshelf is a mail order source of catalogue reprints, books and magazines on collecting, building, and repair.

Musical Instrument Classified - 842 S. Monroe Street, Dept. BD, Arlington, VA 22204. Monthly publication, buy-sell-trade vintage collectable instruments and related items. $12/year. (703) 521-2897.

Orange Blossom Special - P.O. Box 341, Bonsal, CA 92003, c/o Dick Tyner. Quarterly newspaper featuring Western U.S. bluegrass music news and advertising. Free. (619) 758-7205

Sing Out! Magazine - P.O. Box 1071, Easton, PA 18042. Quarterly folk music magazine, music, lyrics, interviews, feature articles on traditional music. $11/year.

University of Tennessee Press - 293 Communications Bldg., Knoxville, TN 37916. Books on music, folklore.

Northern Junket - Ralph Page, 117 Washington Street, Keene, NH 03431. "Each issue brings you interesting articles on controversial subjects in the square and round dance world...traditional squares, contras, history of the dances and general New England folklore, as well as recipes for wives of hungry square and round dancing husbands." Published 5 times/year. $5 for 10 issues, $1 for trial issue. They also hold dance camps.

String Band Music Tablature - Jane Keefer, P.O. Box 721, Salem, OR 97308. Catalogue with sample tab of your style, $1. (503) 362-1320.

Disc Collector Publications - P.O. Box 316, Cheswold, DE 19936. Records and books. Send stamp for list. "Driftwood Records." (302) 674-3149.

National Square Dance Directory - P.O. Box 54055, Jackson, MS 39208, c/o Gordon Goss. International roster of clubs, festivals, callers, etc. Published yearly, $8 postpaid. (601) 825-6831.

Publications on Violin Making and Repair

Violin Identification and Price Guide, Vol. 1 by Roy Ehrhardt. Pages from sales catalogues. Covers American and imported instruments sold in the U.S. from 1800 to the present (1977), year of sale, original price, current price (1977), 1,536 violins, 522 bows, spiral bound, 192 pages. $21.25.

Violin Identification and Price Guide, Vol. 2 by Roy Ehrhardt. Continuation of first volume, 26 page section on French violins imported from 1891–1926, 2,661 violins, 121 bows, spiral bound, 206 pages. $21.25.

Violin Identification and Price Guide, Vol. 3 by Roy Ehrhardt. 152 pages. $12.75.

Cremona Violins and Varnish by Charles Reade. 39 pages.

Violin Bow Rehair and Repair by H. S. Wake. 93 pages, includes plans. 4171 Stettler Way, San Diego, CA 92122.

A Luthiers Scrap Book by H. S. Wake. Bow head repair, fitting a bridge, constructing tools for repair, varnish making, cutting a scroll, much more. Illustrations, 112 pages, eighth printing, 1979, published in San Diego.

The Techniques of Violin Making by H. S. Wake. 112 pages, self published in San Diego. Available mail order from some book and record distributors.

The Violin Maker's Guide by H. E. Brown, 52 pages.

Country Instruments: Makin' Your Own by Andy dePaule. 206 pages, sections on tools, finishing, plans for dulcimer, mandolin, guitar, fiddle, sources for wood and supplies. Oliver Press, Willits, CA., 1976.

Violin Varnish and Coloration by Martins, Roberts, Zemitis. Reviews of other authors' opinions and formulations plus those of the present author. Davis, CA: Amber Publishing Co., 1982. $28 postpaid.

Directory of Contemporary American Instrument Makers. Text edition, lists 2,500 makers of stringed and woodwind instruments. Columbia, MO: University of Missouri Press, 1981, 216 pages, ISBN 0-8262-0322-1. $24.00.

Guild of American Luthiers - 8222 S. Park Avenue, Tacoma, WA 98408. Members receive quarterly journal with "data sheets" on instrument repair and construction, all previously published data sheets available.

Violin Society of America - 23 Culver Hill, Southampton, NY 11968. Annual conventions, international competitions for instrument and bow makers, journal on all aspects of bowed string instruments, repairs, construction, appraisals, playing technique, instrument insurance, etc. $35/year.

Publications on Violin Making and Repair

Practical Violin Making by Edmund Fraser. 23 pages, includes blueprints. $3.40.

Amateur Fiddle Maker's Questions and Answers by H. S. Wake. 47 pages. $8.50.

Full size blueprints - available through **Elderly Instruments** - 1100 N. Washington, P.O. Box 14210, Lansing, MI 48901:

Violin bow - Tourte model, full size with stick bending and hairing instructions. Full frog details. $2.75.

Violin graduating caliper plans - $3.60.

Violin - Antonio Stradivari (c. 1716), 14" (356mm) body length, 12.875" (327mm) open string length. $1.90.

Violin - Joseph Guarnerius (c. 1734), 13.98" (355mm) body length, 12.875" (327mm) open string length. $1.90.

Violin - Jacob Stainer model (c. 1674), 14.06" (357mm) body length, 12.875" (327mm) open string length, includes details for mold plans. $2.75.

Stradivarius Violin - with a complete schedule of dimensions in inches for 4/4, 7/8, 3/4, 1/2, 1/4, etc. sizes. $2.35.

Violin - Amati soundbox pattern, graduations, arches, f holes. $2.75.

Violin - Maggini soundbox pattern, arches, f holes. $2.35.

Medieval Fiedel - flat top predecessor to the viol, tuned like a modern viola. $3.20.

Viola plans - by H. S. Wake. $18.50.

Violin/Fiddle and Bow Making and Repair Courses and Schools

Appalachian State University, Dept. of Music, Boone, NC 28608, c/o Dr. Jack Newton. One semester course in repair, mostly non-fretted instruments, for music teachers. (704) 262-3020.

Boston University Program in Artisanry, 620 Commonwealth Ave., Boston, MA 02215. 4 credit course, intro to the art of luthiery, techniques and skills of instrument making, applied to violin/viola. (617) 353-2022.

Summer Violin Institute, University of New Hampshire, Brook House, 24 Rosemary Lane, Durham, NH 03824. Workshops in violin repair, maintenance, building, bow repair and construction. Room and board available, courses taught by internationally known experts.

The Chimneys Violin School, 614 Lerew Road, Boiling Springs, PA 17007. Four year program in violin, viola, and cello making. (717) 258-3203.

Violin Making School of America, Peter Paul Prier, Inc., 308 East 2nd South, Salt Lake City, UT 84111. (801) 364-3651.

Chicago School of Violin Making, 20 East Jackson Blvd, Chicago, IL 60604. 3½ year course in violin construction, traditional methods and techniques, state approved vocational school. (312) 663-0367.

Musical Instrument Technology Program, Trinidad State Junior College, Box 168, Trinidad, CO 81082, c/o Larry Rice. Every aspect of repairs on brass, wind, string instruments, including business aspects and basic electronics. 2 year course, 24 hours/week toward certificate in Musical Instrument Technology. (303) 846-5582.

Musical Instrument Technology Program, State University of New York, Ag. and Tech. College, Morrisville, NY 13408, c/o John A. Hales. Intensive two year AA program in instrument repair, woodwind, brass, and strings. Workshop experience and repair testing. Fully accredited. (315) 684-7079.

Vermont Instrument Workshop, P.O. Box 115, Post Mills, VT 05058. School devoted to individual instruction in creative luthiery. Workspace, materials and living accommodations provided. (802) 333-4033.

Suppliers for the Violin Making and Repair Trade

Buck Musical Instrument Products - 40 N. Sand Road, New Britain, Pa 18901. Parts, materials, accessories for all acoustic instruments. Catalogue $2. (215) 345-9442.

Custom Pearl Inlay - P.O. Box 338, Waddington, NY 13964, c/o David Nichols. Catalogue $1. (315) 388-7884.

International Violin Co., Ltd. - 4026 W. Belvedere Ave., Baltimore, MD 21215. Instruments, tools, cases, parts, books, etc. (301) 342-3535.

Larry Kass Music Products - P.O. Box 4111, San Rafael, CA 94913. Manufacturer of violin, viola, bass fittings. Wholesale only. (415) 459-3585.

Pearl Works - Rt. 3, Box 122, Mechanicsville, MD 20659. Pearl and abalone products. (301) 884-5389.

Santa Fe Spruce Company - 129 Kearny Avenue, Santa Fe, NM 87501. Engleman spruce. Write for price list and free sample. (505) 983-1622.

Vikwood Ltd. - P.O. Box 554, Sheboygan, WI 53081, c/o Robert Larson. Luthiers specialty woods, free brochure and price list. (414) 458-9351.

Luthier's Mercantile - P.O. Box 774, 412 Moore Lane, Healdsburg, CA 95448-0774. Wood, tools, tuners, finishing materials. 80 page catalogue $4. Free brochure. (707) 433-1823.

Vitali Import Company - 5944 Atlantic Boulevard, Maywood, CA 90270. Supplies for instrument makers, violin catalogue $2.

William's Tool Company - 5531 San Juan Avenue, Citrus Heights, CA 95610. Molds and luthiers tools. Pamphlet 50¢. (916) 967-0780, 3–9 p.m.

Philip H. Weinkrantz Musical Supply Company, Inc. - 3715 Dickason at Oak Lawn, Dallas, TX 75219. Violin related supplies. (214) 526-7833.

Stewart MacDonald Company - Box 900, Athens, Ohio 45701. Banjo, mandolin, and fiddle components, supplies, and kits. (800) 848-2273.

The Fiddle Works - P.O. Box 1250, Mclean, VA 22101, c/o Karen Baker. Fiddle kits, instruction, tapes, books, accessories. Mail order to U.S. and Canada. Free catalogue.

Suppliers for the Violin Repair Trade
As recommended by the faculty of the Violin Institute of The University of New Hampshire
(Revised for 1983)

G. P. Nordenholz - 446 Walton Street, West Hempstead, NY 11552. (516) 483-7170. Accessories.

Metropolitan Music Co. - Mountain Road, RD 1, Stowe, VT 05672. (802) 253-4814. Tools and accessories.

M & M Distribution Co. - P.O. Box 1411, 2465 So. Industrial Highway, Ann Arbor, MI 48106. (313) 665-7711. Tools and accessories.

William Salchow Ltd., Bowmaker - 1755 Broadway, New York, NY 10019. (212) 586-4805. Complete line of tools and supplies for bowmaking.

William Harris Lee & Co., Inc. - 410 South Michigan Ave. Annex, Chicago, IL 60605. (312) 786-0459. Tools and accessories.

Woodcraft Supply - 313 Montvale Avenue, Woburn, MA 01888. (800) 225-1153. Tools.

Joseph Hamerl Geigenlacke (Varnishes) - Postfach 9, 8523 Baiersdorf, West Germany. Varnishes, colors, and resins.

Mohawk Finishing Products, H. Behlen Bros. - Perth Road, Amsterdam, NY 12010. (518) 843-1380. Varnishes, colors, and resins.

Films and Videotapes

The Country Fiddle #1 - Black and white, 8 minutes, 1959, Brandon Films. Filmed by Pete and Toshi Seeger, features Jean Carignan and Mrs. Marion Ungar Thede.

High Lonesome Sound - Black and white, 30 minutes, 1963, Brandon Films or Indiana University. A film by John Cohen, features Roscoe Holcomb and Bill Monroe.

Music Makers of the Blue Ridge - Black and white, 60 minutes, 1965, Indiana University. An NET production, Bascom Lamar Lunsford and musicians near Asheville, North Carolina.

TV videotapes from Broadside TV - 204 E. Watauge, Johnson City, TN 37601:

M7 - *Mountain Music Festival* - a series of tapes on traditional music.

M9 - *History of Country Music* - 8 tapes from a seminar at Clinch Valley College.

M12 - *Music of Many Mountains* - a series including:
12A *Mountain Music* - Pine Ridge, North Carolina, 60 minutes.

12B *Tommy Jarrell* - Famous banjo and fiddle player at his home in Toast, North Carolina, 60 minutes.

12C *Taylor and Stella Kimble* - Fiddle and banjo at laurel Fork, Virginia, 30 minutes.

12D *Mountain Music* - Fiddle, dulcimer, and banjo at Five Forks, Virginia, 30 minutes.

Say Old Man Can You Play the Fiddle - a short film of fiddler Earl Collins playing 6 tunes and making comments about fiddling. Edited by John M. Bishop of Media Generation, 917 East Broadway, Haverhill, MA 01830. (617) 372-0458.

Mark O'Connor Teaches Contest Fiddling Championship Style - on video, Homespun Tapes, Box 694F, Woodstock, NY 12498. Tunes are: "Wild Fiddler's Rag," "Skater's Waltz," "Soppin' the Gravy." VHS or Beta, $55 plus $3.50 postage. (914) 679-7832.

New England Contradancing - produced by National Public Television affiliate Channel 11, Durham, NH. 7½ minutes, features live dancing at the Nelson Town Hall in New Hampshire, and interviews with musician and folklorist Gordon Peery, dance caller Mary Desrosiers, and fiddler Ryan Thomson. Video, 1984.

Portrait of a Free Lance Fiddler - Ryan Thomson. Produced by Natick Cablevision Corporation, P.O. Box A, Natick, MA 01760. (617) 651-2500. 28-minute video featuring musician Ryan Thomson playing solo traditional fiddle tunes, playing with a contra dance band, playing electric lead fiddle with a rock band, playing clawhammer style banjo. 1984.

Fiddler's Organizations

Arizona Old Time Fiddlers Association - Garland Smith, President, 284 N. Arizona Avenue, Chandler, AZ 85224. (602) 963-7674.

Baltimore Folk Music Society - Box 7134, Waverly Station, Baltimore, MD 21218. Membership $7 single, $10 family. Newsletter, dances, concerts.

Brandywine Friends of Old Time Music - box 3504, Greenville, DE 19807. Bluegrass festival, Mountain Music Convention, concerts, newsletter.

California State Old-Time Fiddlers Association - P.O. Box 1703, Oroville, CA 95965, c/o William Kampstra, District 1. (916) 533-0731. Membership $12/year. Newsletter, state and regional contests.

Central California Old-Time Fiddlers Association - c/o Alva Davis, 2805 Charlotte Avenue, Ceres, CA 95307.

Central Valley Fiddlers Plus - P.O. Box 1842, Porterville, CA 93257, c/o E. H. Rather or Alfred Turner. Membership $10 single, $12 couple, $2 minor. Newsletter 50¢ plus postage. (209) 784-1753/8373.

Cornhusker Country Music Club - P.O. Box 42, Louisville, NE 68037, c/o Fred Klopp. Membership $5 single, $7 family. Newsletter. (402) 234-9605.

Fiddle & Guitar Club - 1440 Paramount Blvd., Paramount, CA.

Florida State Fiddlers Association - P.O. Box 713, Micanopy, FL 32667, c/o Thomas Stalely. Membership $10 single, $15 family. Newsletter. (904) 466-3801.

Idaho Old-Time Fiddlers Association - c/o Signal-American, Box 709, Weiser, ID 83672.

Illinois Old-Time Fiddler's Association - 211 West South 4th Street, Shelbyville, IL 62565.

June Apple Musician's Co-Op - P.O. Box 9701, Minneapolis, MN 55440, c/o Bob Bovee. Pop Wagoner, Charlie Maguire, Gail Heil, traditional musicians working together. (612) 338-4558.

Lancaster County Folk Music & Fiddlers Society - 47 East Lincoln Avenue, Lititz, PA 17543.

Michigan Fiddlers' Association - c/o William White, White Brothers String Shop, 4245 Okemos Road, Okemos, MI 48864.

Missouri Fiddlers & Country Music Association - 9245 Whitecliff Park Lane, Crestwood, MO 63126.

Montana State Fiddlers Organization - c/o Bonnie Stark, 3901 Becraft Lane, Billings, MT 59101.

National Old Time Fiddlers Association - c/o John Wilson, P.O. Box 265, Dragoon, AZ 85609.

National Old Time Fiddlers Association - Tri-State Division, Edd Britton, Chairman, 20 West Pleasant Street, Cincinnati, OH 45215.

National Old time Fiddlers Association - 3435 Polley Drive, Vista, CA 92083, c/o Burney Garelick. Membership $15/year, contests, shows, magazine. (619) 727-1280.

National Traditional Country Music Association, Inc. - 106 Navajo, Council Bluffs, IA 51501, c/o Bob Everhart. Music contests, Pioneer Exposition in September at Avoca, IA. (712) 366-1136.

Nevada Old Time Fiddlers Association - 7969 Rodeo Road, Las Vegas, NV 89119, c/o Don Germaine. Membership $15 each, $20 family. Includes national membership, newsletter, meetings, contest. (702) 361-5055.

New Mexico Old Time Fiddlers Association, Inc. - Lois Bucher, Public Relations, 401 Gold Street, Truth or Consequences, NM 87901.

Fiddler's Organizations

New York Old Tyme Fiddlers Association - c/o Alice C. Clemens, R.D. 1, Redfield, NY 13437.

Northeast Fiddlers Association, Inc. - c/o Roger Eastman, 191 Woodlawn Road, Burlington, VT 05401. Newsletter, membership is $4/year U.S., $5 Canadian funds to Don Bernard, Box 764, St. Albans, VT 05478. Newsletter, concerts, sponsors "National Traditional Old Time Fiddler's Contest."

Oklahoma State Fiddler's Inc. - 1824 N.W. 23rd Street, Oklahoma City, OK 73106, c/o Marion Thede. Membership $5/year. Many events, 7 chapters. (405) 525-2757.

Old Time Fiddlers Association of New Mexico, Inc. - Will Irwin, President, 1513 Escalante SW, Albuquerque, NM 87101. (505) 247-2633.

Old Time Fiddlers of Southwest Pennsylvania - Box 457, McLellardtown, PA 15458.

Oregon Old Time Fiddlers Association - Maxine Benson, Secretary/Treasurer, 2140 Ranch Corral Drive, Springfield, OR 97477. Membership $12/year. Newsletter, contest. (503) 746-1083.

Original Michigan Fiddlers' Association - c/o Lois Bettesworth, G-5035 Flushing Road, Flushing, MI 48433.

Santa Clara Valley Fiddlers Association - John Muir Jr. High School, Branham Lane, San Jose, CA.

San Joaquin Valley Fiddlers - Ester Dunn, Editor, P.O. Box 288, Terra Bella, CA 93270.

Scottish Fire - Colin G. Gordon, 1870 Phillips Ways, Los Angeles, CA 90042.

Seattle Folklore Society - 1810 N.W. 65th Street, Seattle, WA 98117, c/o Nancy Katz. Concerts, dances, Seattle Folk Arts School of Traditional Music and Dance, newsletter. Dues $8 individual, $12 household. (206) 782-0505.

Sooner Fiddlers Association - Judy Williams, Editor, 833 N.W. 35th, Oklahoma City, OK 73118.

Southern Arizona Old-Time Fiddlers Association - P.O. Box 5334, Tucson, AZ 85703.

Southern California Old-Time Fiddler's Association - c/o Howard and Joy Moore, Star Route, Box 89, Caliente, CA 93518.

Southern Indiana Fiddlers' Association - c/o Carl Nicholson, Route 3, Salem, IN 47167.

Tennessee Valley Old Time Fiddlers' Association - 305 Stella Drive, Madison, AL 35758.

Texas Old Time Fiddlers Association - P.O. Box 132, Gustine, TX 76455, c/o Vane Elms. Membership $13/year fiddler, $8/year associate. Monthly magazine, 65 contests/year. (915) 667-2561.

U.S. Scottish Fiddling Revival - c/o Brockman, 6365 Lakeview Drive, Falls Church, VA 22041.

Washington State Old Time Fiddlers Association - Roberta Ponischil, Editor, 410 Skylark Drive, Bremerton, WA 98312. Newsletter, meetings, contests. (206) 479-0313.

Bluegrass Organizations

Andirondack Bluegrass League - P.O. Box 901, Corinth, NY 12822, c/o Hank Clothier. Membership $5/year single or family. Monthly newsletter and meetings in the Corinth area, shows, camping weekend, Christmas party. (518) 747-0039.

Arizona Bluegrass Association - 4044 N. 44th Place, Phoenix, AZ 85018, c/o LeRoy Vines. (602) 959-9342.

Arkansas Bluegrass Association - P.O. Box 2178, Little Rock, AR 72203. Monthly meetings and newsletter. $4/year. L.W. Boise, president. (501) 327-6049.

Bluegrass Club of New York - 380 Lexington Avenue, Suite 1119, New York, NY 10017, c/o Doug Tuchman. Membership $5, $7 household, includes monthly newsletter, various events. (212) 687-9000.

Bluegrass & Country Music Makers Association - P.O. Box 249, Darrington, WA 98241, c/o Grover Jones. Meets last Friday/month, sponsors bluegrass festival in July. (206) 436-1006.

Boston Bluegrass Union - 50 Frost Street, Cambridge, MA 02140. (617) 646-6535.

Brazoria County Bluegrass and Gospel Music Association - Route 4, Box 4578, Brazoria, TX 77422. Membership $10/year. Newsletter, monthly meetings, annual April festival. C/o Lee Cade. (409) 798-9890.

California Bluegrass Association - P.O. Box 11287, San Francisco, CA 94101. Membership $8.50/year includes newsletter. (415) 548-9509.

Central California Bluegrass Association - P.O. Box 2033, Orcutt, CA 93455, c/o Joe Quealy. Membership and newsletter $10/year. Meetings, jams, shows. (805) 937-5895.

Central Indiana Bluegrass Association - 6020 Elm Drive, Marion, IN 46952, c/o Audra Demarcus. Membership $5/year. Newsletter, shows, festival. (317) 674-5117.

Central New York Bluegrass Association - 125 Meyers Lane, Liverpool, NY 14088, c/o Bill Knowlton. Meets second Sunday/month from Sept. – May, 2 p.m. at Masonic Temple in Cato, NY. (315) 457-6100.

Chicago Area Bluegrass Association - 1437 W. Howard Street, Chicago, IL 60626, c/o Paul Keller, Bill Landon. Membership $8 single, $12 family. Monthly meetings, jams, concerts. (312) 274-7333.

Eastern Shore Bluegrass Association - P.O. Box 223, Millington, MD 21651, c/o Eunice Price. Membership $5/year. Newsletter, meetings, festival. (301) 928-3613.

Greater Oklahoma Bluegrass Music Society - 2737 N.W. 22nd Street, Oklahoma City, OK 73107, c/o Charlie Clark. Newletter, concerts. Membership $5/year. (405) 943-4106.

Green Country Bluegrass Association - P.O. Box 6565, Tulsa, OK 74156, c/o Bill or Violet Hacker. Membership $3 single, $4 couple/year. Monthly newsletter and shows. (918) 425-5887.

Indiana Friends of Bluegrass - Route 8, Box 86, Greenfield, IN 46140, c/o Paul Cox.. Membership $10/year. (317) 898-9861.

Minnesota Bluegrass & Old Time Music Association - P.O. Box 9782, Minneapolis, MN 55440, c/o Larry Jones. Membership $10 single, $12 family. Newsletter.

Muddy River Bluegrass Association - P.O. Box 1244, Jefferson City, MO 65102, c/o Dan McKown. Monthly meetings and newsletter. (314) 445-3154.

Nashville Bluegrass Music Association - P.O. Box 4781, Nashville, TN 37216. Membership and bimonthly newsletter $10/year U.S. $15 in Canada and overseas.

Northwest Arkansas Bluegrass Association - P.O. Box 2000, Harrison, AR 72601, c/o Mackie McMulley. Bimonthly newsletter, meetings, annual festival. Membership $5/year single, $7.50/year family. (501) 743-3293.

O.K.I. Bluegrass Association - 605 Hulman Building, Dayton, OH 45402, c/o Bernie Phelan. Monthly newsletter. Membership $5/year.

Oklahoma Bluegrass Club - 1001 N. Pine, Oklahoma City, OK 73130, c/o Jerri Hill. Monthly newsletter, concerts. Membership $8/year. (405) 769-3172.

Oregon Bluegrass Association - P.O. Box 1115, Portland, OR 97207, c/o Meg Larson. Newsletter. Membership $10 single, $12 couple, $15 family.

San Diego North County Bluegrass Club - 510 N. Melrose Drive #A5, Vista, CA 92083, c/o Claude Godfrey. (619) 758-0732.

Santa Cruz Bluegrass Society - P.O. Box 2904, Santa Cruz, CA 95063, c/o Glenn Christiansen. Monthly jam sessions, newsletter. (408) 425-4941.

Society for Preservation of Bluegrass Music in America - P.O. Box 95, Lake Ozark, MO 65049. Festival guide and membership $5/year.

Southeast Texas Bluegrass Music Association - 7110 Lewis Drive, Beaumont, TX 77708, c/o Matt and Edy Mathews. Monthly meetings, banjo-fiddle contest, newsletter. Membership $7/year. (409) 892-5767.

Southern Nevada Bluegrass Music Association - P.O. Box 3704, North Las Vegas, NV 89030. Meetings and newsletter.

Southwest Bluegrass Club - 2222 Greenbriar, Irving, TX 75060, c/o Anne Uhr. Monthly magazine, meetings, and festival in June. Membership $7.50/year. (214) 253-5620.

SPBGMA - Bluegrass Music Club of Iowa - RR #1, Greenbriar Estates, Cumming, IA 50061, c/o Donald Taft. Meetings, newsletter, events.

Tri-State Bluegrass Association, Inc. - Box 215, Brunswick, MD 21716. Newsletter, jams, camp-outs. Initiation $8, dues $5/year.

Tri-State Bluegrass Association - RR #1, Kahoka, MO 63445, c/o Erma Spray. Bimonthly newsletter and yearly directory. (314) 853-4344.

Walnut Valley Association - P.O. Box 245, Winfield, KS 67156, c/o Bob Redford. Free publication 4/year. (316) 221-3250.

Washington Bluegrass Association - P.O. Box 490, Toledo, WA 98591, c/o Sue Murphy. Quarterly newletter, concerts, festivals. Membership $10 single, $12 couple, $15 family. (206) 864-2074.

White River Folk and Bluegrass Club - RR #8, Box 313, Muncie, IN 47302, c/o Viola Brooks. Monthly newsletter, meetings, jams, festivals. Membership $5/year. (317) 759-5697.

"My dad was an old time fiddle player, and I remember the first time I played. I was standing at my dad's knees, and he put the fiddle around in front of me, and put the bow up there and put my hand on it. That's how I started."
— **Byron Berline**
Sundance and the
LA Fiddle Band (*Frets*)

"Just keep at it, or that instrument will whip you."
— **Bobby Hicks,**
with Bill Monroe and his
Bluegrass Boys (*Frets*)

When asked whether he'd rather be called a "fiddle" player rather than a "bluegrass" fiddler: "I think so. When you say 'bluegrass' you are putting something in[to] one category and I play what I feel. I don't know if it's anything. If I'm playing with a band, I play to the overall sound of what's going on. I am lucky enough to be broadminded about music. I love all kinds of good music, and I'm going to try to play as much of it as I can."
— **Vassar Clements with**
Bill Monroe, Earl Scruggs
Review, Grand Ole Opry, etc.
(*Frets*)

Music and Dance Camps and Schools

Old Songs Festival - P.O. Box 197, Guilderland, NY 12084. Workshops in fiddle and other traditional instruments, singing, dancing, etc. Dates for 1984 were June 29, 30, July 1. Write for information.

"Root Camp" Fiddle and Dance Workshop at Ashokan - RD 1, Box 489, West Hurley, NY 12491. Dates for 1984 features a "Northern Week," August 19–25, and a "Southern Week," August 26–September 1. Bunkhouse, camping, optional vegetarian meals. Call or write for more information. (914) 338-2996.

Valley of the Moon Scottish Fiddling School - directed by Alasdair Fraser. Contact Jan Tappan, 1938 Rose Villa Street, Pasadena, CA 91107. Dates for 1984 were August 27 – 31 with instructors Alastair Hardie and Dr. Tom Anderson.

Pinewoods Camp, by The Countlry Dance & Song Society of America - 505 Eighth Avenue, New York, NY 10018. Summer camps in Massachusetts of traditional American and ethnic music and dancing, fiddling, etc. The society also offers dances, performances, books, records, and research into music and dance traditions. Many affiliates across the U.S.

The Swannonoa School of Southern Music & Dance - Grey Eagle Rt. 1, Leicester, NC 28748. Associated with Warren Wilson College which offers an "Appalachian Music Program." Summer workshops in fiddle, shape note singing, traditional dancing, banjo, other instruments. (704) 683-4552.

The Swannanoa School of Southern Music & Dance promises to be a unique gathering of musicians and dancers for a week of old tunes and hot times.

The days will be filled with workshops and classes taught by the finest performers and teachers in southern music and dance. The evenings will be a time of informal group singing, music making, and, of course, dances.

We are placing heavy emphasis on the fiddle, with eight great fiddlers playing for the dances, leading daily classes, guest workshops and jam sessions. There will also be special emphasis on clawhammer banjo, back-up guitar, mandolin, string band, southern harmony and gospel singing (including shape note), dance calling, and folklore.

The week will also feature a unique mixture of southern squares, contras and clogging with ragtime dance and turn of the century vintage ballroom dancing to a lively ragtime orchestra.

Saturday will be a celebration with local musicians and dancers joining us for a day of concerts, workshops and jam sessions.

WARREN WILSON COLLEGE

Warren Wilson College is a small liberal arts college in the heart of the mountains of western North Carolina. The college has long been supportive of mountain music and dance. In fact, the Appalachian Music Program at Warren Wilson is the only program in the country where a student can earn a concentration in Appalachian music for their liberal arts degree. The college also has the Mountain Music Archive, which contains tapes, films, and albums of the area's traditional musicians.

The college itself is surrounded by the Craggy Mountains and is located on the banks of the Swannanoa River on a thousand acres. The campus contains a timber operation, a pond for swimming, trails for hiking, open fields for wandering, and a full working farm which supplies most of the food for the cafeteria.

TRADITIONAL MUSIC has become an integral part of Centrum's programming since the first Festival of American Fiddle Tunes eight years ago. The success of the Festival is largely due to the fact that it has always been dedicated to the preservation of obscure and dying traditions. Many featured performers of earlier Festivals are no longer with us, but we are constantly searching for other keepers of those traditions. The blend of these individuals, along with younger, talented enthusiasts, makes the Festival of American Fiddle Tunes unique among Festivals in its offering of week-long workshops, band labs, master classes, repertoire sessions, and concerts, all combined to provide participants with a rare insight into the many and varied facets of what is commonly known as Traditional American Folk Music.

FIDDLE TUNES is renowned for its fine workshops, quality performances, and close camaraderie. The 1984 Festival promises to be better than ever with a faculty representing major regional and ethnic styles, and offering participants a wide choice of options including daily workshops and tutorials in fiddle, banjo, mandolin and guitar, as well as traditional dancing and singing. Participants may also expand their repertoire through the experience of string band playing in daily band labs led by faculty members. Each evening during the early part of the week, select faculty are highlighted in intimate concerts open only to participants, with public performances featured on the weekend, ending with the traditional Saturday night dance under the big top.

THE FESTIVAL OF AMERICAN FIDDLE TUNES
June 27 - July 3

One of America's premier traditional music events presents intensive workshops, all-night jam sessions, and a performance-packed Fourth of July weekend. This year features the traditions of classic Southern string bands with fiddle great Lowe Stokes heading the list of faculty performers. Joining Lowe is fiddler Bob Simmons from the Kentucky-Illinois border. Bob played on the legendary Renfro Valley Barn Dance radio series during the late 1930's and 1940's, including a three-year stint with Clayton McMitchen and his Georgia Wildcats. Festival favorites return to join these fiddlers for a music-filled week. Last year's workshop registration reached capacity in early May, so early sign-up is recommended.

Tuition: $100
Optional dormitory room and board: $125

FIDDLE TUNES FESTIVAL

Festival of American Fiddle Tunes - Centrum, Fort Worden State Park, P.O. Box 1158, Port townsend, WA 98368. Summer workshops in fiddle, banjo, dancing, singing, mandolin, guitar, etc. Room and board available, staff from around North America, many styles of traditional music.

Augusta Heritage Arts Workshop - Davis and Elkins College, Elkins, WV 26241, c/o Doug Hill. Intensive summer workshops in traditional music, dance, folklore, and crafts. (304) 636-1903.

Ralph Page Dance Camps - 117 Washington, Street, Keene, NH 03431. Square dance weekend, 1st weekend of November. Folk dance weekend, 1st weekend of May. 5 day folk and square dance camp in September, 5 day folk and square dance camp last week of December. Send name and address to get on mailing list.

Village School of Folk Music -
  645 Osterman Avenue, Deerfield, IL 60015. (312) 945-5321.
  545 N. Milwaukee Avenue, Libertyville, IL 60048. (312) 367-1191.
  125 N. Buffalo Grove Road, Buffalo Grove, IL 60090. (312) 537-3020.
c/o Bob Gand. Music stores, classes and private lessons. All folk instruments.

Records and Reviews

THIS SECTION contains reprints of advertisements of folk and fiddle records. It is organized by record and distribution companies and samples of their offerings. Within each listing by company, records of particular fiddle styles have been grouped together. To locate information about certain fiddlers, bands, styles of fiddling, and accompanying musicians, see the index on page 129.

Since these listings are only a sample of the available recordings, readers desiring more information are urged to contact the various firms listed, and also those in the "General Listing of Sources" section on pages 67–68.

Roundup Record Reviewers:

RC	Bob Coltman
SH	Steve Harris
LD	Laura Dickerson
JT	Jack Tottle
PK	Pete Kairo
DK	Dan Kahn
WAR	Wendy A. Ritger
MPW	Mark Wilke
SJA	Sarah Abrams
LN	Laura Nagan
RFG	Robert F. Gear
RED	Bob Doucet
GKJ	Glenn K. Jones
EW	Evanne Weirick
GT	George Thomas
CS	Cynthia Stoddard
SB	Scott Billington

Roundup Records
P.O. Box 154
N. Cambridge, MA 02140
Address Correction Requested
Forwarding Postage Guaranteed

THE EAST TEXAS SERENADERS   (COUNTY 410)

Fiddle, tenor banjo, guitar, cello

ACORN STOMP/OZARK RAG/SHANNON WALTZ/COMBINATION RAG/
BABE/SWEETEST FLOWER WALTZ/ARIZONA STOMP/3-IN-1 TWO STEP/
DEACON JONES/SERENADERS WALTZ/EAST TEXAS DRAG/BEAUMONT
RAG/ADELINE WALTZ/MINEOLA RAG.

The times brought to life in fragile, raggy beauty
by this LP were a brief moment, but what a moment: the
spontaneous generation of old-time string band music in
the southwest. While string band playing was becoming
a way of life in the 1920s south, bands were few in
Texas. The Serenaders, based around Tyler, were about
the only band they knew. In a few years what would
later be called Western Swing would sweep Texas, and
this lilting, fetching older music (shakily credited
with playing a part in WS development) would be gone
by 1940, overridden by something much more forward.
Which is a shame, because this music gets inside you
as bolder stuff often doesn't do.
Fiddler Huggins Williams, born of a Tennessee father,
shows some of that state's treatment of a tune in his
deft, pungent noting. But he was a mixer of many other
influences: blues, limber rags, a touch of gentle jazz,
sweet clear Texas touches on the hoedown and surely
some of the most poignant, beautifully conceived old
time waltz playing ever done. Restrained sureness
characterized the guitar and the rarely flourished banjo.
The personality of the band is the delightfully tubby
cello, endlessly evoking another time and place. The
ensemble is hesitant yet impulsive. I don't think in
these days when technique has become a trap there are
any string bands left with this naive ventursome quality,
the ungainly older rhythms and experiments with expressive phrasing only additing to the Serenaders'
charm. Their music is fun to hear, makes you think
about people you danced with years ago, and when the
record's over you wonder where the time went.

                      RC $5.00

2nd ANNUAL BRANDYWINE MOUNTAIN MUSIC CONVENTION '75 TRA-
DITIONAL MUSIC OF WEST VIRGINIA (Heritage XII).
Heritage is one of the few labels specializing exclusively in Old Timey Music and doing a good job at it,
too. This album is an excellent cross section of Old
Time Mountain Music as played at Brandywine '75. It
features tunes such as "Yew Piney Mountain" by seasoned
master, Wilson Douglas, as well as "Wake Up Susan" by
The Morris Brothers (John and Dave, not Wiley and Zeke).
Ola Belle and her family make an appearance for one
priceless cut, "I've Endured." Tracy Schwarz and Mike
Seeger do two little-heard tunes, "Deceiver" and "Box
the Fox." Phoebe Parsons does a poem and a song sort
of an Arkansas Traveler idea, but much different. Highwoods String Band is in their usual good-time form playing "Dusty Miller," "Texas Gales," and "George Booker."
Ira Mullins fiddles "Cluck Ole Hen" with a fine old-time
sound and Jenes Cottrell does a neat version of "The
Devil and the Farmer's Wife," half-spoken, half-sung
with a banjo accompaniment. A recommended album for any
Old Time Music fan. The quality of the recording (done
by NPR) is as good as can be expected from a live recording.

                           -SH $4.00

OLD ORIGINALS VOLS. 1 and 2 (sold separately) (Rounder
0057/0058)
Volume 1: JAKE GILLY/WALLS OF JERICHO/YOU NEVER MISS
YOUR MAMMA/ROUSTABOUT/SALT RIVER/SHOOTIN' CREEK/OLD TIME
FIRE ON THE MOUNTAIN/TWIN SISTERS/BONAPARTE'S MARCH INTO
RUSSIA/DINEO/BREAKIN' UP CHRISTMAS/FLYIN' INDIAN/
STILLHOUSE/TURKEY IN THE STRAW/HOP LIGHT LADIES/TOMMY
LOVE/SHORTENIN' BREAD/RICH MOUNTAIN/SANDY RIVER BELLES/
POSSUM TROT/SARO/TRAIN ON THE ISLAND/OLD VIRGINIA MARCH
Volume 2: FANNY HILL/FORKED DEER/HOLLIDING CINDY/WAVES
ON THE OCEAN/TRAP HILL TUNE/SALLY ANN/PINEY WOODS GAL/
EVENING RAINBOW WALTZ/DID YOU EVER SEE THE DEVIL UNCLE
JOE/BELLE ELECTION/MOLLY PUT THE KETTLE ON/OLD MOLLY
HAIR/SARO/AIN'T GONNA WORK TOMORROW/QUIT THAT TICKLIN'
ME/TWIN SISTERS/GOING HOME/HOUSE CARPENTER/PEARLY BLUE/
CHICKEN IN THE BREAD TRAY/WALLS OF JERICHO/CUMBERLAND
GAP/RAMBLING HOBO/CRIPPLE CREEK/NANCY BLEVINS
For years we've wanted field recordings; suddenly
we're knee deep in them. Good regional collections have
recently appeared from the Ozarks, from Kentucky, West
Virginia and elsewhere. This set, covering the
musically unique area of southwestern Virginia and the
bordering area of North Carolina, is top-notch. Mainly
it focuses on instrumental music, though stray lyrics
come through here and there, and there is a shortened
ballad. The performers and men and women in their
sixties and older (a few familiar names: surviving
members of the Shelor Family and Floyd County Ramblers
who recorded in the '20s-30, and John Rector, the
fiddler, not the banjo picker).
What makes these tracks so good? Almost without
exception the musicians play in styles untouched, or
nealy, by the commercial music developments of the last
few decades. There's no bluegrass here, no pop touches
at all. In one case where a tune was learned from Flatt
and Scruggs it has been beautifully renaturalized into
a creditably oldtimey piece. The music is precisely
not smooth, not polished; there isn't a touch of the
contest and festival style that has reduced much
fiddling and picking today to mush. The players play
lightly, almost shyly -- their music is out of date and
they know that, and of course they are past their
prime -- but with a fierce individuality, a concern for
the noting and phrasing of a tune, an almost lost
individualized feeling for rhythm, "time," a sort of
plucky adventuring in home-made sound. Only the best
field recordings have this, and collectors Carter and
Owen are both lucky and skillful to have found it in
such abundance. Their informative notes and photos
help show the musicians in the round and convey a sense
of the distance and time this music has had to travel
to come to us.

ANY OLD TIME STRING BAND (Archoolie 4009)

LET ME FALL/DEAR COMPANION/TURKEY BUZZARD/CHINQUAPIN
HUNTING/I WISH I'D STAYED IN THE WAGON YARD/MA CHER
BEBE CREOLE/DIXIELAND ONE STEP/HOME IN PASADENA/LONG
LOST LOVER BLUES/VALSE DE ORPHELIN/C-U-B-A/FREE LITTLE
BIRD/I'VE GOT WHAT IT TAKES/I BID YOU GOODNIGHT
From the name, you might think this is an old time
string band. Well, sort of or sometimes. The instru-
mentation certainly is. Most string bands are all men.
This one is all women. The vocals and picking are all
competent and what is just as good, quite spirited.
(Example from the notes - under the credits for "Let
me Fall" it lists one as "guitar & raucous shouts.")
Besides the string band tunes, though, they do jazz
("Dixieland one-step"), Cajun (much Balfa Brothers
influence), Blues from Bessie Smith and Lottie Kim-
brough, a hymn from the Bahamas and a Bing Crosby
song about the ways to escape Prohibition (C-U-B-A).
Aside from "I've got what it takes..." which loses a
lot in the transition from Bessie Smith to anything or
anybody else, everything on the album is fresh and good.
I listened to it everyday for the first week I had it.
I am trying not to be too effusive and write an objective
review but I really love this album. Buy it. Listen to
the difference women's harmonies make on traditional
songs. Sing along. Dance around your kitchen. Enjoy!

                      LD $5.00

FIDDLIN' ARTHUR SMITH & HIS DIXIELINERS   Volume 1
(County 546)

GOIN' TO TOWN/A LONESOME DAY TODAY/CHEATHAM COUNTY BREAK-
DOWN/FLORIDA BLUES/I'M BOUND TO RIDE/FIDDLER'S BLUES/
STRAW BREAKDOWN/K.C. STOMP/TAKE ME BACK TO TENNESSEE/
DICKSON COUNTY BLUES #2/ADIEU FALSE HEART/BONAPARTE'S
RETREAT/I'VE HAD A BIG TIME TODAY

FIDDLIN' ARTHUR SMITH & HIS DIXIELINERS   Volume 2
(County 547)

INDIAN CREEK/CHITTLIN COOKIN TIME IN CHEATHAM COUNTY/
PEACOCK RAG/THERE'S MORE PRETTY GIRLS THAN ONE/SUGAR TREE
STOMP/PIG AT HOME IN A PEN/FIDDLER'S DREAM/HOUSE OF DAVID
BLUES/FREIGHT TRAIN MOAN/RED APPLE RAG/THE GIRL I LOVE
DON'T PAY ME NO MIND/BLACKBERRY BLOSSOM/IN THE PINES/
SMITH'S RAG

Fiddlin' Arthur Smith is one of a handful of old-time
country musicians who stand alone in a uniquely important
musical niche. His popularity was immense during the twenties and thirties among those who heard him on the Grand
Ole Opry. Roy Acuff, who succeeded Arthur on the Opry,
called him "the King of Fiddlers" and the album notes include similarly superlative accolades from Bill Monroe and
Kenny Baker. Many other influential bluegrass fiddlers
cite Arthur's influence.

Arthur composed fiddle tunes and songs and sang in a
relaxed and engaging manner. His fiddling style was truly
remarkable. It was as different from previous fiddlers
as, say, Clarence White's guitar style compared to earlier
bluegrass guitarists. Arthur's fast tunes were full of
fire, joy, and adventuresome technique. His slower tunes
had a moving bluesy quality.

In an important sense, Fiddlin' Arthur Smith is a link
between bluegrass (which these recordings pre-date) and
old-time country music. His "In the Pines" is remarkably
similar to Bill Monroe's later recording and Smith's
"Fiddler's Blues" is based around a phrase nearly identical
to Monroe's melody for "Blue Grass Stomp." The Stanley
Brothers' versions of "Pig in a Pen" and "Bound to Ride"
sound like they came from Arthur's. Among other Smith originals which have become favorites of bluegrass fiddlers
are "Florida Blues," "Peacock Rag," and "Red Apple Rag."

But, the reason these releases are most welcome is
not for the filling of a chunk of musical history. It is
because Arthur's music still comes through with wonderful
freshness, spirit, and excitement. There are lots of great
fiddle tunes, the majority of his own composition, and a
variety of songs ranging from infectious humor to soulful
country love songs. The Delmore Brothers accompany him
on most cuts, and blend beautifully both instrumentally
and vocally. Both albums are rare treats and are highly
recommended to anyone with an ear for either old-time country music or bluegrass. This set is clearly one of the
most significant and enjoyable re-issues in years.

(An added bonus is the excellent booklet included
with each album. Prepared by Charles Wolfe and Barry Poss,
it contains many pictures and first-rate historical information.)

                                    J.T. $5.00 each

ARKANSAS SHEIKS, "Whiskey Before Breakfast" (Bay #204).
Seems I've heard that title somewhere before. Oh-well...
The Arkansas Sheiks are a wonderfully good-humored old-
timey string band that seem to enjoy their music, which
encompasses traditional jazz tunes, fiddle tunes, west-
ern-swing and round-singing. The tunes with hammered
dulcimer (Whiskey Before Breakfast, Billy Martin, Growl-
ing Old Man/Drowsy Maggie, Carpenter's Reel, Boatman/
Cherokee Shuffle) are foot-tappers that could make
Ebenezer Scrooge start dancin'. The round (Sherburne)
is again another tune sung without accompaniment that
makes one feel like cuttin' a rug. Alvin Yardley Tune
has a western swing ragtime feel that makes it one of
my favorites. Brother Ephus is one of those country
humor call-and-response tunes that reminds you of the
games you used to play as a kid. A genuinely good time
album. I recommend it highly.

                                    -PK (\$4.50)

THE HOLLOW ROCK STRING BAND (Kanawha 311)
KITCHEN GIRL/CLOG/WALTZ/DINAH/RICHMOND COTILLION/HOG-
EYED MAN/JOHN BROWN'S MARCH/GREEN FIELDS OF AMERICA/
HOP LIGHT LADIES/JAWBONES/BETTY LIKENS/CABIN CREEK/
FOLDING DOWN THE SHEETS/MONEY MUSK/DEVIL ON A STUMP/
OVER THE WATERFALL/FIDDLER'S DRUNK AND THE FUN'S ALL
OVER

First issued around a decade ago, this LP has the
distinction of being a collector's classic in its own
time -- partly because it has usually been unavailable,
but also due to its sheer excellence. This album
almost by itself began an amazing decade of infatuation
with the rare and idiosyncratic in tunes and songs --
the Second Wave of old time playing which has produced
a number of fine revival groups and some good recorded
field collections of authentic regional music to build
on the fine Library of Congress efforts of the 30s and
40s. Alan Jabbour, noted scholar, handles his fiddle
with likable rawness and fine spirit, with stylistic
debt to the late Virginia oldtimer, Henry Reed. Tommy
Thompson here began to build his formidable reputation
with note-perfect, mellow note-for-note unison frailing.
Bert Levy's mandolin usually takes a rhythm role but
both he and the late Bobbie Thompson (guitar) step out
into countermelody at times. The ensemble has a light,
quick, deft sound that arrested its early hearers and
sounds just as fresh today. Compared to more recent
productions in similar styles and approaches, Hollow
Rock easily ranks with the best. Old friends like
"Cabin Creek" (aka "Barlow Knife") and jammers'
favorite "Over the Waterfall" have a scampery, delightful disciplined looseness that comes with having put
something new and fine together. The music is frisky,
done with skill and potency and enough raggedness to
make it live and breathe. I hope Kanawha can keep up
with the demand; I'm just taking a head count of all
the people I know who have wanted this LP and couldn't
find it for/years. Taking the best tradition offers
and showcasing it with a tight ensemble sound (in its
own way an innovation), Hollow Rock gives us rare
tunes beautifully performed and standing the test of
time.

                -RC $4.50

MAJOR CONTAY AND THE CANEBRAKE RATTLERS: Flying Crow 104
OLD FAMILIAR TUNES $5.50

Side One: Johnson Gal/Davy/I'm S·A·V·E·D/Sweet Milk and Peaches/
A Lazy Farmer Boy/Merry Girl/George Washington/Negro
Suppertime

Side Two: Come Over and See Me Sometime/Belle of Lexington/Billy
Grimes, The Rover/Got No Honey Babe Now/Eight of
January/Give Me Back My Fifteen Cents/Drink Some Cider/
Indian War Hoop

The members of this young string band claim to be "purveyors of
forgotten style." This recording, from 1978, is far from for-
gettable. The Rattlers' style seems to fall somewhere between
the collector's fetishism of the New Lost City Ramblers and the
unbridled enthusiasm of the Highwoods/Backwoods String Band. Two
things which make them especially likable are their preference
for top-notch obscure material and each member's multi-instru-
mental skill. It is hard to tell who is playing what on each cut.
Somehow, though, even without a bass, the band always sounds
tight, authentic and right at home.

The opening "Johnson Gal," from Mississippi's Leake County
Revellers, features appropriately deadpan vocals and flying
fiddle by Mark Farrell with leader Pat Contay playing some
excellent old-timey mandolin. "Davy" (e.g. "Green Corn") is
from West Tennessee's Weem's String Band, and is graced by a
tasteful bowed cello part. "S·A·V·E·D" (the staid Georgia
Yellow Hammer's version, not the veritable spelling bee recorded
later by the Blue Sky Boys) is aptly sung by Bill Dillof. Narmour
Smith's medicine-show romp is enhanced by the addition of mandolin
and banjo. Carter and Young's risque "Lazy Farmer Boy" (e.g.,
"Who Wouldn't Hoe Corn") is faithfully reproduced with twin
fiddles. Then come a rousing, twin banjo revival of Da Costa
Woltz and friends' "Merry Girl," an Arkansas hoedown admonition to
"go to H---(allelujah)" and a tasty, triple-fiddle spree on
another rare Mississippi tune originally sung by the Nations
brothers.

Side two opens with the Yellow Hammers' scrappy invitation and
commentary, after a nice a cappella intro. Next up is Galax
fiddler Emmet Lundy's beautiful "Belle of Lexington." On this
tune the twin fiddles of Tom Legenhausen and Steve Friedberg are
very tight, as Dillof chips in a unison mandolin line of hammered-dulcimer clarity. A "Billy Grimes" ballad from southwest
Virginia is followed not by the Doc Boggs classic that has been
done to death but by a (North Carolina) drifter's reflections on
marriage. The often re-hashed "Eighth of January" sounds quite
new with the addition of Contay's squeaky harmonica. After the
Binkley Brothers' "Fifteen Cents" comes a down-home drinking
song--words and guitar runs from Riley Puckett, fiddle arrange-
ment from Jimmy Johnson's boys. The finale is Hoyt Ming and His
Pepsteppers' immortal instrumental. Like the original, it sounds
as likely to have come from the jungles of Borneo as from Native
Americans.

The Rattlers deserve congratulations on their thoroughness. They
have clearly taken great pains to be faithful to the music they
admire, right down to a plunkity twenties guitar sound. The
thirteen-page 10 x 10 insert has some great memorabilia, serial
numbers of all the source 78's, and a series of quotes to explain
the band's name, as well as the usual lyrics and personnel data.
The Rattlers' music has just about everything that the 78's do
except the surface noise.

RECOMMENDED.

--DK

THE OLD VIRGINIA FIDDLERS   (County 201)

MIDNIGHT SERENADE/LEATHER BRITCHES/TOMMY LOVE/COON DOG/
SCHOTTISCHE/WALKING IN MY SLEEP/MISSISSIPPI SAWYER/JENNY LIND
POLKA/SUSANNA GAL/SARO/GEORGIA CAMP MEETING/ROCK THE CRADLE
JOE/HOP LIGHT LADIES/PATRICK COUNTY BLUES

Another excellent County re-issue--this one features home
recordings from the late forties that document the unique fiddle tradition of Patrick County in the Virginia Blue Ridge,
just east of Grayson and Carroll Counties of string band fame.
The Spangler brothers, J. W. and Dudley, do the honors here.
Under the tutulage of their legendary father, Wallace, both
boys played a straight-ahead, yet intricate style quite distinct from that of surrounding areas. Good notes by Barry
Poss and Tom Carter here, and remarkable versions of "Leather
Britches" and "Mississippi Sawyer".

D.K. $5.00

IN THE FIELD: SOUTHEAST TENNESSEE FIDDLERS
                            (Pine Breeze 005)
Field recorded fiddling with banjo and guitar accom-
paniments
ELDIA BARBEE: Cumberland Gap, Flatwoods, Liza Jane,
George Gann, LEE TRENTHAM: Mississippi Sawyer, Bona-
parte's Retreat, Sockeye, Pine Ridge Breakdown, HOMER
CHASTAIN: Greenback Dollar, Cotton Eyed Joe, Cindy,
Old Joe Clark, BLAINE SMITH: Big Ball's Uptown, Girl
I Left Behind, Buckin' Mule, Irish Washerwoman
    Recording traditional music in the field -- because
so much has now been done -- has become more than a
question of merely multiplying performances. That's an
issue on side 1 of this well-recorded student collection
done in the Chattanooga area. The well-known Eldia
Barbee is a fluent longbow fiddler strongly influenced
by Lowe Stokes, playing with authority and charm; yet
in these recordings, at least, I missed that quality
of individuality that makes us sit up and listen to
a fiddler. Nor does Trentham come alive much on disc,
though he is competent enough, bowing in the older
jiggy manner and then throwing in Pee Wee King licks
on his Bonaparte's Retreat for an unnerving combination of traditional and modern. He doesn't sound particularly together, and at a guess has developed his
playing more in isolation from dancers than the other
three men who play here.
    Side 2 is a whole different story -- it sounds
like a different record. Both Chastain and Smith play
with style and nuance well beyond the average. Chastain has a fine loose swingy expressive style which
becomes positively stately at times, carried along by
infallible rhythm. He likes tunes with simple struc-
tures so he can make plenty free with them, and he
knows when to understate a phrase for a beautiful old-
time sound. Smith, surprisingly, plays a viola, but
like a fiddle, so it doesn't sound deeper, only harsher.
His style is agreeable, full of slithers and swoops,
strikingly archaic over the raw, demonstrative clawhammer picking of Florrie Stewart.
    It's hard to sum up the record. I take issue with
the Side 1 accompaniments by Pine Breeze instructor
Ron Williams -- seems to muddy the waters of tradition
somehow, and that may have been a factor in the less
liberated feel of that side. The record could use
some rarer tunes; but what the men on Side 2 do with
their common tunes, like Smith's joyously re-originated
"Big Ball", sounding like one of those Hoyt Ming Mississippi fantasias, is great stuff. And one tune I urge
on the listener is the oddly recast "Irish Washerwoman"
by a man evidently impatient with jigs. The Pine Bree-
zers have a devotion to traditional music that is lauda-
ble, have found some good traditional musicians -- and
need only, perhaps, to develop a surer sense of what
makes a well-paced record. Much good material is here;
and side 2, plus Barbee's pleasant styling, certainly
make this one, for all its unevenness, worth the price.
                            -- RC $4.50

OSCAR AND EUGENE WRIGHT Old-Time Fiddle and Guitar from West Virginia (Rounder 0089)
Side One: STONEY POINT, GENTLE ANNIE, AGGRAVATIN' PAPA-SHADY GROVE, WALKING IN THE PARLOR, SUWANEE RIVER, DANNY BCY, DUCKS ON THE POND, NO HOME CRIED THE LITTLE GIRL, SHORTENING BREAD, DAVID DUGGER-STONEY RIDGE STOMP
Side Two: PROTECTING THE INNOCENT, CHATTANOOGA BLUES, SNOWBIRD OF THE ASHBANK, HELL UP HICKORY HOLLER, ANNIE LAURIE, CUMBERLAND GAP, SHELVING ROCK-KATY HILL, BANKS OF THE WABASH, KITCHEN GIRL, FORKS OF THE SANDY, WEEVILY WHEAT

This father and son from the mountains of Southern West Virginia perform pure tradiational mountain music in a variety of styles. Eugene, in his fifties, plays fiddle and accompanies his father on guitar.

Oscar, who is over eighty, plays fiddle, banjo, and guitar. He sings occasionally, though this is chiefly instrumental music. Oscar fiddled with Charlie Poole's band a few times in his youth, and learned "Forks of the Sandy" from Posey Rorer, Poole's fiddler. Other influences include Arthur Smith and Henry Reed. Radio has exposed Oscar and Eugene to pop music - for example, "Danny" - and blues, as reflected in Eugene's guitar fingerpicking on "Chattanooga Blues."

Oscar's fiddling excellence is showcased on several solos, and there are some interesting guitar-fiddle duets. Eugene's guitar in these, played in a bluegrass flatpicking style, is appropriate and tasteful, even though it is far from the standard accompaniment for his father's traditional fiddle tunes. Those pieces where Eugene fiddles with Oscar's frailed banjo backup are more traditional fare. There's fine banjo work on songs like "Cumberland Gap" and "Hell Up Hickory Holler."

The rest of the record is devoted to sentimental songs, most of which have been in the Wright family since before Oscar's time. In three guitar-fiddle duets, "Annie Laurie," "Little Annie," and "Danny Boy", Eugene plays fiddle in what I suppose to be an old parlor style, heavy with double stops, grace notes, and trills. His father's guitar work, on "Annie Laurie" especially, is fascinating. It's a unique style: single not arpeggios, usually in a repetitive pattern, punctuated irregularly by strums. These duets, as their familiar names suggest, are sweet and flowery, and a great contrast to the stark simplicity of the old time fiddle pieces. Oscar accompanies his own singing with guitar on several songs, further demonstrating his peculiar style. On "No Home Cried the Little Girl" he throws in some complex Spanish-sounding rhythmic patterns. Really original guitar playing for a man who only knows two keys!

Both Oscar and Eugene Wright play mainly for their own entertainment. Here we are granted a visit to their very intimate musical world.
-W.A.R. $5.50

HIGHWOODS STRINGBAND "No. 3 Special" (Rounder 0074)

COTTON-EYED JOE/YOU AIN'T TALKIN' TO ME/CUFFEY/WAY OUT THERE/ SLEEPING LULU/GYPSY GIRL/PIG ANKLE RAG/C. & N.W. RAILROAD BLUES/DEVILISH MARY/BETTY LIKEN-KITCHEN GIRL/MAGGIE WALKER BLUES/WAGONER/MEETING IN THE AIR/SAIL AWAY LADIES

Whoopee! For a good time, call these guys. Highwoods reputation as the best young old-time string band is indisputable on this record. Those who've heard their first two (Rounder 23 & 45) will note that this release combines the giddly asides and excitement of the first with the fine sound quality of the second. They have the tightest twin fiddles going in Potts and Koken, MacBenford's rowdy banjo, and hearty vocals from everyone especially Jenny (!) Cleland. The most notable change in the band's sound is Doug Dorschug's guitar, which has gone from a tentative imitation of Riley Puckett to a flowing, supple style of his own which many bluegrassers would envy. Sources are all noted. The liner photo says it all on this one, however. Recommended.

D.K. $5.00

EMMETT LUNDY "Tunes from Grayson County, Va." (STRING 802)

JULIE ANN JOHNSON/TALKING ABOUT GREEN LEONARD/ FISHER'S HORNPIPE/ FLATWOODS/ EVENING STAR WALTZ/SUGAR HILL/ HIGHLANDER'S FAREWELL/SHEEP SHELL CORN/PINEY WOODS GAL/ TALKING ABOUT HIS FIRST FIDDLE/CHAPEL HILL MARCH/FORKY DEER/ MOLLY PUT THE KETTLE ON/WAVES ON THE OCEAN/DEAF WOMAN'S COURTSHIP/DUCKS ON THE MILLPOND/LOST GIRL/BONAPARTE'S RETREAT /TALKING ABOUT THE FIDDLE & THE DEVIL/SUSANNA GAL/WILD GOOSE CHASE/CLEVELAND'S MARCH/BELLE OF LEXINGTON

In these priceless selections we come, perhaps, as close to hearing the roots of fiddling as we ever will. Lundy's fiddling is drawn from roots early in the 19th century, well before the bulk of commercial 78 recordings now being discovered. These are the best of the historic, and previously unavailable 1941 Library of Congress recordings of this obscure legent of Virginia fiddling who made two commercial recordings with Ernest Stoneman, didn't like them, and never did any more. The performances here are informal, unpolished, with the mistakes left in, but for sheer leather and nerve they put fancier fiddling in the shade. This is good music caught at home where it has been living for a century, with all the interest that high-powered modern fiddling lacks: rusty, angular noting done leisurely, with a lofty disregard for later convention. As the excellent notes make clear, Lundy was emerging from an ancient free-form tradition when he joined with his sons' banjo and guitar for these sessions. You hear the fiddle, still wild and melodically liberated, in the process of being tamed and simplified to fit accompaniment. It's an exciting mating. Then there's Lundy's wonderful talent for finding just the unexpected decoration to the melody, the rhythmic adventure, the booming, ringing, hollow, sometimes errie timbre. A landmark fiddle record --indluding a few brief conversations--that tells us where the good music's been coming from. RECOMMENDED.

R.C. $5.00

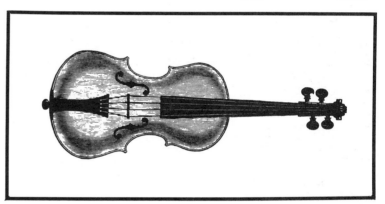

THE RED CLAY RAMBLERS "Merchants Lunch" (Flying Fish 55)

MERCHANTS LUNCH/BEEFALO SPECIAL/WOMAN DOWN IN MEMPHIS/MOLLY PUT THE KETTLE ON/MILWAUKEE BLUES/MELANCHOLY/RABBIT IN THE PEA PATCH/I'VE GOT PAINS/KILDARE'S FANCY - SHIPS ARE SAILING - HIGH YELLOW/DANIEL PRAYED/FORKED DEER/HENHOUSE BLUES/SWEET AND LOW

The Red Clay Ramblers began as an old timey string band and this is a tradition they still uphold well (MOLLY PUT THE KETTLE ON, and the early bluegrass numbers MILWAUKEE BLUES and RABBIT IN THE PEA PATCH) but over the years they have added honkey-tonk piano, trumpet and penny whistle so that their repertory now includes various jazzy blues numbers (WOMAN DOWN IN MEMPHIS, Fat's Wallers SWEET AND LOW and others). There are good arrangements of traditional Irish music (KILDARE'S FANCY...) several original numbers such as the tribute to that all-American animal the Beefalo, the ultimate procrastination song I'VE GOT PLANS (or is it just an excuse for a current lifestyle?) and the title song, about a trucker in a sleazy luncheonette and his trials and tribulation.

In concert or on record my favorites by the Red Clay Ramblers are their a capella gospel numbers, and DANIEL PRAYED didn't let me down.

Despite the diversity of styles the coherence of the group has never changed. This is a good-time album. Recommended.

L.D. $5.00

OLD TIME FIDDLE BAND MUSIC FROM KENTUCKY   Morning Star 45003,
                                                           45004, 45005 ($6.50
                                                           each)

Volume 1, "Wink the Other Eye": Jimmie Johnson's String Band:
Gate to Go Through, Soap in the Washpan, Old Blind Dog, Washington
Quadrille; Hack's String Band: Wink the Other Eye, Pretty Little
Girl; Taylor's Kentucky Boys: Soldiers Joy, Gray Eagle, Forked
Deer; Leonard Rutherford: Richmond Blues, Monroe County Quickstep,
Cumberland Gap, Let Her Go I'll Meet Her; Madisonville String
Band: B Flat Rag

Volume 2, "Wish I Had My Time Again": Ted Gossett's String Band:
Fire in the Mountain, Fox Chase, 8th of January, Bow Legged
Irishman; Green Bailey: Fate of Ellen Smith, If I Die a Railroad
Man; Doc Roberts: Brick Yard Joe, Old Buzzard; H. L. Bandy: Going
Across the Sea, Sail Away Ladies; Cobb & Underwood: Black Snake
Moan; Hatton Bros.: Wish I Had My Time Again; Taylor, Burnette &
Moore: Knoxville Rag; Lonesome Luke & Farm Hands: Wild Hog in the
Woods
                                                                The
Kentucky String Ticklers are a smooth ragtime band with heavy-
knuckled piano and beautifully bluesy fiddle, and the once
mysterious Blue Ridge Mountaineers turn out to be Cincinnati
radio figures Ma and Pa McCormick with taut, dense fiddle
reeling in one of the rarest of the rare and also one of the
best. To close the wild Saturday night of the set, Morning
Star choice a holiness-style sacred vocal with simple fiddle
and guitars that brings the listener back somewhere near earth
again.

Probably the best LP for the general listener is Volume 1; the
fiddler in search of rare material will streak for Volume 3, and
Volume 2 has the most variety. But all three are indispensable.
Backed by the extraordinary taste and knowledge of authorities
Richard Nevins and Gus Meade (the blow-by-blow account of Meade's
sleuthing to discover the origins of the musicians, many of whom
were not even known to be from Kentucky till he tracked them
down, is not the least fascinating of the production details),
plus period photos, the set taken together is eno'jh to cause
today's oldtime music revivalists to redefine what they are doing,
while everybody else just grooves on the music's passion, grace
and power. Nevins in his notes speaks of its "excitement,
innocent warmth, loose, calm assuredness . . . satisfying balance
of sanctity and sensuality." Those well-chosen words barely convey what joys are waiting in these grooves for you.
VERY HIGHLY RECOMMENDED

                                        --RC

John McCutcheon: Front Hall 021
Barefoot Boy with Boots On $6.00

Loggerman's Breakdown--Dulcimer Reel/Barefoot Boy with Boots On/
Little Pink/Laural Branch--Ways of the World--Sugar in the Gourd/
Pay Day/Deep Settled Peace/Under the Double Eagle/Forked Deer/
Urst Wedding March--Fanny Poer--Planxty Irwin/Little Moses/Free
Little Bird/West Virginia Mining Disaster--Which Side Are You On?/
Peekaboo Waltz--Niskayuna Ramble/Ninety Years Old

McCutcheon was one of the more prolific artists on the fine June
Appal label.

In his notes here he remarks how many "favorites" he has among
the many styles, instruments, tunes, and traditional musicians
he has known. The only thing special about this record might
be the way McCutcheon over-extends himself, were it not for
the fine playing of Paul Van Arsdale on hammer dulcimer. In
his first appearances on record, Van Arsdale contributes some
sprightly playing on two little-known traditional tunes and two
nice originals. The body of the album is pleasant enough, with
McCutcheon playing nine instruments in a dizzying variety of
styles. He seems to do best at more subtle, understated material.
The enclosed notes are very thorough with reference to each of
McCutcheon's sources. Ruth Rappaport plays fine piano on the
hammer dulcimer tracks. A nice record all-in-all with little-
heard tunes and styles.

                                        --DK

BUDDY THOMAS, "Kitty Puss--Old Time Fiddle Music From
Kentucky" (Rounder 0032).
Refreshingly good; it might be called "The Joy of Fiddling," keeping clear of fiddling's cliches and bringing to light some of its meanings and secrets. The re-
clusive Thomas died early and recorded little; the notes
give a moving tribute to a man who just poured himself
out in music. It is magnificent stuff in more or less
the Doc Roberts manner, that carolling, vigorous sound,
a little Irish in its lilt and detail, with a zing and
catchiness found nowhere else. There are four or five
distinct styles here, all consummately done, and all but
a few of the tunes are fine obscurities out of the old
times that will make any fiddler's mouth water. Give it
to your favorite fiddler for Christmas, but don't say
anything about the fantastic crosstuned fiddle solo on
Sweet Sunny South; let that be a surprise. ALSO: Nine
Miles Out of Louisville/Frankie/John Rawl Jamieson/
Sheeps and Hogs Walking Through the Pasture/Georgia Row/
Briarpicker Brown/Stillhouse Branch/Blue Goose/Yellow
Barber/Possum Up a Simmon Tree/Kitty Puss/Martha Camp-
bell/Turkey in a Peapatch/Big Indian Hornpipe/Brown Button Shoes.

                                        -RC   ($4.00)

ROUNDER

0004 Clark Kessinger with Gene Meade

Fiddle tunes and waltzes by this world's champion old time fiddler, known to fans around the world. *Rickett's Hornpipe; Rose o' My Heart Waltz; Bitter Creek; When I Grow Too Old to Dream Waltz; Red Bird; Tenn. Waltz; Three o'Clock in the Morning; Wild Horse; Waltz You Saved for Me; Sunny Side of the Mt.; Lost Indian; Good Night Waltz.*

0005 Snuffy Jenkins & Pappy Sherrill: 33 Years of Pickin' & Pluckin'

Old time fiddle and banjo tunes from the Carolinas. Snuffy is credited by Earl Scruggs, Don Reno, and others, as the biggest influence on their styles. Pappy is a prime old time fiddler. "A really valuable—indeed historical—record. . . . This LP is as good as anything from the past."—Old Time Music. *Texas Quickstep; Mountain Top/Shout Lula; Run Boy Run; Cherry Blossom Waltz; I Want My Rib; Alabama Jubilee; Nancy Rowland; Milk Cow Blues; 50 Year Ago Waltz; Kansas City Kitty, C&NW Railroad Blues; Lonesome Road Blues; Shortnin' Bread; Model T. Blues; Coney Island; Beaumont Rag; When the Bumble Bee Backed Up to Me and Pushed; Dreamy Georgiana Moon; Aunt Liza's Favorite; Wagoner.*

0010 The Fuzzy Mountain String Band

Popular string band from the Durham/Chapel Hill area, presenting here a selection of rare fiddle and dance tunes. A number of these tunes have become standards due to this record. "The Fuzzy Mountain String Band is one of the best I've heard."—Dick Spottswood in Bluegrass Unlimited. *Shooting Creek; Double File; Old Sledge; Gal I Left Behind Me; Sally Ann; 28th of January; Green Willis; Piney Woods; Ebenezer; Old Mother Flanagan; Last of Calahan; Wild Hog in the Woods; Magpie; Keep the Ark a Movin; Pretty Little Dog; Protect the Innocent; Poor Johnnie Has Gone to The War; Frosty Morning; Camp Chase; Bonaparte's Retreat.*

0023 The Highwoods String Band: Fire on the Mountain

Wild old time string band music, largely from Galax and North Georgia traditions. This group has literally set mountains on fire, and have probably the most devoted audience of any group in old time music in the last ten years or more. *Fire on the Mountain; Grey Cat on the Tennessee Farm; Nancy Rowland; Hopalong Peter; Last of Callahan; On a Cold Winter's Night; My Own House Waltz; Walking in the Parlor; Lee Highway Blues; Bully of the Town; Who Broke the Lock; Ways of the World; Free Little Bird; Old and Grey; Liberty Off the Corn Licker Still.*

0024 The Hollow Rock String Band

Alan Jabbour, Tommy Thompson, and Jim Watson in an album of fiddle tunes collected from a variety of lesser known southern mountain fiddlers. Hollow Rock's first album of many years ago remains a much sought after classic. *Shelvin Rock; Route; Jenny Lind Polka/Year of Jubilo; Sally Ann; Isom Waltz; West Fork Gals, Leather Britches; Red Fox; Shady Grove; West Virginia Rag; Boatin Up Sandy; Billy in the Low Land; Granny; Rose Division Schottische, West Virginia Gals; Shootin Creek; British Field March; Peekaboo Waltz; Sandy River Belle; Birdie.*

0027 Hazel & Alice

Old time and bluegrass music by Alice Gerrard and Hazel Dickens. Solid traditional instrumentation and singing combined with a mixture of original and older songs. "This marriage (if that's the word) between country music and feminism is more fruitful than we could have hoped, and a credit to both."—Old Time Music. *Mining Camp Blues; Hello Stranger; Green Rolling Hills of West Virginia; A Few More Years Shall Roll; Two Soldiers; Sweetest Gift a Mother's Smile; Tomorrow I'll Be Gone; My Better Years; Custom Made Woman Blues; Don't Put Her Down You Helped Put Her There; You Gave Me A Song; Pretty Bird; Gallop to Kansas.*

0029 The Smokey Valley Boys

Old time string band music from the Mt. Airy, N.C. area; the band has made quite a habit of winning about every contest in range with their powerful, hard-driving style. Benton Flippin on fiddle, Gilmer Woodruff on banjo. "Exciting, even riotous music."—Old Time Music. *Lost Indian; Benton's Dream; Whoa Mule; Fortune; Breakin Up Christmas; Pole Cat Blues; Salt River; Grey Eagle; Richmond; Sally Ann; June Apple; John Brown's Dream; Liberty; Fiddler's Reel.*

1032 Georgia Yellow Hammers: The Moonshine Hollow Band

From northern Georgia's Gordon County, the Yellow Hammers recorded fiddle breakdowns, sentimental songs, blues, pop numbers and gospel quartets—even a couple of Sacred Harp tunes, and comedy skits. The diversity of their music is reflected in this collection of some of their finest recordings originally made between 1924 and 1929. *The Moonshine Hollow Band; Whoa, Mule; Pa, Ma, and Me; Fourth of July At A Country Fair; Johnson's Old Grey Mule; Picture On The Wall; Tennessee Coon; I'm S-A-V-E-D; G Rag; Peaches Down In Georgia; Raise Rough House Tonight; Song Of The Doodle Bug; When The Birds Begin Their Singing In The Trees; Warhorse Game; The Old Rock Jail Behind The Old Iron Gate; Black Annie.*

1033 Tennessee Strings

Anthology of Tennessee string band music from the 1920s and 1930s. Representative groups include: Tom Ashley with Gwen Foster, Charlie Bowman with the Hill Billies, Johnson Brothers,

0035 The Fuzzy Mountain String Band: Summer Oaks and Porch

Second LP by the Fuzzies. More good fiddle tunes, banjo and dance music by this popular group. *West Fork Gals; Fire on the Mt./Breaking Up Christmas; Bonaparte Crossing the Rhine; Snowbird on the Ashbank; Roustabout; Santa Anna's Retreat; Barbara's Fancy; Shortening Bread; Dusty Miller; Falls of Richmond; Quince Dillon's High D; Trude Evans; Loch Lavan Castle; Ducks on the Millpond/Sugar Hill/Back Step Cindy; Peter Francisco; One More River to Cross; Barlow Knife; Fisher's Hornpipe.*

0037 J.P. and Annadeene Fraley: Wild Rose of the Mountain

Old time eastern Kentucky fiddle tunes on fiddle and guitar. A very good introduction to authentic old-time music. "Lively, lyrical"—Playboy. "Few fiddlers have been recorded in recent years that own such handsome tone, such easy capability with the bow."—Old Time Music. *Cluckin Hen, Going Back to Kentucky' Birdie; Red Headed Irishman; Mud Fence; Swing Nine Yards of Calico; Run Johnnie Run; Wild Rose of the Mt.; Miller's Reel; Little Liza Jane; Granny Take a Look at Uncle Sam; Sail Away Ladies; Forked Deer; Roosian Rabbit, White Rose Waltz;I Dusty Miller; Going Down the River; Fun's All Over.*

0045 Highwoods String Band: Dance All Night

A second album of the Highwoods String Band, recently returned from their tour of Latin America. Even more unforgettable than their first album. *Dance All Night; Goodbye Miss Liza; Money Musk; Been All Around This World; Carroll County Blues; My Dixie Darling; Forked Deer; Old Jimmy Sutton; Wild Bill Jones; Hawks and Eagles; Mountaineer's Love Song; There's More Pretty Girls Than One; Tater Patch; Way Down the Old Plank Road.*

0047 Wilson Douglas

Traditional old time fiddler from Ivydale, West Virginia who learned many of his tunes from the late French Carpenter. Banjo by Speedy Tolliver, guitar by Doug Meade. *Cotton Eyed Joe; Rocky Road to Dublin; Little Rose; Walking in the Parlor; Elzic's Farewell; Yew Piney Mountain; Shelvin' Rock; Camp Chase; West Fork Girls; Brushy Run; Old Christmas Morning; Chicken Reel; Paddy on the Turnpike; Forked Buck; Old Mother Flanagan.*

0074 The Highwoods Stringband: No. 3 Special

Highwoods' new album is a collection of pretty much the same kind of material which has become associated with them through their concert appearances and previous two albums: foot-stomping old time tunes and lilting vocals from the tradition of old-time country music. With their good-time, happy-go-lucky style, the Highwoods is always a winner requiring repeated listenings repeatedly enjoy their down-home humor. The band consists of double fiddles, old time banjo, guitar, and bass. *Cotton Eyed Joe; You Ain't Talkin' to Me; Way Out There; Sleeping Lulu; Gypsy Girl; Pig Ankle Rag; C. & N.W. Railroad Blues; Devilish Mary; Betty Liken; Kitchen Girl; Maggie Walker Blues; Wagoner; Meeting in the Air; Sail Away Ladies.* **Eight-track tape available.**

0128 Backwoods Band

Probably the most exciting old-time band to enter the scene in 1979, this group of veteran musicians (Mac Benford, Eric Thompson, Susie Rothfield, Claudio Buchwald & Joe Fallon) has chosen to take up the baton left by the Highwoods Stringband and carry on the living, vital tradition. With an eclectic base, and some original tunes, the Backwoods Band adds new dimensions to the solid, toe-tapping danceable core of old-timey American country music. *Fortune; Nancy Jane; Falls Of Richmond; Rocks And Gravel; Fish In The Millpond; Merry Girl; Lay Down Baby; Stay All Night; Cowboy Girl; The Oklahoma Rooster; Sad And Lonesome Day; Ryestraw; Build Me A Cabin; Paddy On The Turnpike.*

1001 Blind Alfred Reed: How Can a Poor Man Stand Such Times and Live?

A reissue album of 78s cut by this West Virginia fiddler and topical songster, recordings made in the late 1920s. Several of Reed's songs have become known through the efforts of various revival groups. "An entirely captivating experience. To hear his music is to be swept back into the 1920s and faced with a countryman's philosophy of life and morals . . . a record without which no collection of old time music, nor understanding of the old time tradition, is complete."—Old Time Music. *Walking in the Way with Jesus; Black and Blue Blues; Why Do You Bob Your Hair Girls; Explosion in the Fairmont Mines; You Must Unload; Prayer of the Drunkard's Little Girl; Always Lift Him Up and Never Knock Him Down; Beware; How Can a Poor Man Stand Such Times and Live; Woman's Been After Man Ever Since; We've Just Got to Have Em That's All; I Mean to Live for Jesus; Why Don't You Bob Your Hair Girls—No. 2; There'll Be No Distinction There.*

1003 Fiddlin' John Carson: The Old Hen Cackled and the Rooster's Going to Crow

The title song is generally considered to be the very first record that started off the entire commercial country music industry, cut in 1923. Sixteen numbers here by the irascible Fiddlin' John and Moonshine Kate. "Rounder's anthology offers a balanced portrait of Fiddlin' John in the variety of his ways. The material draws from his best, and this album rescues him from an undeserved obscurity."—Sing Out. *Little Old Log Cabin in the Lane; There's a Hard Time Coming; It's a Shame to Whip Your Wife on Sunday; Old Hen Cackled and the Rooster's Going to Crow; Bachelor's Hall; Smoke Goes Out the Chimney Just the Same; Whatcha Gonna Do When your Licker Gives Out; Georgia's Three-Dollar Tag; Do Round My Lindy; Honest Farmer; Gonna Swing on the Golden Gate; Corn Licker and Barbecue—Part 2; I'm Nine Hundred Miles from Home; I'm Glad My Wife's in Europe; Sugar in the Gourd; Engineer on the Mogull.*

1004 Burnett & Rutherford: Ramblin' Reckless Hobo

Spirited old time hillbilly fiddle and banjo songs and instrumentals from southern Kentucky by Dick Burnett, Leonard Rutherford, and friends. Originally recorded 1926-1930. *Ladies on the Steamboat; Cabin with the Roses at the Door; Going Around the World; Taylor's Quickstep; Lost John; Blackberry Blossoms; There's No One Like the Old Folks; Ramblin' Reckless Hobo; Knoxville Rag; My Sweetheart in Tennessee; My Sarah Jane; Billy in the Low Ground; Going Across the Sea; Short Life of Trouble; Two Faithful Lovers; Little Stream of Whiskey.*

1005 Gid Tanner and the Skillet Lickers: Hear These New Southern Fiddle and Guitar Records

1924-1934 recordings, featuring Gid, Riley Puckett, Lowe Stokes, Clayton McMichen, Bert Layne—the whole crew. Georgia swamp opera pure and simple! Exciting, wild string band music. *Run Nigger Run; Sleeping Lulu; Settin in the Chimney Jamb; Uncle Bud; John Henry; I'm Satisfied; Pass Around the Bottle and We'll All Take a Drink; Cumberland Gap; Roll 'Em on the Ground; Slow Buck; Keep Your Gal at Home; Watermelon on the Vine; Ryestraw; Tanner's Boarding House; Flatwoods; Sugar in the Gourd.*

1010 Ed Haley: Parkersburg Landing

This album consists of home recordings made in 1946 by Ed Haley, a blind Kentucky fiddler who never made a commercial record. Of an exceptionally high order, this collection of recordings will certainly be welcomed by devotees of authentic American fiddle music. An exciting release from perhaps the greatest of the old time fiddlers never to record (commercially). *Parkersburg Landing; Humphrey's Jig; Stackolee; Cherokee Polka; Cuckoo's Nest; Wake Susan; Cherry River Rag; Flower of the Morning; Grey Eagle Jig; Man of Constant Sorrow; Forked Deer; Lost Indian; Done Gone; Dunbar.*

1023 Gid Tanner and the Skillet Lickers: Kickapoo Medicine Show

Another great album by this well-known Georgia old-time string band. The talents of Gid, Riley Puckett, Clayton McMichen and the rest of the Skillet Lickers are represented here in an album that gives an indication of the breadth and scope of their repertoire. A couple of previously unissued cuts, including one solo banjo number by Gid supplement the title skit and the wild fiddle band numbers. Produced by Charles Wolfe and Mark Wilson. *Nancy Rollin; The Farmer's Daughter; I Ain't No Better Now; Never Seen the Like Since Gettin' Upstairs; The Arkansas Sheik; You Got to Stop Drinking Shine; You Gotta Quit Kicking My Dawg Around; Cumberland Gap on a Buckin' Mule; Paddy*

6008 Ed Reavy

One of the most important composers of Irish music in this century, Ed Reavy has been based in Philadelphia for some 40 years now and yet his music has spread far and wide; many of his tunes have become part of the staple repertoire of most traditional Irish musicians in Ireland itself. Ed is a first-class fiddler and is represented here on 5 tracks; the other selections are Ed Reavy compositions played by a number of Irish musicians including Billy McComiskey, Martin Mulvihill, Eugene O'Donnell and many more. *The Wild Swans At Coole; Reilly Of The White Hill; The Shoemaker's Daughter; Lad O'Beirne's; Lovely Lough Sheelin; Love At The Endings; Bridget Of Knock; The Ireland We Know; Fling; The Road To The Glenn; Reavy's No. 9; Maudebawn Chapel; Packey's Place; The Castleblayney Piper; The Slaney Bog; In Memory Of Coleman; The Lone Bush; Love At The Endings; The Letterkenny Blacksmith; Johnny McGoohan's; Tom Clark's Fancy; The Boys Of The Lough; Pat Clark's; The Shanvaghara; The Hunter's House; The Flock of Wild Geese.*

3006 The Boys of the Lough: Second Album

This popular group from the British Isles is featured here in an American release of their Trailer LP. One of the most successful revival groups to have ever stormed this country. *Da Lerwick Lasses (Shetland Reels); An Goirtin eornan (Irish air); Sally Munro; Patsy Campbell; Gravel Walk; Lough Erne; Gold Ring Halting March; Lovely Nancy; Merrily Kiss the Quaker's Wife; A Yow Cam' Ta Wir Door Yarmin; Lass with the Bonny Brown Hair; Lowrie Tarrell; Mason's Apron.*

6006 Irish Traditional Instrumental Music From Chicago

Companion piece to Rounder 6005, this album was recorded by Miles Krassen and Larry McCullough and documents the Irish musical culture of Chicago. Uilleann pipes, fiddles, piano, accordion, flute and concertina are the instruments featured sometimes solo and in various combinations. Featured artists include: Joe Shannon, John McGreevy, Eleanor Neary, James Keane, Sr., Frank Thornton, Terry Teahan, Maida Sugrue, Jimmy Thornton, James Keane, Jr., and Liz Carroll. *New Steampacket; Bucks of Oranmore; Milliner's Daughter; Scatter The Mud; Fasten*

7005 Carl MacKenzie: Welcome To Your Feet Again

A beautifully arranged collection of traditional fiddle music, featuring the full range of Scottish music: slow airs, hornpipes, marches, jigs, reels, strathspeys, etc. One of the most impressive and lyrical fiddle albums available. Piano by Doug MacPhee. *Kennedy Street March; Doug MacPhee's Strathspey; Joe's Reel; Miss Wedderburn's; Tom Dey Strathspey; Roderick MacDonald's; The Earl of Crawford's Reel; Devil's Delight Reel; "A" and "D" Reel; Jerry's Beaver Hat Jig; Dan R. MacDonald's Jig; Bee's Wing Hornpipe; Spellan's Inspiration Hornpipe; Mary Clare Hornpipe; Scottish Air; Miss Jessie Smith Strathspey; Dan R.'s Favourite Strathspey; Lady Mary Stopford Reel; Uist Lasses Darling Reel; Portland Fancy Jig; Rosewood Jig; The River Bend Jig; Miss Maxwell's; Back of the Change House Reel; Dolmar Reel; Robert Cormack, Aberdeen; Happy Go Lucky Hornpipe; Vendome Hornpipe; Owny's Best Jig; Wilfred's Fiddle Jig; Penny Hill Jig; Welcome to Your Feet Again; Colin MacKay's Reel; Colin MacIntosh Reel.*

MICHAEL COLEMAN, "Legacy" (Shanachie 33002).
A reissue Event, full of music that will make you rise
from your chair. One can fault this record only for its
failure to present a badly needed full biography of Coleman; in every other way it is a joy: the first chance
for the 70s to hear the artist who practically recreated
Irish dance music in the 20s and 30s. Coleman's fiddling took an art which had stiffened with time and gave
it new soul and distance, defining it for thousands of
players to come. His Sligo fiddling practically sings
with grace, relaxed ease and sinew, a gala spirit that
speaks even to people who think they don't like Irish
fiddling. There is a rare duet with piccolo on McDonald
Medley, and Stirling Castle-Miss Ramsey's is remarkable
for its tone and magnificent rhythmic sweep, but every
tune is great. Coleman has been hearsay or faint memory
for too long. No fiddler or Irishperson should be without it, and if you are neither, don't deny yourself a
magic treat anyway.
SELECTIONS: Trim the Velvet/The Gray Goose/Kerryman's
Daughter-Bird in the Tree/Jackson's Jigs/Lord Gordon's
Reel/Jackson's Reels/Dougherty's Jigs/Kerry Reel-Per-
shire Hunt/Tobin's Fancy/Greenfields of America-Swal-
low's Tail.
                                        -RC ($4.5

KATHLEEN COLLINS (Shanachie 29002).
An American-born woman who learned violin to please her
Irish immigrant father, Collins caught fire when exposed
in her early 20s to Sligo music and the posthumous genius of Michael Coleman. Within a few years she won the
celebrated Dooney title, the test of Sligo style. She
is no slouch! From the rigor of early training in the
grimly correct classical manner of this highly perfect-
ed art, from years of demanding performance as an Irish
dancer and dance teacher, she has won free into a striking mixture of Sligo's lilt and Galway's fluidity. Her
style is commanding and graceful, marrying the old eco-
nomy of expression and delight in ornament with today's
flavorsomeness and dynamism, and she has her own arch,
hesitant wryness and understatement. A lovely introduction to the Irish fiddle for those new to it, and for
the devotee a fine revisit.
SELECTIONS: Dowd's Reel-Star of Munster/Monsignor's
Blessing-Limerick Lasses/Humours of Ballyloughlin/Paddy
Ryan's Dream-Coleman's Cross/Rosemay Lane-The Orphan/
Sergeant Early's Dream-Fahy's Reel/Connelly's Reel-
Mullingar Races/Reavy's Reel-Jenny's Welcome to Charlie/
Jug of Punch-Eddie Kelly's Reel/Sean Ryan's Jig-Father
Kelly's Jig/Morning Dew-Woman of the House/New Century
Hornpipe-Sean Ryan's Hornpipe/Private Ass & Cart-Jack-
son's Reel.
                                        -RC ($4

KEVIN BURKE "If the Cap Fits..."   (Mulligan 021)

A KERRY REEL/MICHAEL COLEMAN'S/THE WHEELS OF THE WORLD/
JULIA DELANEY/DINNY DELANEY'S/THE YELLOW WATTLE/THE MAS-
ON'S APRON/LAINGTON'S REEL/PADDY FAHY'S JIG/CLIFFS OF
MOHER/THE STAR OFMUNSTER/JOHN STENSON'S no 1&2/BIDDY
MARTIN's/GER THE RIGGER/BILL SULLIVAN'S POLKA/PADDY
CRONIN'S/TOSS THE FEATHERS plus 9 more... With: (!)
Kevin Burke (of course), Paul Brady, Donal Lunny, Micheal
O Domhnaill, Jackie Daly, Gerry O'Beirne, Peter Browne
    A great fiddle album! With a bunch of top Irish
musicians working to back him up, Kevin delivers large
amounts of the subtle mastery that is obscured when he's
heard with the high-powered BOTHY BAND. Side two features a medley of tunes one into the next without a
break for almost the entire side. The backing musicians
change as he flows into each new tune, but it is really
his excellent playing that propels this lengthy medley
to a breathless close. Any Irish music lover will like
this album for its traditional mood. Any fan of the
BOTHY BAND will want it. And any fiddle player - Irish
or not - would be interested in this exuberant record.

                              — MPW $5.50

THE BOYS OF THE LOUGH (Shanachie 79002)
Focals, fiddle, flute, mandolin, guitar, jewsharp,
concertina
TTHE BOYS OF THE LOUGH/SLANTY GART/IN PRAISE OF JOHN
MAGEE/WEDDING MARCH FROM UNST/THE BRIDE'S A BONNY
THING/SLEEP SOOND I' DA MOARNIN'/FAREWELL TO WHISKY/
OLD JOE'S JIG/LAST NIGHT'S JOY/THE GRANNY IN THE
CORNER/THE OLD OAK TREE/CAOINEADH EOGHAIN RUA/THE 9
POINTS OF ROGUERY/DOCHERTY'S REEL/FLOWING TIDE/ANDREW
LAMMIE/SHEEBEG & SHEEMORE/THE BOY IN THE GAP/MCMAHON'S
REEL/JACKSON & JANE/THE SHAALDS OF FOULLA/GARSTER'S
DREAM/THE BRIG
    In their six short years together the Boys have
made their enchanting brand of music a phenomenon,
spawning hosts of imitators here and abroad. Yet their
first LP has continued to be hard to find in the U.S.
Here it is reissued for us: recordings from their
very early days, eclectic yet uncannily faithful
blends of Irish, Scots and Shetlands music, varied by
praiseworthy vocal -- they are that rare thing, good
traditional singers as well as instrumentalists. Yet
they take the right liberties, building their instrumental virtuosity into delicate layers of sound that
extend tradition and make it personal and living in
ways that seem right. Of all their work I like this
the best; it has the feeling of something new being
born. For those new to the Scots-Irish folk renaissance,
McConnell's master fluting are the first things you
notice; but it is Dick Gaughan, who with Paul Brady
and a few others has solved the problem of how to make
a guitar fit Irish music, and the use of the thump and
knock of Robin Morton's bodhran that give their music
its strange authority. Here are all sorts of selections
they have since made into standards -- and a personal
favorite of mine, the haunting "Sheebeg & Sheemore."
The Boys' many fans won't need to be told how good this
is. For those new to the Scots-Irish folk renaissance,
few LPs can be so heartily recommended for color,
craftsmanship and sheer good listening.
                        -RC $5.00

Seamus and Manus McGuire: Folk-Legacy FSE-78
Humours of Lissadell $6.00

Side 1: Brennan's Favourite, Tongs by the Fire/Hand Me Down the
         Tackles/Anach Cuain/Rose in the Heather, Father Tom's
         Wager/Seamus McManus/Humours of Lissadell, Winter
         Apples/Da Slocklit Light, Smith o'Couster, Da Grocer/
         O'Mahoney's, McFadden's Handsome Daughter

Side 2: Love at the Endings, Ryan's, Maid of Mt. Kisco, Hunter's
         Purse/The Banks/Shaney Mulhern, Morning Sunrise/Ur Cnoc
         Cein-Mhic-Cainte/Lament for President Garfield, Down the
         Broom/The Fisherman's Widow, Sweet Biddy Daly/Derwent-
         water's Farewell, Larry Redican's

Two brothers from Sligo have recorded a fine sampling if fiddle
tunes, accompanied by Terry Rudden on guitar. Seamus, who's
also a member of the group "Hang the Piper," shows the warmth
and delicacy of his playing in the slow air, "Un Cnoc Cein-
Mhic-Cainte," though his tone in the two other airs is reedy
rather than rich, as it should be. He can, however, perform a
lively reel with great merriment--for example, in the inaptly
titled "Lament for President Garfield" (the only American tune
on the album). Seamus' classical training and style stands in
some contrast to his brother's background, which is basically
traditional. The tone Manus achieves is more focused, and the
style smoother and more slippery; listen to "Down the Broom."
Together they produce a few real gems: "Seamus McManus," a
truly charming and joyous Canadian waltz; "The Banks," a ballroom type of hornpipe; and the title piece, which is fast,
intricate, and interesting. A sheet of notes is included.
                                                 --SJA

MUSIC FROM SLIABH LUACHRA

VOL. 1 KERRY FIDDLES (Topic 12TS309)

THE TOP OF MAOL & HUMOURS OF BALLYDESMOND/FISHERMAN'S HORNPIPE
& BYRNE'S HORNPIPE/MUCKROSS ABBEY & MULIVIHILL'S REEL/CRONIN'S
HORNPIPE & STACK OF BARLEY/O'DONNELL'S LAMENT/DANNY AB'S SLIDE/
FRIEZE BRITCHES & PAUDEEN O'RAFFERTY/CHASE ME CHARLIE & TOM
BILLY'S FAVOURITE/KENNEDY'S FAVOURITE & WOMAN OF THE HOUSE/
APPLES IN WINTER, MAID ON THE GREEN & THRUSH IN THE STRAW/
OLD MAN ROCKING THE CRADLE/HUMOURS OF GALTYMORE, CALLAGHAN'S
REEL & THE NEW-MOWN MEADOWS, CALLAGHAM'S HORNPIPE & THE RIGHTS
OF MAN/JOHNNY WHEN YOU DIE, THE SWALLOW'S TAIL & MISS MACLEOD'S
REEL.

VOL. 2 THE STAR OF MUNSTER TRIO (Topic 12TS310)

DUBLIN PORTER & MOUNTAIN LARK/LARK IN THE BOG/MOUNTAIN ROAD
AND PADDY CRONIN"S REEL/KNOCKNABOUL & BALLYDESMOND POLKAS/
BOIL THE BREAKFAST EARLY & BUNKER HILL/THE RED-HAIRED BOY/
LUCY'S REEL & THE CLARE REEL/BILL BLACK'S & O'DONOVAN'S
HORNPIPES/JOHN MAHINNEY'S REEL #1 & NO NAME REEL/GRANDFATHER'S
THOUGHT & MADAM IF YOU PLEASE/NO NAME REEL/NAPOLEON'S RETREAT/
CONNIE THE SOLDIER & HUMOURS OF GLEN/PALATINE'S DAUGHTER/JIM
MAC'S HORNPIPE/CHERISH THE LADIES/THE HARLEQUIN/THE OLD BUSH
& WITHIN A MILE OF DUBLIN.

VOL. 3 THE HUMOURS OF LISHEEN (Topic 12TS311)

HUMOURS OF LISHEEN & ART O'KEERE'S JIG/BLUE RIBAND & MERRY
GIRL/FRISCO HORNPIPE/BIDDY CROWLEY'S BALL/BOLD TRAINOR O &
NO NAME SLIDE/TAP THE BARREL & JENNY TIE THE BONNET/CAILIN
AN TI MHOIR/NO NAME POLKA/FREDDY KIMMEL'S HORNPIPE & HOME
BREW/PADRAIG O'KEEFE'S POLKA/POL HA'PENNY HORNPIPE/JOHN
MAHINNEY'S JIG #2 & DUCKS & THE OATS/I LOOKED EAST & I LOOKED
WEST/NO NAME SLIDE & WORN TORN PETTICOAT/TAIMSE I M/CHODLADH/
NO NAME SLIDE/JULIA CLIFFORD'S & BILL THE WAIVER'S POLKAS/
NO NAME JIG/JOHNNY COPE/JOHN CLIFFORD'S POLKA/BEHIND THE BUSH
IN THE GARDEN & GOING FOR WATER.

This is an event comparable to the landmark recordings of U.S.
artists like the Hammons Family and Ed Haley, recovering a
vast quantity of fine music from one of Ireland's last traditional strongholds. Sliabh Luachra is the Irish name for
the Blackwater River district on the Kerry-Cork border, and
the music is the not-well-documented Kerry style of playing.
The set thus far (and a projected fourth volume featuring
flute) follows the activity of a phenomenal musical line of
inheritance beginning with the legendary itinerant fiddle
teacher Padraig O'Keefe, reflecting in tune after tune the
sounds of a time and a place and a circle of musicians.
    Vol. 1 presents O'Keefe himself and two star pupils,
Denis Murphy and his sister Julia Clifford, and is all fiddling. O'Keefe's reflective, spacious, lonesome style goes
well back into the last century, and is caught here in some
magnificent recordings made in 1952 by Seamus Ennis for the
BBC Sound Archives. Murphy and Clifford own a brighter, more
pellmell sound, with the strong rhythms and infectious gaiety
that owe much to dance playing--uncomplicated but sure and
satisfyingly snappy. Later, in the next volume, it will
become clear that what the set is all about is Julia Clifford's growth and development as a fiddler. For the moment
it is O'Keefe who predominates, with his astounding nuances
of timbre and tone.
    Vol. 2 follows Clifford in her incarnation as dance
fiddler with husband John (accordion) and son Billy (a master-
ful flutter to be featured in Vol. 4) in recordings made in
1964 and 1976. The Cliffords began in the 1940s in London's
dance halls, and the Star of Munster Trio was the culmination
of a dream, a band of their own. This music is led by Julia
Clifford's strong, arresting, personalized solo fiddling.
There are a number of duets with Billy's flute, and duets
and trios dominated by John's tromping, romping bravura
accordion, not subtle or intricate but brawny and adventurous
and played for the fine fun of the thing. With songs, reels,
polkas, airs, everything but waltzes, this is good diversified
stuff.
    Vol. 3 features John and Julia, with the accent on
Julia's expressive fiddling, soloing on nearly two-thirds of
the LP. Reg Hall Plays piano to good effect on some pieces;
side 2 is almost all Julia by herself, and she develops the
full sweep of her grand style, amounting to awesome command
of her idiom, a quiet virtuoso who has learned to make her
instrument a speaking bridge between then and now. Add to
this her loyalty to a repertoire full of rare tunes and sup-
prising turns, and this is the work of a woman who deserves
to be influential and widely heard.
    If I had to choose one of these I'd pick Vol. 1 for the
oldtimey fiddling, but Vol. 3 undoubtedly has the best tunes
and is musically the most delightful. They're all outstanding,
together spanning a range and variety of instrumental music
from a single region which is a model for similar collections.
HIGHLY RECOMMENDED.   R.C.

6005   Irish Traditional Instrumental Music
       from the East Coast of America:
       Volume One

Recorded by Mick Moloney, this and its companion volume
(Rounder 6006) constitute the first anthology of traditional Irish
music from the United States. Mick's volume concentrates on the
East Coast, primarily Philadelphia, New York and Boston.
Featured artists include: Tim Britton, Eddie Cahill, Charlie Coen,
Jack Coen, Gus Collins, Brian Conway, Paddy Cronin, John
Fitzpatrick, Maureen Fitzpatrick, Mike Flynn, Maureen Glynn,
James Keane, Gene Kelly, Tony de Marco, Bill McComiskey, Sean
McGlynn, Brendan Mulvihill, Martin Mulvihill, Eugene O'Donnell,
Mike Preston, Mike Rafferty, John Vesey and Mick himself. *The
Congress Reel; The Green Groves of Erin; Pigeon on the Gate;
Boys of the Lough; The Banks of Newfoundland; The Woodford
Jig; Within a Mile of Dublin; The Pike Island Lassies; Barrel
Rafferty's Reel; The Stranger Hornpipe; The Golden Slipper; The
Boys of Ballisodare; The Duke of Leinster; Money Musk; Keel Row;
The Maid and the Cherry Tree; The Wexford Lassie; McGovern's
Favorite; The Oak Tree; The Widow's Daughter; The Flogging
Reel; The Ballinakill Hornpipe; The Bridge Hornpipe; An Phis
Fhliuch; O'Farrell's Welcome to Limerick; Paddy Kelly's Reel; Lad
O'Beirne's; Spellan the Fiddler; The Golden Eagle; Buckley's
Reel; The Copper Plate; The Coal Miner's Farewell to Kilroe; The
Congress Reel; The Clar Hornpipe; The Concert Reel; Miss
McLeod's; The Rookery; Saddle the Pony.*

Gardening Tip:
"Young tomato plants can
be nicely supported with
stakes made from defunct
violin bows."
Submitted by Steven Brown of
Schenectady, New York

DE DANANN "Selected Jigs Reels & Songs" Shanachie 79001

TOM BILLY'S, RYAN'S JIG, THE SANDMOUNT REEL, THE CLOGHER
REEL/LOVE WILL YE MARRY ME, BYRNE'S HORNPIPE/THE BROKEN
PLEDGE, JENNY'S WELCOME TO CHARLIE/THE BANKS OF THE QUAY,
CRUCAHARAN CROSS/THE FLOWER OF SWEET STRABANE/THE
FLOWERS OF SPRING, JACKIE SMALL'S JIG/THE LOG CABIN,
BEAN A' TI AR LAR/CAROLAN'S DRAUGHT/THE BANKS OF RED
ROSES/OVER THE BOG ROAD/THE HAGS PURSE, THE COLLIERS
JIG/BARBARA ALLEN/DEAR IRISH BOY, JOHNNY LEARY'S POLKAS.
    This is the second album from the fine Irish group,
De Danann, which has toured the United States several
times to wide acclaim in the folk world. Frankie Gavin
(fiddle, whistle and flute) and Alec Finn (bouzouki)
already have an album of Irish traditional music to
their credit (Shanachie 29008). Gavin, a musician of
excellent taste and ability, has played the fiddle
since he was ten and has emerged with a style of playing
full of warmth and authority. Johnny McDonagh brings
the bodhran to life as few people can. In his solo on
"Over The Bog Road" McDonagh produces an astounding
spectrum of sounds and rhythms on his instrument.
Charlie Piggot is the multi-instrumentalist of the group,
playing tenor banjo, mandolin, whistle, ten-key melodeon and bouzouki.
    The group is joined on this album by Johnny
Moynihan (ex-Sweeney's Men, Planxty member) who plays
whistle, mandolin, harmonica--and the bouzouki, which
he first introduced into Irish music. But it is
Moynihan's vocals, his unique and haunting style, that
comprise one of the special pleasures of this excellent
album.
                              L.N. $5.00

KEVIN BURKE "Sweeny's Dream" (Folkways FW8876)

SIDE ONE: LOVE AT THE END/HUMOURS OF LISSADELL/SWEENY'S DREAM/
MURPHY'S/SLIGO MAID, WOMAN OF THE HOUSE, SAILOR'S BONNET/
THE STRAYAWAY CHILD/COLLEGE GROVES/TOSS THE FEATHERS/KING OF
THE FAIRIES/MASON'S APRON, LAINGSTON'S HORNPIPE.

SIDE TWO: BUNCH OF KEYS, GIRL THAT BROKE MY HEART/BONNIE
KATE, JENNIE'S CHICKENS/RISE A MILE/BRENDAN MCGINCHY'S,
SWEENY'S BUTTERMILK/THE TURTLE, CHICKEN IN THE SAUCEPAN/
THE KID ON THE MOUNTAIN/POLKA'S GEORGE WHITE'S FAVORITE,
COLEMAN'S CROSS/

This is one of the best fiddle releases in recent times ranking
along with Tommy Peoples record on Schanachie. Kevin Burke is
in fact People's replacement in the Bothy Band. Although
Burke lacks some of People's abandon, it is difficult not to
compare their quite similar styles and to speculate if this
had something to do with the Bothy Band choosing him as Tommy
Peoples' replacement.

Kevin Burke recorded this album while spending time in the
United States in 1972. While here he met and played with a
number of American musicians including recording with Arlo
Guthrie. The supporting players are Alan Balaran and Brian
Heron, (Heron was with the Incredible String Band). Also
Alan Podber and Hank Sapoznik, all of these people played
with an empathy to Burke's style which is a strong and distinct one, the over all sound and drive in his playing does
compare, I think, with Tommy Peoples but Kevin Burke is his
own man throughout the album, and the energy is tireless and
unflagging.

I think that fiddlers and fiddle fans of any persuasion would
enjoy this album in addition to those addicted to the Irish
Genre.

This is one that is a must for someone who doesn't want to
buy a lot of albums. It is so easily one of the best.

                    R.F.G. $4.50

VINCENT GRIFFIN (Topic 338)
"Traditional Fiddle Music From County Clare"

      Fiddling with piano (harp on one tune)

REELS: FAHEY'S 1 & 2/PADDY RYAN'S DREAM/MAMMY'S PET/MARTIN
ROCHEFORD'S SLIGO MAID/LORD MCDONALD'S/BALLINASLOE FAIR/THE
REELS/MCFADDEN'S FAVORITE/THE NEW YEAR'S IN/YOUGHAL QUAY/LORD
GORDON'S/DR. GILBERT/THE QUEEN OF MAY/THE NIGHT IN ENNIS/THE
MAID BEHIND THE BAR/CROWLEY'S/LADY ANNE MONTGOMERY/DOWN THE
BROOM/GATEHOUSE MAID; JIGS: PADDY FAHEY'S/CLIFFS OF MOHER/
COLEMAN'S/TRIP TO SLIGO/GARRETT BARRY'S; HORNPIPES: NEW CEN-
TURY/CUCKOO; AIR: SE BHFATH MO BHFUARTHA

   The trouble with Irish fiddle music is certainly not quality; indeed it is so vigorously fought that the merely competent are soon forgotten. That's the trouble: the competition.
Scads of Irish fiddle LPs are on the market now, decent enough,
but beginning to sound alike. But this is different. The best
fiddling takes you into the fiddler's mind, and that is what
makes Vincent Griffin a surprise and a delight. His is the
work of a careful stylist with a liking, not so much for the
chipper and light, as for the melancholy--hear his plaintive
lilts and slithers on, for example, "Crowley's Reel". Griffin,
1974 all-Ireland champion, likes his minor keys and this is a
feast of them. He treats his noting with a heavy, liquid bow,
drawing the notes out broad and blue. Even on the hornpipes
there is this thoughtful quality, hoarse with color and wayward
and slippery. Only the lone air is a disappointment for its
failure to realize the possibilities of fiddle and harp, but
that's a small complaint on a superb, and different, Irish fid-
fle LP in which every note is given room to have its say.
RECOMMENDED.

            R.C. $5.50

THE BOYS OF THE LOUGH "Good Friends-Good Music" (Philo 1051)

The Boys with: Tony McMahon (accordian), Barney Mckenna
(banjo), Vincent Griffin (fiddle), Finlay MacNeill (vocal,
pipes), Tom Anderson (fiddle), Willie Johnson (guitar), Jimmy
Cooper (dulcimer), Louis Beaudoin (fiddle), Willie Beaudoin
(guitar), Sylvia Blaise (piano), Jay Unger (fiddle), Lyn Hardy
(guitar), Kenny Hall (mandolin, guitar), Eamon Curran (Uileann
pipes), Robbie Hughes (Uileann pipes), Tommy Gunn (lilting,
fiddle), Brendan Gunn (fiddle), Tony Smith (fiddle), Pat
Hanley (flute), John Joe Maguire (flute).

Side One: BRETON WEDDING MARCH/THE WILD IRISHMAN & THE SCHO-
LAR/DOWN THE BROOM & THE GATEHOUSE MAID/GAELIC MOUTH MUSIC/
FAREWELL TO GIBRALTER & CAPTAIN HORNE & THE HIGH ROAD TO LIN-
TON/FAR FROM HOME & DA ROAD TO HOULL/HILLSWICK WEDDING &
ROBERTSON'S REEL/CADAM WOODS & THE BONNIE LASS OF BON ACCORD/
LA GRANDE CHAINE & THE NEWLYWEDS REEL

Side Two: KITCHEN GIRL & THE NEW RIGGIT SHIP/CANADIAN WALTZ/
HOP HIGH LADIES/DENNIS MURPHY'S HORNPIPE & LEATHER BRITCHES/
THE HUMOURS OF ENNISTYMON & THE FIRST HOUSE IN CONNAUGHT &
ROLL HER IN THE RYE GRASS/KITTY'S GONE A-MILKING & MASTER MC-
DERMOTT'S/THE FLAIL & PADDY DOORY'S & THE PRIDE OF LEINSTER/
THE MIDSUMMER'S NIGHT & THE TINKER'S DAUGHTER & THE CROCK OF
GOLD

    This, The Boys of the Lough's sixth album, is quite pro-
bably their most exciting and satisfying one to date. Not only
are they in fine form but they are joined by well over a dozen
musicians from the British Isles and America, with styles as
diverse as French Canadian, old timey string band, and, of
course, Irish, Scottish, and Shetland Islands. This fusion of
backgrounds coupled with the skill of the musicians makes for
a surprising, exuberant collection of tunes, all in the spirit
of sharing that is one of the finest aspects of traditional
music at its best.

                    R.E.D. $4.50

PADDY KILLORAN'S BACK IN TOWN (Shanachie 33003)

SLIGO MAID'S LAMENT & MALLOY'S FAVORITE/THE LUCK PENNY &
COACH ROAD TO SLIGO/MULLINGAR RACES & BOYS ON THE HILLTOP/
TANSEY'S FAVORITE & THE HEATHERY BREEZE/GEESE IN THE BOG/
JOLLY TINKER & PRETTY GIRLS OF MAYO/AH SURELY & THE STEPPLE-
CHASE/MACGOVERN'S FAVORITE & TOM WARD'S DOWNFALL/HARVEST
HOME & CONDERRY HORNPIPE/HUMORS OF LISADELL/MAID OF MT. KISCO
& THE HUNTER'S PURSE/MCDERMOTT'S & MEMORIES OF SLIGO/ROARING
MARY & MAID OF CASTLEBAR/FARRELL O'GARA & SILVER SPIRE REEL

If you haven't heard of Paddy Killoran you needn't be ashamed.
Overshadowed during his lifetime by his swingy, dynamic countryman, Michael Coleman, Killoran till now has been an obscure
legend, a name on sought-after 78s, a fading memory in the New
York Irish community that doted on his beautiful clear fiddling
30 and 40 and 50 years ago. But I don't know but that I prefer him even to Coleman. Killoran's trademark was an attack
so light, quick, easy and melodic it makes you jump and star-
tle and starts songs in your head. His astonishing imagination can be judged on an overdone piece like Harvest Home,
which he turns into a treat with fresh surprises. He's backed
here by piano sometimes and guitar sometimes, and in the
best tracks of all he is paired with fellow Sligo fiddler
Paddy Sweeny. These powerful fiddle duets had an incalcul-
able influence on Irish duet playing in America, as they were
among the first, and the best, to reach record. But in every
piece Killoran has his special touch, his unusual notion trans-
lated into sound. As with Coleman and a rare few other Irish
fiddlers in this century, he has the magic of a time when the
memory of the old home was still fresh and every note was a
poignant tribute, a reminder and a farewell. RECOMMENDED.

            R.C. $4.80

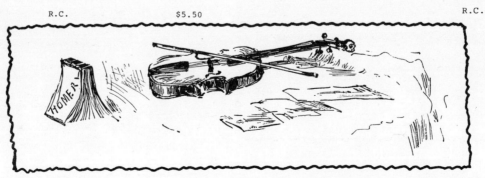

WESTERN SWING VOLUMES 4 AND 5 (Old Timey 119, 120; $5.50 each)

Vol. 4: Tune Wranglers: My Sweet Thing, It Don't Mean a Thing/
Modern Mountaineers: Getting That Lowdown Swing, You
Got to Know How to Crack & Swing/Jimmie Revard: Tulsa
Waltz/Hank Penny: It Ain't Gonna Rain No Mo', Mississippi
Muddle/Claude Casey & Pine State Playboys: Pine State
Honky Tonk/W. Lee O'Daniel: Lonesome Road Blues/
Washboard Wonders: It Ain't Right/Crystal Springs
Ramblers: Tired of Me, Down in Arkansas/Shelly Lee
Alley & Alley Cats: Try it Once Again/Ted Daffan's
Texans: Worried Mind, Blue Steel Blues/Milton Brown:
Baby Keeps Stealin'

Vol. 5: Tune Wranglers: I Believe in You/Light Crust Doughboys:
Tom Cat Rag, Blue Guitars/Buddy Jones: Mean Old Lone-
some Blues, Settle Down Blues/Farr Bros.: Kilocycle
Stomp, Cajon Stomp/Milton Brown: I'll Be Glad When
You're Dead, Stay on the Right Side Sister/Universal
Cowboys: Hot Mama Stomp/Jimmie Davis & Brownies:
High Geared Daddy/Honky Tonk Blues/Nite Owls: El
Rancho Grande/Bill Boyd: Thousand Mile Blues/Bob
Skyles & Skyrockets: Hot Tamale Pete/Ocie Stockard:
Bass Man Jive

The manifold glories of this agreeable country jazz are all here.
It took a while for reissue companies to get much beyond Bob
Wills and his atypical western swing; but this fine series of
WS classics does much to redress the balance and is just getting
better and better. These are stunning albums--don't pass them
up if inflation's left you any money at all.

Volume 4 is tightly coherent despite its anthology format and
its astounding range of WS styles--blues, boogie, hoedown, waltz,
fast march and washboard scrub. It comes close to jazz in the
exciting fiddling of J. L. Chatwell with the Modern Mountaineers,
who also use Emil Hofner's neat steel work, a sozzled-sounding
tenor sax, Smokey Wood's deft piano and a natty vocal. Revard
is eclectically cowboyish in his classic waltz, which has lived
on in tradition for its sheer lyrical beauty, and the Tune
Wranglers have a hot raggy feel to their headlong fiddling and
scratchy banjo.

The focus of both LPs is on the 1930s, before the World War
II ear synthesis of styles and the coming of sophistication
to country music, when the individuality and inventiveness of
territory bands like these were necessarily submerged. So
we're hearing a lot of hot new ideas fresh from the minds and
fingers of the musicians--like the odd, quaintly pop-
flavored minor skiffle piece by the Washboard Wonders with
its Cab Calloway touch. It's worth remembering these guys
were doing these things in the same time and space as the
Blue SkyBoys and Monroe Brothers! Most modern of the groups
here are, doubtless, Penny's and Daffan's--the former with a
densely knot sound and turnabout instrumental solos, the latter
anticipating honkytonk--but all the groups are exploring
everything they can think of, and that's exciting, and moving
to hear.

Texas Sand: Anthology of Western Swing (Rambler 101)
TUNE WRANGLERS, ROY NEWMAN & HIS BOYS, MILTON
BROWN & HIS BROWNIES, CLIFF BRUNER, PRAIRIE RAMB
LERS, JIMMIE REVARD & HIS OKLAHOMA PLAYBOYS, JOHNNY
TYLER & HIS RIDERS OF THE RIO GRANDE, CURLY WIL-
LIAMS & HIS GEORGIA PEACH PICKERS, THE SUNSHINE
BOYS, JESSE ASHLOCK, "T" TEXAS TYLER & HIS OKLAHOMA
MELODY BOYS
Side One: TEXAS SAND/EVERYBODY'S TRYING TO BE MY
BABY/IDA! SWEET AS APPLE CIDER/THAT'S WHAT I LIKE
ABOUT THE SOUTH/DEEP ELM BLUES/LET ME LIVE AND LOVE
YOU/I NEVER SEE MY BABY ALONE
Side Two: SOUTHERN BELLE (FROM NASHVILLE TENNESSEE)/
LONESOME BLUES/OLD WATERFALL/TEXAS STOMP/NO GOOD
FOR NOTHIN' BLUES/BETTY ANN/TEX TYLER RIDE

> "Sand in my coffee, sand in my tea
> When I die they're gonna bury me
> Deep in that shifting, drifting Texas sand."

Good times is what it's all about--from the
hilarity of "I Never See My Baby Alone" (Johnny
Tyler) to the sublime whimsy of "Texas Sand" (the
Tune Wranglers), these guys all show they know how
to have fun. There's not a less than sweet moment
in this collection of reissues from eleven Western
swing bands, recorded between 1935 and 1950.
   There's a few real rib-ticklers; "Everybody's
Trying to Be My Baby," "Deep Elm Blues," and "I
Never See My Baby Alone" have the most outrageous
lyrics. These are balanced out by the several
sentimental tunes featuring honey-dripping singing
in that real Western Swing style: the Tune Wranglers' "Texas Sand," Jesse Ashlock's "Betty Ann,"
and of course Milton Brown's selection, "Ida!
Sweet as Apple Cider" fall into this group. Each
band has great instrumentation. Some famed musicians play in various bands. Cliff Bruner's fiddle
solos on "Ida!" and "That's What I Like About the
South" are highlights of the album. Pianists Moon
Mullican and Eddie Whitley are both featured on a
couple of songs, and steel guitar aces Speedy West
and Bob Dunn put in fine appearances.
   Roy Newman's group is the most jazz-oriented,
featuring some gutsy clarinet, and there are electric guitar solos in some of the later recordings.
Hints of the coming of rock & roll are here, but
are more apparent in the rocking rhythm of songs
like "Everybody's Trying..." than in the electric
guitar's shy presence in these pieces.
   It is almost unfair to single out one song
in an album with so much that's superior, but one
of special note is Milton Brown's piece. Brown's
sure delivery and the way his band works together
should convince you of his lasting stature. (If
interested in further convincing, listen to Taking
Off (String 804) devoted solely to Brown and his
Brownies.)
   There's a lot of scope here--from the rough,
back-woods Prairie Ramblers' "Deep Elm Blues" of
1935 to "Tex Tyler's Ride," a slick, Hollywood 1950
recording, but it's all got that unmistakable Western swing. Excellent sound quality. Record collectors note: it's pressed on clear vinyl.
                                    -WR $5.00

AN AMERICAN IN TEXAS   Lespedeza Record Co.
                                 $6.00

(Same personnel and instrumentation except add fiddle.)

Side one: As the Crow Flies/You Keep Me Holding On/Sad As It
          Seems/The Last One to Know/Green Tree/At Least Two
          Ways

Side two: Bluebird/Too Far to Fall/An American in Texas/Don't
          You Know--Can't You See/Walking Angel/Deeper Than
          Love

With roots in such seemingly diverse musics as Prof. Longhair's
New Orleans piano of the 1950s, Lionel Hampton's small·band swing
and jive tunes of the late 1930s, Texas swing, and the best of

STOMPIN' AT THE HONKY TONK   (String 805)

Side one: CLIFF BRUNER'S TEXAS WANDERERS-SUGAR/TEXAS
WANDERERS-RACKIN' IT BACK/CLIFF BRUNER'S TEXAS WANDERERS-
KANGAROO BLUES/PORT ARTHUR JUBILEERS - PUSSYWILLOW/CLIFF
BRUNER'S TEXAS WANDERERS - ONE SWEET LETTER FROM YOU/
PORT ARTHUR JUBILEERS - JEEP'S BLUES/SHELLY LEE ALLEY
AND HIS ALLEY CATS - HOUSTON BLUES/CLIFF BRUNER AND HIS
BOYS - JESSIE
Side Two: BAR-X COWBOYS - ROCKDALE RAG/LEON 'PAPPY'
SELPH AND HIS BLUE RIDGE PLAYBOYS - FLORENE/TEXAS WAN-
DERERS - DEEP ELM SWING/ CLIFF BRUNER AND HIS BOYS - NEW
FALLING RAIN BLUES/DICKIE MCBRIDE AND THE VILLAGE BOYS -
TULSA TWIST/PORT ARTHUR JUBILEERS - JONES STOMP/MODERN
MOUNTAINEERS - WHO'S CRYIN' SWEET PAPA NOW/BOB DUNN'S
VAGABONDS - STOMPIN' AT THE HONKY TONK
     Those devotees of western swing excited by the early
music of Bob Wills and Milton Brown should check out
this latest collection on Tony Russell's String label.
Drawing from the wealth of recordings made by Houston-
based bands, from the old-timey string band approach
of the Bar-X Cowboys to the cool sophistication of Cliff
Bruner's groups, this fine anthology gives a vivid
account of the wild goings-on there must have been around
Houston in the late 30's-early 40's.
     Ex-musical Brownie fiddler Cliff Bruner hogs the
limelight here, and his band, which includes Bob Dunn
(also from Milton Brown's group) on stell-guitar and Leo
Faley on mandolin, turns in some fine performances, especially on "New Falling Down Blues" and the bawdy "Kangaroo
Blues."
     In addition to his work with Bruner, Dunn fronts his
own band (Bob Dunn's Vagabonds) and is featured with the
Texas Wanderers (basically the same band as Cliff Bruner's
Texas Wanderers minus Cliff). Anyone familiar with Dunn's
work with Milton Brown will be further staggered by his
drunken, knock-about steel-guitar solos with this band.
Indeed, no one does it like Dunn!
     Further highlights are those sides by the Port Arthur
Jubileers (that "blue and lonesome" accordian solo on
"Jeep's Blues" is just too much!), "Houston Blues" by
Shelly Lee Alley and His Alley Cats and the magnificent
"Who's Cryin' Sweet Papa Now" by the Modern Mountaineers.
     If you thrilled to String's excellent BEER PARLOR
JIVE (String 801) or any of Old Timey's western swing
anthologies (OT 105, 116, 117), then prepare to be floored
by this peach of collection!

                              GKJ $5.50

JOHNNIE LEE WILLS "Tulsa Swing" (Rounder 1027)

IN THE MOOD/RIDIN' DOWN THE CANYON/COWBOY'S DREAM/SOUTHLAND
SWING/DON'T LET YOUR DEAL GO DOWN/KEEP A LIGHT IN THE WINDOW
TONIGHT/NEVER ALONE/FOUR OR FIVE TIMES/LEATHER BRITCHES/SALLY
GOODIN/BUFFALO GALS/SILVER DEW ON THE BLUEGRASS TONIGHT/SMOKE
ON THE WATER/BOOGIE WOOGIE HIGHBALL/LOVE YOU SO MUCH/BLACK-
EYED SUSAN BROWN/FARTHER ALONG/SMITH'S REEL

     Western swing, a unique mixture of swing and fiddle music,
has become synonymous with the name Wills. When Bob Wills
formed his first band in the 1930's, he asked his brother,
Johnnie Lee, to play tenor banjo for him. For six years they
travelled across Texas popularizing their new style of music.

In 1940, Johnnie Lee Wills got his own band together and,
while Bob was touring California, Johnnie Lee and his band were
enjoying much success in Texas and Oklahoma. There was always
a lot of interplay between the two bands, they shared the same
manager and publishing company and were constantly swapping
personnel.
     This record is made up of songs from a series of radio
shows done in 1950-51 and typifies the kind of music through
which the band made its reputation. Many of the musicians included were former members of Bob Wills' band (Leon Huff, vocals; Don Harlan, clarinet).
     "Tulsa Swing" features western swing at its peak of devel-
opment. The instrumentation of Johnnie Lee's band tended to
be more traditional than that of Bob Wills' band. They both
used the twin fiddles and clarinet, but Bob also experimented
with brass and reeds. On the other hand, Johnnie Lee was ob-
viously influenced by the Bop movement of the 40's and experimented with these concepts rather than instrumentation. Sound
quality is excellent.

                         E.W. $5.00

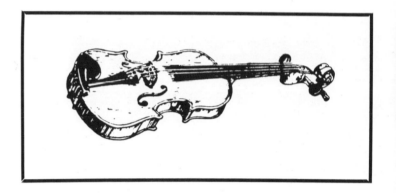

Operator's Special Various artists (String 807)
Side One: Jimmie Revard & his Oklahoma Playboys-SWING
ME/Johnnie Lee Willis & his boys-MILK COW BLUES/The
Tune Wranglers-SHE'S SWEET/Leaford Hall & his Texas
Vagabonds-BLUE MAN/Buddy Jones-ROCKIN ROLLIN MAMA/
Doug Bine & his Dixie Ramblers-RAMBLERS STOMP/Ocie
Stockard & his Wanderers-NICKEL IN THE KITTY/Bob Styles
& his Skyrockets-RUBBER DOLLY
Side Two: Sons of the West-PANHANDLE SHUFFLE/Hoyle Nix
& his West Texas Cowboys-A BIG BALL'S IN COWTOWN/John
Lee Wills & his Boys-TOO LONG/Bob Skyles-JIVE AND SMILE/
Buddy Jones-MEAN OLD SIXTY FIVE BLUES/Smoky Wood & his
Woodchips-WOODCHIP BLUES/Adolph Hofner & his San
Antonians-SOMETIMES/Jimmy Revard-IT'S A LONG LONG WAY
TO TIPPERARY
     Add to the growing list of exciting Western
Swing anthologies this new one on String, the same
label that's given us the Milton Brown, Beer Parlor
Jive, and Stomping At The Honk Tonk albums, all
first class documentations of the genre. Unlike
Stomping which devoted itself to the Houston based
bands, Operator's Specials (a term used by record
dealers for releases aimed at the juke box trade)
covers a broader area, presenting bands from South and
West Texas, Oklahoma, and Louisiana, and crossing all
sorts of stylistic ground as well; from the romping
Bobs Wills inspired dance music of Nix's "A Big Balls
In Cowtown" ("Come in mama, the hogs have got me!")
to the more sophisticated "Nickel In The Kitty", with

it's twin fiddle intro and more pop flavored vacals.
     Jim Revard opens and closes the album with more
of his usual good-time music;"Swing Me" is distinguished by the blues fiddle of Ben McCay, the inspired steel
playing of Emil Hofner, and some great vocals by Eddie
Whiteby.
     Johnnie Lee Wills, whose band show-cased the
talents of such Western Swing luminaries as guitarist
Junior Barnard and pianist Millard Kelso (both would
later be members of Bob Wills' Texas Playboys), are
well represented by "Too Long" and by Johnnie's big
hit and signature tune, "Milk Cow Blues", which is
highlighted by Kelso's piano break and the bluesy
fiddling of Cotton Thompson.
     Of particular interest is the weird brand of
Western Swing played by Bob Skyles and his Skyrockets;
what with the wild, jazzy soloing and pairing of a hot
horn section - clarinet/tenor sax, trumpet, trombone,
tuba - and the crazy, driving trap drumming of Clifford
Kendricks, the Skyrockets sound, at times, like
Oklahoma counterparts to the hot New Orleans jazz players.
     Other notables (on a record of nothing but not-
able music) are the low down Jimmie Rodgers inspired
singing of Buddy Jones on the rowdy "Rockin Rollin
Mama" and "Mean Old Sixty Five Blues", (Both feature
Moon Mullican on piano), the double entendre, and absolutely unsubtle "Woodchip Blues" by Smoky Wood,
whose vocals suggest a black influence,(possibly even
Fats Waller - listen to the spoken ending of the song)
and a foot stomping version of "Ain't She Sweet" by
the Tune Wranglers. Packaging, notes & sound quality
are outstanding. Terrific!
                              -Glenn Jones $6.00 ·

                         100

MILTON BROWN AND HIS MUSICAL BROWNIES   "Taking Off"   (String 804)

Side One: CHINATOWN, MY CHINATOWN/ST. LOUIS BLUES/IN EL RANCHO
GRANDE/TAKING OFF/IF YOU CAN'T GET FIVE TAKE TWO/FAN IT/
LITTLE BETTY BROWN/SOME OF THESE DAYS

Side Two: SWEET GEORGIA BROWN/TEXAS HAMBONE BLUES/WASHINGTON
AND LEE SWING/MY MARY/GOOFUS/HONKYTONK BLUES/SWEET JENNIE LEE/
THERE'LL BE SOME CHANGES MADE

   Tony Russell's fine String label has released the first
album devoted solely to the music of Milton Brown and his Musical
Brownies. Those devotees of western swing who have collected the
various Old Timey and String anthologies where the Brownies'
cuts were the highlights of those collections will hardly need
any introduction to this giant of western swing.
   Brown began his career singing with Bob Wills in 1930,
first with Wills Fiddle Band, later as the Alladin Laddies, and
finally as the Light Crust Doughboys who began broadcasting in
Fort Worth. A disagreement with W. Lee O'Daniel who sponsored
the Doughboys, and jealousy between Wills and Brown, led to
Brown's resignation, and in 1932 he formed his Musical Brownies
and began broadcasting on KTAT. Gathering excellent musicians
and putting his experience with Wills to use, he developed a very
successful and popular dance band, one that would go far in its
four short years of existence toward popularizing western swing.
In 1936 Brown died after an automobile accident, and his friend
and biggest rival, Bob Wills, went to claim the title of King of
Western Swing.
   This reissue of sixteen of the Brownies' songs are mostly
from sessions recorded in 1935 and 1936. Also included are two
selections from 1937, recordings made after Brown's death and
though both cuts are good ("Honkytonk Blues" and "There'll Be
Some Changes Made"), it soon proved that the band was unable to
manage without Brown's leadership and the bank broke up in 1938.
The Brownies' repertoire was nothing if not eclectic and styles
here range from the Tex-Mex influenced "In El Rancho Grande,"
hot dance tunes complete with calls ("Little Betty Brown"), to
such popular standards as "Chinatown" and "Sweet Georgia Brown,"
all done with the spiciness that characterized nearly all of
Brown's work.
   Most of the musicians were highly talented, but Cecil Brower's
really swinging jazz style fiddling stands out as does the inde-
scribable steel guitar solos of the amazing Bob Dunn which are like
nothing done with a steel guitar before or since--(really crazy
stuff!!)--listen especially to the title song and his solos in
"Some of These Days" and "Washington and Lee Swing." Both Brown
and Wills professed to have been greatly influenced by black musicians and singers; the influence, I think, is more discernable in
the Brownies' music and especially Brown's singing. Brown was a
fine singer and it is easy to see how his leaving the Light Crust
Doughboys upset Wills. His singing here shines most on "St. Louis
Blues," "Some of These Days," and the sentimental "My Mary." In
addition, we have some humorous songs: "Goofus," the somewhat
bawdy "If You Can't Get Five Take Two" and "Fan It" all feature
some terrific lyrics and fine soloing; sounds as if the Brownies
were having quite a time! "Taking Off," besides being an excellent collection, also boasts excellent sound quality (very clean
and clear), is well 'annotated' by Tony Russell and has a pleasing
cover too--what more can I say: an exceptional album of music by
one of the greatest of the early pioneer western swing bands!!

G.K.J. $5.00

DEVIL WITH THE DEVIL   Rambler 102
                                              ($5.50)

CLIFF BRUNER'S TEXAS WANDERERS: The Right Key (But the Wrong
Keyhole)/I Ain't Gonna Give Nobody None o' This Jelly Roll;
BLUE RIDGE PLAYBOYS: Gimme My Dime Back; TUNE WRANGLERS: They
Go Wild Over Me/I'm Wild About That Thing; LIGHT CRUST DOUGH-
BOYS: Gulf Coast Blues; ROY NEWMAN: I Can't Dance (I Got Ants
in My Pants)/The Devil with the Devil; JIMMIE REVARD & OKLA.
PLAYBOYS: Cats Are Bad Luck/Cake Eatin' Man; MODERN MOUNTAINEERS:
When My Baby Comes to Town; MILTON BROWN: Easy Ridin' Papa;
TEXAS WANDERERS: Wonder Stomp; BILL BOYD: Jig

The emphasis is on hot, jazzy phrasing in these western swing
reissues from nine bands working between 1935 and 1939, when WS'
musical experiment was in full flower. Focusing on the hot and
bluesy to the exclusion of WS' many other kinds of music is, of
course, only part of a very colorful mosaic, but it sure does
make one neat LP, Rambler's second release (the first was also a
WS anthology, Texas Sand), the record pressed in natty red wax
to match the cover. It's satisfying and flawless, full of
fiddlers intoxicated with jazz' headlong fingering and syncopated
phrasing, pianists lost in the wonders of boogie, guitarists
inspired by Bob Dunn's lap steel inventions, and vocalists rough
and smooth working in single- and double-entendre. The result is
something like what you might have heard on an oiltown jukebox if
the distributor really knew what he was doing.

Western swing is seldom, as its name implies, just fast. The
heat in the Bruner band, for example, opens up to let in some
lazy fiddle phrasing and Leo Raley's fine vocal and electric
mandolin leads. The Tune Wranglers, whose signature is their
cheerful willingness to bash along through a melody, offer all
at once a wafer-thin, otherworldly tenor banjo solo. And
dominating the Blue Ridge Playboys' work is the scrawny urchin's
voice of Pappy Selph, which seems to hark back to a cross
between oldtime music and vaudeville. This is the secret of
WS' wide appeal: its ability to stop on a dime and start up
something different, giving the flavor of moving in several
directions at once without ever losing track.

Most jazzy on the LP are Roy Newman's bands, the first with twin
fiddling and Holly Holton's charmingly dirty clarinet plus a
really original vocal duet trading echoes with Earl Brown's
scat jazz vocal. The title piece is all drama and minor key.
At the other end of the spectrum is the marriage of coarse and
mellow that is Revard, nicely overdone as always, with the rich
grace of a dowager doing the Black Bottom. The album's breeziest
moment is the Texas Wanderers' long sax lead over a spiderwebby
steel guitar--tossing it to an equally lightfingered fiddle.
Milton Brown's incredible ease is, as always, the master's
touch--he must have been the despair of all the WS bands. But
it is Bill Boyd who has the last word and it is dynamite. One
of his occasional forays into pure steam, "Jig" seems to have
been designed for fiddler Carroll Hubbard who, beginning with a
slow sweet Paul Whiteman phrase, proceeds to demolish, at a
thousand miles an hour, every fiddler who ever picked up a bow.
Somehow the band, with Knocky Parker's piano professorship in
the vanguard and Marvin Montgomery playing the banjo of his
life, manages to do it. You have never heard a record end quite
like this. But it was good from the start. Even people who
don't like Western Swing are likely to like it.

YANKEE INGENUITY   "Kitchen Junket" (Fretless 200A and 200B)

WOODCHOPPER'S REEL - EDDIE'S REEL/SHANDON BELLS - THERE CAME
A YOUNG MAN/JOYS OF QUEBEC/PLANXTY GEORGE BRABAZAN - DOMINICAN
REEL/GROWLING OLD MAN AND THE GRUMBLING OLD WOMAN/PAINTER'S
POLKA/MOUTH OF THE TOBIQUE - MACKILMOYLE REEL/ANGUS CAMPBELL
- TOP O' THE HILL/FAIRY TODDLER JIG - CHARLIE HUNTER/REDDE
MONTREAL - SET DEA BAIE ST PAUL/COLORED ARISTOCRACY - RAGTIME
ANNIE/STAR OF THE COUNTRY DAWN

Peter Larnes: piano, guitar, 5-string banjo; Hank Chapin:
acoustic bass; Donna Hinds: fiddle; Jack O'Conner: mandolin,
fiddle, tenor guitar, tenor banjo; Tony Parkes: piano, calls;
Joan Pelton: Bodhran.

     Yankee Ingenuity is a traditional New England dance
band. The fiddle tunes come from Ireland, England, Scotland,
French Canada and the United States. It is infectious, lively
music at its best and I defy anyone to remain still while
listening to these records.
     There are two versions of the same record: one with
calls, one without. I find either to be good listening but
in the end I prefer the calls: this music makes the most sense
in its proper context of a dance.
     Tony's calls are clear, concise and often witty. He
keeps dancers on their toes and although he doesn't sing the
calls his phrasing flows, rather fights, with the music.
     Donna Hinds' fiddling has never been better: <u>Joys of
Quebec</u> proves to be a showcase for the whole band but it is
Donna who continues to drive with an especially fluid bow.
     The band uses occasional stop time devices and switches
leads between the fiddle, mandolin and tenor banjo, to achieve
variety within each tune. The results are excellent. The
record makes sense as casual listening (good luck remaining
casual!) or as a learning-dancing tool.

                    G.T. $4.50

APPLEJACK WITH BOB MCQUILLEN: CONTRADANCE MUSIC NEW ENGLAND STYLE
Green Linnet SIF 1028 ($6.00)

Side A: Scotty O'Neil: Prelude, Sarah's Jig, Joanie's Jig,
          Shelley's Reel, Joey's Hornpipe, Larry's Walrz, Deer
          Run North, Michael's Hornpipe, Andy's Hornpipe, Jill's
          Jig, New England Winter, The Dancing Bear

Side B: Chips from the Block, Scotty O'Neil, Woodland Dream,
          Ralph Page, Sanella's Swinger, Laurie's Hornpipe,
          Boil the Sap, Paul's Jig, Ralphy's Red Hat, Applejack's
          Reel

Jill Newton: fiddle; Laurie Indenbaum: fiddle; Andy Toepfer:
guitar; Michael McKernan: mandolin, mandola, 5-string and tenor
banjos. With Bob McQuillen: accordion, piano, and all compositions.

Ready for a surprise? This is it! From Vermont, four musicians
who've been playing New England dance music since 1975 have
recorded an album of tunes by Bob McQuillen that will make your
heart dance. Terrific double-fiddling dominates, supported by
skilled playing from the others and exciting arrangements.
"Larry's Waltz" is as sweet as the best maple syrup, "Ralph
Page" bounces like a sparkling superball, and "New England
Winter/The Dancing Bear" is simply magnificent. Take your pick
of the rest--you can't lose here. RECOMMENDED.

                    --SJA

New England Contra Dance Music (KM 216)
Side 1: HULL'S VICTORY/MEDLEY:KITTY McGEE;A HUNDRED
PIPERS/DOUBLE FILE/MEDLEY:ROSS'S REEL;BATCHELDER'S
REEL/SWING AWAY/MY HOME WALTZ/MEDLEY: SALAMANCA REEL;
THE HUNTER'S PURSE;TARBOLTEN
Side 2: MEDLEY: TURNPIKE SIDE;TOBIN'S FANCY/MEDLEY:
GOIN' UPTOWN;AVALON QUICKSTEP/MEDLEY: FAREWELL TO
WHISKEY;HITLER'S DOWNFALL/WESTPHALIA WALTZ/MOUNTAIN
RANGER

     This is an anthology of New England contra
dance music played by several fine groups of musicians: Strathspey, Arm & Hammer String Band, and
Alan Block & George Wilson. Contra dances were
New England first cousins to the English country
dances, with a somewhat less stately pace and
rowdier nature. The tunes are from the British
Isles and this country, and both the music and
dance have an infectious feel to them. If you've
never contra-danced, you owe it to yourself to try,
and if you've never heard contra dance music, this
is a fine place to begin.
                    -RED $5.50

Allan Block "Alive and Well and Fiddling" (Living Folk 104)

GRUB SPRINGS/FLOP-EARED MULE/EAST TENNESSEE BLUES/HARD
TO LOVE/MONEY MUSK/DOWN AMONG THE BUDDED ROSES/CIDER MILL/
BUNCH OF RUSHES/AIN'T NO USE IN YOUR HIGH-HATTIN' ME/
JOHNSON GALS/RIGHTS OF MAN & OLD TEMPLE HOUSE/SANDY RIVER
BELLE/THE CRUEL MOTHER/PADDY ON THE TURNPIKE/THE TWO
BROTHERS/SUNNY HOMEIN DIXIE/QUINCE DILLON'S HIGH D TUNE.

     Allan Block has been a familiar figure at festivals,
dances and concerts throughout New York and New England
for a number of years. Those who have heard him will be
glad to know that this, his long, over-due second album
captures much of the spontaneity and life that characterize
his performances. The selections were culled from tapes
of 'live' concerts, and although the sound quality is not
the best the musicianship is first-rate. Allan is an
eclectic fiddler, though he leans to old time string
band tunes, and he is graced with the ability to draw
the utmost out of his fellow players. Here he is joined
by a number of fine musicians from the Boston area, John
Schwab, Claudio Buchwald, Dick Fegy, Lorraine Lee, Andy
May, and Nancy McDowell.

                    -RED $4.00

6004   The American Swedish Spelmans Trio

Edwin Johnson, his son Bruce and his grandson Paul Dahlin (all from Minneapolis) represent three generations from one family of Swedish fiddlers. Here they offer up a fine album of Swedish fiddle music—polskas, gånglåts, marches, waltzes, and more. *Te Budum Och Sommaren; Polska Från Rättvik; Brudmarsch Från Rättvik; Vals Från Rättvik; Polska Efter John Eriksson; Efterkålken; Vals Efter Timas Hans; Gånglåt Från Rättvik; Polska From Dalarna; Vals Från Ore; Gärdebylåten; Knuts Livstycke; Midsommarpolskan; Vandringen I Varlden; Skinnbracka Med Lukku; Gånglåt Efter Sens John; Horgalåten; Dal Jerks Gånglåt; Fjusnäs Valsen; Polska Efter John Ericksson; Visby Gånglåt; Polska Från Våstbjörka; Stens Vals; Vals Från Gardebyn.*

The Swedish Fiddlers (Folkways 8471)
9 polkas, 4 waltzes, 2 bridal marches, 2 walking tunes
     The release of this record makes three of the best Swedish fiddle albums anywhere available to Roundup readers. It was recorded at the Delsbo gathering, a fiddler's convention similar to Galax or Union Grove (in times past) over here. Energetic playing both on and off the stage is represented. The listener is presented with a balanced cross section of regional styles and individual techniques. The best "spelmans" on both the conventional violin and the key-fiddle (a sort of violin-hurdy-gurdy-dulcimer of medieval origin) are featured. The high points of this set include the opening three tracks which are played by all assembled with overwhelming clarity. It's easy to believe some of the wilder legends Sam Charters recounts in his notes, of dancers entranced by the playing of crazed fiddlers, when one listens to these ensemble performances, especially the "Rullspolka." On side two, Rojas Jonas Eriksson renders a version of "Gratlaten" (cryin' song) that is a virtuoso review of the evolution of Swedish traditional music. Of the other records mentioned at the top of this review, Philo 2017 presents all key-fiddle duets by the peerless Eric Sahlstrom and similar notes by Charters to those in the Folkways set. Rounder 6004 boasts fiddle trios led by the redoubtable Edwin Johnson, an immigrant to Minnesota. All three records present some of the most rhythmically bewildering and tonally rich fiddle music played anywhere. Each has received heady praise in Sweden. Try the Rounder or Philo for focus on one instrument. This new Folkways is ideal for variety and atmosphere and a bargain compared to their "ethnic" offerings.
                                                                 DK $5.00

THE DANCING BOW - SWEDISH FIDDLE MUSIC (Sonet 201)
                                                  (2-LP)
50 polkas, waltzes, quadrilles, and native dance rhythms with violins, key fiddle, wooden shoe fiddle and some zither accompaniment
     This generous selection of melodies is gorgeous in sound and the most satisfying collection of Swedish fiddling yet recorded. The wealth of fiddlers (something like three dozen of them) creates a variety of approaches and sounds -- sameness is no problem here. The tradition is that of the ancient spelmen -- wandering musicians who led a catch-as-catch-can life devoted to their music.
     What sort of music is it? Not "hot" in any sense -- nor, despite the name "polska," do most of the pieces have the slightest resemblance to polkas. Rich in melody and the characteristic countermelody, frequently in minor or eerie major, the music is as wandering as its tradition, adopting strict tempo as an option, not as a rule. The key fiddle's hurdy-gurdy-like sound is deep and resonant, slightly mechanical with tremulous high overtones. The paired fiddles create an echoing, evocative sound that is utterly strange and compelling and takes you places. There are passages reminiscent of classical repertoire, and there are a few up-tempo standards, but most of the arrangements cast a spell by their stark simplicity overlaid by the complexity of one or several other voices: lovely wayward melodies, exploring possibilities in sound against an ancient pattern.
     I can't imagine any fiddler who wouldn't want to put these sides on the turntable to wonder over, and to learn from. For the general listener this is a package of ravishing sounds that do things to the ear and the mind: strings coming alive as voices so lifelike that you lean toward the speaker trying to learn somehow what they are saying. The players range in age from young men like Bjorn Stabi and Ole Horth, familiar to Americans from their tour and Nonesuch LP, to grand old men of the tradition like Eric Sahlstrom. This collection makes you hungry for more such high-quality recordings from the European national traditions. RECOMMENDED.
                          -RC 2 LP set $11.00

ERIC SAHLSTROM w/ GOSTA SANDSTROM, "Fiddle Music From Uppland" (Philo 2017).
Up until now the only widely available U.S. release of Swedish fiddling has been a well-performed, but Dolby-muted set of Dalarna tunes by two young performers (Nonesuch H-72033). This album is the first in a series that Philo records has leased from Sonet of Sweden's extensive survey of national fiddle traditions. The intricacies of the "spelman's" bowing technique and harmonies make Swedish fiddling one of the most bewitching listening experiences that life has to offer. Hopefully, Americans will turn a good ear to this recording. The key fiddle (used by both musicians here) has evolved from the 14th century to an instrument that is shaped like a dulcimer, is fretted like an autoharp and sounds like a fiddler's dream. Sahlstrom is Uppland's master key fiddle builder and is considered one of Sweden's most versatile stylists. All but three of the nineteen(!) pieces he performs here are waltzes and polkas. His permutations of 3/4 time and ornamentation will boggle the minds of even Texas fiddle aficionados. The sound quality puts Nonesuch to shame. Samuel Charters' notes are lengthy but superlative, particularly with reference to the "spelman's" magical powers in peasant folklore. This album won a Grammy in Sweden and deserves one here. Philo will release as many of the Sonet series as Pete Public will pay for -- er, uh, --that is, listen to, and Rounder has a record of Swedish-American fiddling in the can. Hopefully we'll soon be able to review some examples of large fiddle ensembles and/or schottische performances. For now, top marks to this album and I'm keeping my fingers crossed for more like it.
                                             -DK ($4.)

The Rounder 7000 series features Canadian music, especially the vigorous violin music of Cape Breton Island in Nova Scotia. For years, the "iron curtain" of trade restrictions has prevented the U.S. from hearing this wonderful traditional music, whose roots are intimately tied to the sources of our own Appalachian culture. In Cape Breton, fiddle music still retains the zest and vitality of pioneer life, coupled with a technical skill that is virtually unparalleled in folk music.

7001   Joseph Cormier:
Scottish Violin Music from Cape Breton Island

This is the first record ever issued in the United States of the exciting and complex music of Cape Breton, Nova Scotia. A must for any fiddle fan, and first in a series of albums featuring this fiddle style. *Haggis; Glenville's Dirk; Bird's Nest; Mrs. Scott Skinner; Smith's A Gallant Fireman; Andy's Reel; Paddy on the Turnpike; Strathspey in E; Backs Hornpipe; The Trumpet; Iron Man; Put Me in the Box; Muileann Dubh, Miss Lyle's Strathspey; Lassies of Glenaodale; A Salute to Winston Fitzgerald; Tom MacCormack's Capers; Glencoe Bridge March; Lieutenant Howard Douglas; Medley of Old Time Reels; Bonnie Lass O Bon Accord; Devil in the Kitchen; Duntroon Reels Medley.*

7002   Graham Townsend:
Le Violon/The Fiddle

A varied anthology of fiddle music by Canada's best known instrumentalist, featuring Scottish, Irish, Canadian and southern styles with appropriate backup. An excellent introduction to fiddle music for the novice, and a sure source of many hours of appreciation for the initiated. Full biographical notes included. *Black Jack Whiskey; Gigue De Joliette; La Galope De Ste.-Blandine; La Galope Malbaie; Mississippi Cajun; Irish-American; Tom Ward's Downfall; Miss Monahan; Roxborough Castle; Mary Walker; Eighth of January; Bill Cheatham; Archie Menzie's; The Spey in Spate; Mason's Apron; Back Up & Push; Crazy Creek; Erin's Fancy; My Dungannon Sweetheart; The Tarbolton; Paddy on the Turnpike; Pride of the Ball; Plaza Polka; Lochaber Gathering; Marchioness of Huntly; Major Manson; Isle of Skye; Ronfleuse Gobeil; Le Reel de Champlain; The A Minor Reel; Reel du Pecheur.*

7010   Tom Doucet:
I Used To Play Some Pretty Tough Tunes

Nova Scotian fiddler Tom Doucet established quite a name for himself at Boston area dances in the 1920s and 1930s. Presented here are some of the best of his recordings from that early era, another look into another time. All drawn from home recordings. *Temperance Reel Medley; Panhandle Swing; Blue Belles Of Scotland; Tom's E-Flat Clog/Banks/Autocrat; Superior Medley; Mrs. Dundas of Arniston; Lancers; Erin Reel; Joanne Reel; Shrips Clog; High Level Hornpipe; Fred Allen's; Irving's Clog/Cotton Eyed Joe; St. Lawrence River; Durham's Bull; Decision Reel; Shepard's Reel Medley; St. Elmo's Clog.*

7013   Winnie Chaffe:
Highland Airs of Cape Breton

Popular Winnie Chaffe demonstrates the mainland Scottish influence in Cape Breton, featuring many beautiful slow airs and strathspeys played with a highly developed technical skill. The classical beauty of this LP will surprise many accustomed only to the hectic and raucous aspects of traditional fiddling. Forthcoming Summer 1978.

7004   Joe Cormier: The Dances Down Home

A vivacious collection of traditional jigs and reels, arranged for a real "down east square dance" and played by one of Cape Breton's masters of rhythmic drive. It is impossible to listen to this record without being moved to dance. Fine accompaniment on piano and bass. *MacDonald's; King George the IVth; Miss Anderson; Braes O' Elchies; Margaret Chisholm's; Sheehan's; Loch Earn; Donald Cameron's; Sou'west Bridge; The Flaggon; Go About Your Business; Dan R.'s Favorite; Brig O'Feugh; Donald Stewart the Piper; Come Under My Plaidie; Delnabo; Malcolm Finlay; Keep It Up; Prince Charlie; Charlie Hunter's; Fancy Hornpipe; Gillian's; The St. Kilda Wedding; Archie Menzie's; Fisher's; Mr. Bernard; Miss Hutton's; Miss Johnson of Pitworth; Mrs. Walpole; The Earl of Hyndford; Blind Norrys.* **Eight-track tape available.**

7007   Graham Townsend:
Classics of Irish, Scottish and French Canadian Fiddling

Classic selections from Coleman, Skinner, Allard, etc. played by one of the world's most acclaimed violin virtuosos. Truly incredible technique displayed here, plus Graham's intuitive grasp of traditional form. Graham's own personal favorite of the thirty odd recordings he's made. Forthcoming Spring 1978.

7008   Jerry Holland

Deft and confident performances by Cape Breton's newest virtuoso (only twenty-one at time of recording). A full complement of original compositions further display Jerry's incredible musical talent in the field of Scottish music. Piano by Joey Beaton. *My Friend's; Joey Beaton's; Lady Madelina Sinclair: Lord Blantyre; Miss Wedderburn's; Hiawatha; Newcastle; President Garfield; Rhea Steele and Ann Marie MacDonald; Mark Wilson's; Traditional Jig; Cape Breton's; Temperance; Malcolm Finlay; Molly McGuire; Miss Maxwell; The Laddie With the Pladdie; Miss Ratray; Lasses O'Ballantrae; Carnie's Canter; The New Fiddle; The Tipsy Sailor; Jessie Ann's Favorite; Miss Barker; The Rocket; Gillian's; Return From India; Glen Rinnes; Loch Leven Castle; Miss Lyall; Ferry Bridge; Ivy Leaf; Garfield Vail; Mrs. Wallace; Red Shoes; The Old Man and Old Woman (Old Style); Maggie Brown's Favorite; Farewell to Catawba; Jimmy Mackinnon of Smelt Brook; Auby Foley; Auby Foley's Hornpipe; Mary Clare.*

7012   Joe MacLean

His old 78's read 'Joe MacLean and his Old-Time Scottish Music," a description that fits these brand new recordings every bit as well. A fine fiddle record by one of Cape Breton's best loved musicians. Forthcoming Spring 1978.

7011   The Beatons of Mabou

Mr. and Mrs. Donald Angus Beaton join their sons Kinnon and Joey in a program of real "close to the floor" fiddle music. Donald Angus is one of the last figures in Cape Breton playing the old-fashioned "gaelic" way and best demonstrates the original Celtic heritage that underlies all of our modern violin music. A very valuable recording historically as well as being one of the most invigorating and driving fiddle records ever recorded. Forthcoming Spring 1978.

0118 Mark O'Connor:
On The Rampage

For the most part, "On The Rampage" is Mark O'Connor's first jazz fiddle album with an introductory album note from Stephane Grapelli on Mark's impressive fiddle work. O'Connor, though only seventeen years old, seems to have virtually limitless musical awareness. Here he is accompanied mainly by Sam Bush and John Cowan of the Newgrass Revival, with guest appearances on one cut by Grisman and Rice; he personally takes care of most of both fiddle and guitar parts. O'Connor is presently guitarist with the Grisman Quintet. *Come Ride With Me; Mark's Ark; Midnight Interlude; On The Rampage; Ease With The Breeze; Rampology; The Dark Rain; Soft Gyrations; Tubular Explosions; Disco Fiddle Rampsody.*

0122 Norman Blake:
The Rising Fawn String Ensemble

The Rising Fawn String Ensemble is the first of Norman Blake's next three albums, all to be released on Rounder. Norman's previous two for us are now both classics and ground-breaking in many respects. While many musicians with the considerable reputations Norman has justly come to enjoy would have begun to stagnate musically from resting on the laurels of previous accomplishments, he along with Nancy Blake and sterling fiddle player James Bryan have instead continued to evolve in new directions, extending their musical explorations to include British Isles tunes complementary to their originals and their impeccably-chosen American traditional material. *Devil Chased Me Around The Stump; Charlie Gaither; Medley; The Promise; Tin Foil And Stone; Three Ravens; Handsome Molly; Jeff Davis; Medley; Old Ties; Coming Down From Rising Fawn, Number Two.* **Cassette tape available.**

Richard Greene RAMBLIN' (Rounder 0110) $5.50

"Ramblin'," "New Orleans," "Caravan," "Bach Violin Concerto in E Major," "Limehouse Blues," "Steven Foster Medley," "You Are My Sunshine," "Uncle Pen in the Pines," "The Walls of Time"

Few musical sensibilities and talents are broad enough to encompass both Bach and bluegrass, let alone versatile enough to do justice to the different technique required. Richard Greene--a fiddler unlike any other--is one of those rare few. For his musical "Ramblin'," he has chosen accompanists well-matching his own range of expression: Andy Statman, Tony Rice, Dan Crary, Larry McNelly, Buell Neidlinger, with Maria Muldaur and Peter Rowan admirably acquitting themselves on vocals.

In the sixties, Richard became known for his instrumental prowess with groups as various as Bill Monroe and His Bluegrass Boys, Earth Opera, Sea Train, and the Blues Project, of which Peter Rowan, David Grisman, and Bill Keith--to mention but a few--were also veterans. A couple of years ago, Rounder issued Richard Greene's first solo album of fiddle tunes, entitled "Duets," with everyone from David Nichtern to Tony Trischka to J. D. Crowe. "Ramblin'" illumines yet new dimensions of Richard's violin work as it has unfolded in the interim.

CS

BARRY DRANSFIELD Bowin' and Scrapin' (Topic 386)
RATTLING ROARING WILLIE/METAL MAN/FIDDLER'S PROGRESS/
WHO KNOWS WHERE THE TIME GOES?/MY LAGAN LOVE/SHEFFIELD
HORNPIPE/PET OF THE PIPERS/UP THE AISLE/SWEDISH WEDDING
MARCH/WEDDING SONG/BRIDIE'S WEDDING/NORWEGIAN WEDDING
MARCH/WEDDING MORRIS/SANDY BELL'S/OBLIGED TO FIDDLE/
PLANXTY DAVY/SPANISH CLOAK/BUSHES AND BRIARS/SWEDISH
AIR/O'CAROLAN'S CONCERTO/RECITATION UPON A GENTLEMAN
SITTING ON A CREMONA VIOLIN/SALLY GARDENS/CLONMEL RACES

Has Barry Dransfield ever made a bad record? If so it's not in my collection. It could be argued that Fiddler's Dream--Robin & Barry Dransfield's foray into electric folk--was not so hot, but there were bits of brilliance and it definitely showed potential (they abandoned that direction because of the cost and trouble of an electric touring band). Besides the records listed below--all recommended--Barry has played with the Albion Country Band and was part of the wild bunch that rocked it on the mini-classic, Morris On.

In an era of multi-national record companies and a Music Industry that plugs singers (?) into format rhythm sections and mass markets the results, _true_ musicians like Barry really stand out (if they aren't lost in the shuffle!). There is much fine fiddling on this gem and bits of doggerel, indicating that behind the tunes is a heart and a soul and a very entertaining minstrel! Recommended for all, especially friends of the fiddle, violin, cello, bowed(!) mountain dulcimer, and African gimbri.
                                                    -MPW $5.50

For further listening:
The Rout of the Blues (Leader/Trailer 2011) Robin & Barry
    $5.50
Lord of All I Behold (LTR 2026) Robin & Barry $5.50
The Fiddler's Dream (Transatlantic 322) Robin & Barry
    $5.50
Popular to Contrary Belief (Free Reed 018) Robin &
    Barry $5.50

RICHARD GREENE "Duets" (Rounder 0075)

ALABAMA JUBILEE/METHODIST PREACHER/DANNY BOY/THE YOUNG MAN WHO
WOULDN'T HOE CORN/TWINKLE LITTLE STAR/LITTLE RABBIT/TENNESSEE
WALTZ/NICK'S NOODLE/COLORED ARISTOCRACY/ANOUMAN

Contemporary-minded fiddle fans will find this album almost too good to be true. Greene's prolific career, ranging from Bill Monroe and Red Allen to Seatrain, Muleskinner and The Blue Velvet Band, has earned him a reputation as the most eclecticly _soulful_ of fiddling's new generation. This record is a tremendous showcase of his talents, as he squares off, one-on-one, against Banjo (Tony Trischka and J.D. Crowe), Guitar (Tony Rice and Dave Nichtern), Mandolin (Grisman) and even electric piano. Greene throws in licks from Joe Venuti, Chubby Wise, Yehudi Menhiun, Doc Roberts, Stephenne Grappelli, Benny Martin, Kenny Baker and a few dozen of his own. The tunes range from incredible flat-out duels with Trischka (especially "Little Rabbit") to the beautiful nocturne which closes the album. Everything is delivered with the passion, verve and incredible timing that are Greene's tradeworks.

D.K. $5.00

SCOTTY STONEMAN WITH THE KENTUCKY COLONELS Live in L.A.-
1965 (Briar 4206)

OKLAHOMA STOMP/ONCE A DAY/EIGHTH OF JANUARY/ANY DAMM THING/
DOWN YONDER//SALLY GOODIN//A WOUND TIME CAN'T ERASE/CHEROKEE
WALTZ/CACKLIN' HEN/GOODNIGHT IRENE

This release, long-awaited by bluegrass cultists,
spotlights the music's most eccentric fiddler at the height
of his powers. The late Scot Stoneman was not a happy man,
except--we are told--when he played. His surreal tone and
wild licks have defied description and delighted listeners
for years. His tragic off-stage excesses are regretted by
even the most jaded. In his four months with the Colonels
he found a band somewhat tolerant of his stage antics, and
in Clarence White a sympathetic musician who could keep
time (!) with his playing, and complement his talents.
This album is well-packaged, with outstanding commentary
by Richard Greene and Pete Rowan. I regret that Briar has
insisted on including five vocal cuts by Scotty, among them
the tasteless "Any Damm Thing," which dilute the intensity
of his fiddling. The sound quality is what you'd expect.
But WOW! The power and looney genius of the instrumental
tracks is over-whelming. Richard Greene is not fooling
when he places this music years ahead of "Newgrass."

D.K. $5.00

**0140   J. D. Crowe, Bobby Hicks, Doyle Lawson, Tony Rice,
Todd Phillips:
The Bluegrass Record**

In one of the most impressive re-groupings in recent bluegrass
history, Rice, Crowe, Lawson, and Hicks have accomplished one
of those well-nigh impossible feats—recapturing much of the
musical fire and magic of their earlier time together, Rice and
Lawson back with Crowe again. Bobby Hicks is the new fiddle
ingredient and cooks beautifully. They have carried the
significance of their musical reacquaintance one step further by
revitalizing and reinterpreting a number of classic 1950's
bluegrass numbers. *Blue Ridge Mountain Home; We Can't Be
Darlings Anymore; Molly and Tenbrooks; I Believe In You,
Darling; Model Church; On My Way Back To The Old Home;
Gonna Settle Down; Toy Heart; Pain In My Heart; Chalk Up
Another One; River Of Death.* **Cassette tape available.**

**0016   Vassar Clements:
Crossing the Catskills**

Vassar's fiddle playing is now as well known to rock audiences
as to bluegrass fans. This is the first album devoted to his
characteristic style, and he gets free play here, though keeping
it country style. Backed by Dave Bromberg, Mike Melford and
Everett Allan Lilly. *Paddy on the Turnpike; Liberty; Norwegian
Wood; Wild Bill Jones; Faded Love; Half and Half; Stumble;
Corina Corina; Florida Blues; Good Woman's Love; Bill
Cheatham; Crossing the Catskills.*

0046   Mark O'Connor

An album of fiddle tunes by the 12 year old National Junior
Fiddle Champion, called a "genius" by Roy Acuff. Texas style
fiddling. Mark is backed by Charlie Collins and Norman Blake.
*Dusty Miller; Kelly Waltz; Cuckoo's Nest; Don't Let the Deal Go
Down; Dreamer's Waltz; Sally Johnson; Billy in the Lowground;
Festival Waltz; Brilliancy; I Don't Love Nobody; Roxanna Waltz;
Say Old Man.*

0117   Blaine Sprouse

Blaine Sprouse commands the reputation of being one of the very
hottest of younger bluegrass fiddlers around today. Somewhat of
a fixture around the Nashville pickers' scene, this is Blaine's first
fiddle album and was assisted in production by the able hand of
Butch Robins. *Red Wing; Arkansas Traveler; Long Cold Winter;
Kansas City Kitty; The Waltz You Saved for Me; Turkey in the
Straw; Snowshoes; Whitehorse Breakdown; April's Reel;
Beaumont Rag; Missouri Waltz; Orange Blossom Special.*

0100   Byron Berline: Dad's Favorites

This is Byron Berline's first solo album, although he has recorded
extensively with Country Gazette and with Sundance. This is his
first fiddle album and is a tribute to his father, a first-rate old-time
fiddler. Byron is accompanied by numerous outside musicians,
all of equal note, including members of Sundance, as well as
Dan Crary, John Hickman, John Hartford, Doug Dillard, among
others. *Coming Down from Denver; New Broom; Grey Eagle;
B&B Rag; Redbird; Ragtime Annie; Limerock; Stone's Rag;
Miller's Reel; Arkansas Traveler; Sweet Memories Waltz;
Birmingham Fling.* **Eight-track tape available.**

**0127   Kenny Kosek & Matt Glaser:
Hasty Lonesome**

In acoustic picking circles, Kenny Kosek and Matt Glaser have
long been respected as the ace fiddlers they are—Kenny going
back to his Country Cooking and Breakfast Special days and Matt
coming up with fellow-pickers on the order of Bela Fleck and
Russ Barenberg. Both are among the New York-based group of
musicians who have been creating a new body of music for the
acoustic, jazz-influenced string band. The musicians'
irrepressible sense of fun and humor strongly tinges the album,
as well as their eclecticism. *Hasty Lonesome; Le Chamoix
Cornu; K-Town Fling; Lonesome Fiddle Blues; Deep Elum Blues;
B-Fiddle Medley; Marx Brothers Medley.*

MARTIN, BOGAN, AND THE ARMSTRONGS That Old Gang of Mine
(Flying Fish 056)

Side One: YES PAPPY YES/IN THE BOTTOM/MARIE/ICE CREAM
FREEZER BLUES/THAT OLD GANG OF MINE
Side Two: JAMAICA FAREWELL/I'D DO MOST ANYTHING FOR YOU/
NAGGING WOMAN BLUES/SHEIK OF ARABY/STREETS OF OLD CHICAGO

This new one by "the last of the old-time black
string bands" (to quote Howard Armstrong) is unquestion-
ably one of the most exciting new releases of the season!
Everything we've come to expect from this fine band--
their consummate skills as musicians, their good humor--
(listen to Armstrong's fiddle solo on the low-down "Ice
Cream Freezer"!)--and the tastefulness they lend to whatever they touch, no matter how maudlin or familiar; all
this, and more, is well evidenced here. Lovingly produced
by Steve "City of New Orleans" Goodman (who adds his dis-
criminating flat-picking to some of the proceedings), this
album is somewhat unusual for the group in that it presents
Carl Martin, Ted Bogan, and Howard and Tom Armstrong in
various different settings, as well as in the familiar
quartet setting of their last two albums.
     The songs performed here by the basic ensemble (with
Goodman occasionally sitting in) include "Yes Pappy Yes";
the crowd-pleasing "Ice Cream Freezer" (which Armstrong
will usually introduce at their concerts as "Harlem's
National Anthem"--his advice: "Keep your mind above your
gluteus maximus"), done here to natural low-down blues
perfection; the sentimental title song, beautifully sung
by Ted Bogan; "I'd Do Most Anything for You" (Carl's
vocals here); and "The Sheik of Araby (!)" which features
the trio harmonies of the whole group.
     Sitting in with the band on "In the Bottom" and
"Marie," along with Goodman again, is (the outstanding)
Jethro Burns on mandolin, Jeff Gutcheon on piano, Hugh
McDonald on bass, and Sheldon Plotkin on drums; and believe me, "these guys really cook!"
     In addition to the above mentioned "I'd Do Most Any-
thing for You" and "Sheik of Araby," side two features
each member of the group's individual talents: Ted Bogan
sings and fingerpicks his way through what is surely one
of the loveliest versions of "Jamaica Farewell" ever recorded. He is very sympathetically backed by Howard Levy
on vibes and harmonica--just beautiful! Levy also demonstrates his talents as a blues pianist when he backs Carl
Martin's vocals on "Nagging Woman Blues"; he leaves no
doubt that he knows what Carl has got on his mind! Howard
Armstrong lays down his fiddle to do some excellent guitar
fingerpicking on his nostalgic "Streets of Old Chicago."
He is backed by Jim Tulio on upright bass, and together
they provide a heart-stirring finale to this excellent
album.
     Those familiar with the group's other album covers
will be further pleased by Howard Armstrong's cover art--
I only wish that Flying Fish included some session photos
of the group(s) in action as well, but no matter. This
album gets my highest recommendation (satisfaction guaranteed!!) and the next time these gents come around, do
yourself a favor and go see them. Nobody can provide
such a solid combination of good music and good times
as "that old gang of mine."

                                        G.K.J. $5.00

2003 Martin, Bogan, and Armstrong:
      Barnyard Dance

First album by this extremely popular black string band,
featuring guitar, fiddle, and mandolin. The three have been
playing together since 1931. "One of the finest and most
important 'rediscovery' albums in a long time."—Journal of
American Folklore. *Lady Be Good; Carl's Blues; Corinna
Corinna; Barnyard Dance; Cacklin Hen; Sweet Georgia Brown;
French Blues; Mean Mistreatin Mama; Old Man Mose; Alice
Blue Gown; Knox County Stomp.*

LOUISIANA CAJUN MUSIC VOL. 1, "From the Southwest
Prairies" (Rounder 6001).
Made in 1964-66 when Cajun music was still nearly unknown in the north, these field recordings catch the
music at a somewhat less cosmopolitan stage: fine, raw
and stringy. Three of the Balfa tunes are available on
their two Swallow albums, but these performances by the
most genial and winning of all Cajun groups are different, less polished and more straightforward, the fiddles
licking and curling around the heavy voice and the rock-
steady beat. Less known are Pitre and Nacquin, the former a fine band led by Pitre's fiddle or accordion, using modern instruments cleverly to underscore the ponder-
ous, searing feel of the oldtime sound. The vocals are
some of the best anywhere, drawled and passionate and
abandoned; Les Flammes d'Enfer is The Flames of Hell,
and their music has a tinge of that. One Pitre and all
the Nacquin pieces are vocal with just fiddle; Nacquin
has a swinging, dynamic tenor and his old-French repertoire is a good link to what came before the modern
style. Bring on Volume 2!
BALFA FRERES: Danse de Mardi Gras/Lacassine Special/
Valse du Bamboucheur/Hackberry Hop/Valse des Platains/
Lake Arthur Stomp/Parlez-Nous a Boire. AUSTIN PITRE &
EVANGELINE PLAYBOYS: La Valse d'Orphelin/Les Flammes
d'Enfer/T'as Fini de Me Voir. EDIUS NACQUIN: Hack a
'Tit Moreau/Si J'aurais des Ailes/La Ville de Monteau/
Ou t'etais Mercredi Passe.
                                        -RC $4.0

Fiddle Styles

Facundo Gonzalez: NEW MEXICAN VIOLINISTA (Folkways FE 4062;
$6.50)

Spanish Colonial Dances: Una Polka, Valse, La Cuna, Dance,
Valses, Shotis, Gaviota/Matachines Music: La Procesion/El
Monarca, El Toro, La Malinche

It's hard to know how to approach the music of this sturdy
78-year-old solitary fiddler, relic of a tradition almost
unrecorded and now nearly forgotten. The music is largely
European in origin, not much influenced by native musical
ideas, and served as entertainment for the scattered
residents of what were historically the northern reaches of
Mexico. Sr. Gonzalez retains little of the fluidity heard
in the fiddling of an El Ciego Melquiades or any of the
1930s border fiddlers. He learned his art by playing with
a guitarist for dances, and so we can think of him as a
slightly less unconventional Melquiades; but for years he
has preferred to play by himself for himself at home. This,
and his aging, have made his dances jerky and slightly
shrill. You would not be able to dance to this record. In
his doughty, sometimes wayward essays at the rhythms and
harmonies he remembers, Gonzalez captures a certain lin-
gering charm abandoned by New Mexico's more contemporary
fiddlers with their electric pickups. But the European
material holds few surprises and he has lost his grip on it.
The music of the Matachines costume dance, done at Christmas-
time, in its lesser familiarity seems to call forth his best
and most spirited playing; for a few minutes his bowing arm
is surer and his fingers transcend their age and there is
something like life in the playing. I wonder whether the
record wouldn't have been musically better had someone
found Gonzalez a guitarist to play traditional rhythm. As
it is, this is an expression of an old man's private memory
of common-type material, haltingly performed, interesting,
but a shadow of its former self.

                                        RC

FOUR GIANTS OF SWING (Joe Venuti, violin; Eldon Shamblin, guitar;
Curly Chalker, pedal steel guitar; Jethro Burns, mandolin)
S'Wonderful (Flying Fish 035)

With S'Wonderful, Flying Fish has extended its concept
of jazz/western swing fusion, begun several years ago with
Hillbilly Jazz, to its ultimate realization. The players on
this session are simply the best round, and all four were crea-
tors of the swing styles now enjoying a renaissance through
newer groups and players like the Central Park Sheiks and Lew
London. The ageless Joe Venuti takes the lead for most of
the thematical statements (most of the tunes are standard
Ellington or Gershwin compositions), while everyone is given
a featured solo, including outstanding playing by younger
pianist Robert Hoban.
All in all, Flying Fish has outdone itself, and listeners who enjoyed the label's previous efforts in this direction will respond to S'Wonderful with great enthusiasm.

                                S.B. $4.50

EDDIE LANG & JOE VENUTI (Columbia JC2L24
"Stringing the Blues"

GOIN' PLACES/DOIN' THINGS/PERFECT/CHEESE & CRACKERS/STRINGING
THE BLUES/I'M SOMEBODY'S SOMEBODY NOW/TWO TONE STOMP/BEATING
THE DOG/TIGER RAG/WILD CAT/HANDFULL OF RIFFS AND 21 OTHERS

JOE VENUTI "Sliding By" (Sonet 734 - $5.50)

SLIDING BY/RED VELVET/THAT'S A PLENTY/BUT NOT FOR ME/CLARINET
MARMALADE/LOVER/BLACK SATIN/RHAPSODIE/SOPHISTICATED LADY/
SWEET GEORGIA BROWN

The two record set on Columbia is a fitting tribute to
two extraordinary jazz pioneers. Guitar and violin were re-
garded as somewhat dubious lead instruments in jazz in the
early days. It was Lang and Venuti, along with Lonnie Johnson
and Stuff Smith, who brought string instruments to the center
stage, and added a whole new batch of licks to boot. Their
influence, of course, was seminal to the work of Django Reinhardt and Stephane Grapelli. But you don't need to know any
of that to enjoy the thirty-two hot sides in this collection.
Included are samples of their own brilliant duets, four of
Johnson & Lang's best efforts, Lang's work with King Oliver,
Tom Dorsey, and Bing Crosby (a fine scat vocal on "Some of
These Days"), and Joe Venuti's Blue Four with Lang, Jimmy
Dorsey, Adrian Rollini and Don Murray. The closeness between
Lang and Venuti (they grew up together--Lang started out as a
violinist...) is as evident on their sides together as
their irrepresible swing. Venuti's tone and sheer exuberance
--even on the ballads--mark his place as an innovative, perhaps unequaled, master.
The Sonet recordings are by a still puckish, seventy-
eight year old Venuti. A pickup-mike is strapped to his box,
so the sound is rather electric, but the old tone and inventiveness are still there. The back-up includes "young"
friends Dick Hyman and Bucky Pizzarelli. Venuti gets so into
these fine old standards that he even sings a few choruses
with bassist Major Holley.

                    D.K. $5.00

JOE VENUTI 1927 to 1934 Violin Jazz (Yazoo 1062)

Side One: SENSATION/APPLE BLOSSOMS/RAGGIN' THE SCALE/
SATAN'S HOLIDAY/A MUG OF ALE/HEY! YOUNG FELLA/WILD CAT/
Side Two: THE WILD DOG/SWEET LORRAINE/KICKIN' THE CAT/
JIG SAW PUZZLE BLUES/HIAWATHA'S LULLABY/FOUR STRING JOE/
GOIN' PLACES

Joe Venuti was the first and arguably the finest jazz
violinist. Classically trained, he brought to the instrument a superb technique and inventive flair. His duets
with guitarist Eddie Lang are as fresh and exciting today
as they were when recorded back in the late '20's and early
'30's.
These cuts are vintage works, reflecting all the bounce
and spirit of the times, coupled with a gloss and elegance
rarely heard in popular music then. Along with Lang, there
were a number of top musicians of the day present at these
sessions, such as Jimmy Dorsey, Adrian Rollini, and Frankie
Trumbauer. Venuti shines throughout, of course, and his
musical rapport with Lang was phenomenal.
Also recommended: Eddie Lang & Joe Venuti, Stringing
the Blues (CSP JC2L 24) and Eddie Lang, Jazz Guitar Virtuoso (Yazoo 1059).

                        R.E.D. $5.00

JEAN-LUC PONTY/STEPHANE GRAPPELLI (Inner City 1005).
A summit meeting between the two Gallic masters of jazz
violin that proves disappointing to those of us not comfortable with high voltage. The album was recorded at
Fremontel in December of 1973, shortly after Ponty completed a year on the road with Frank Zappa. Though all
the compositions here date from that tour, the overall
sound is that of the Mahavishnu Orchestra. Not surprisingly, the only musicians who don't pale in this particular comparison are the stars of the show, both of
whom improve considerably on Jerry Goodman's passive
mimicry of McLaughlin. Why the grand master should have
to do the whole album on Ponty's terms is beyond me, but
Stephane gets in his usual amazing licks amid the din.
Ponty, while a good composer, remains self-conscious as
an improviser. His playing can be explosive and grip-
ping--witness "Golden Green," "Valerie" and half of "Bow-
ing-Bowing." Too much of the time, though, Ponty cat-
hauls and wah-wahs, his mediocrity surpassed only by the
sidemen.

                                -DK ($4.50)

HOT SWING FIDDLE CLASSICS 1936-43 (Folklyric 9025)

Stuff Smith: HOPE GABRIEL LIKES MY MUSIC/PUTTING ALL MY
EGGS IN ONE BASKET/AFTER YOU'VE GONE/ROBINS AND ROSES/
I GOT A HEAVY DATE
Emilio Caceres: I GOT RHYTHM/HUMORESQUE IN SWING TIME//
JIG INC/RUNNING WILD
Svend Asmussen: HONEYSUCKLE ROSE/MELANCHOLY BABY/IT DON'T
MEAN A THING/MY BLUE HEAVEN/SOME OF THESE DAYS

This record focuses on three giants of jazz violin,
less widely known than Venuti or Grappelli, but no less
amazing and distinctive. Stuff's sides show him at his
peak, during his stint at New York's Onyx Club. They capture some of the earliest and best electric violin sides.
Smith grew up with an earful of Louis Armstrong and his
playing has a horn-like ring and an inventive flair that
Satch would be proud of. Every solo sizzles with energy,
enhanced by a smoking band and Stuff's scat vocals.
Texan Caceres, showing a classical background, wails
away like Isaac Stern gone berserk. His sweet tone forms
a ringing bridge between Smith and the versatile Swede.
Svend Asmussen's sides sound like nothing I've ever heard.
At times he matches Venuti's verve--with a touch of his
own. Then again, he can sound so smooth and fluid that
you'd swear Sidney Bechet or (as the notes suggest) Benny
Goodman was playing. Every track of this record features
Class-A violin backed by a jumping rhythm section. Sound
quality is standard for the 30's. RECOMMENDED

                                D.K. $5.00

SHANACHIE RECORDS Corp.

KNOCK-NA-SHEE　　　29017

Talented young group featuring fiddles, flute, guitar, mandolin, and vocals. *"....Jo Allen's flute playing is exquisite. It is clear and bouncy, and her phrasing is excellent. Marty Somberg's fiddle playing is equally energetic and weaves around Jo's and Mark Simos' melodies and accompaniment....rowdy, yet quiet and relaxing....It's a great record."* --RUTH RAPPAPORT, RECORD ROUNDUP

ANGUS CHISHOLM - Early Recordings　14001

This album consists of all the commercial recordings made by Angus Chisholm, the finest exponent of traditional Scottish fiddling ever to record. His exquisite tone was the product of bowing almost too good to be believed, and an amazing left hand that literally shakes the notes out of the fiddle. His playing is the standard all Cape Breton music is measured by.

BILL LAMEY　　　14002

Along with the late Angus Chisholm, Bill Lamey best exemplifies the ancient Scottish music which managed to survive far better on Cape Breton island than in its homeland. Lamey's music is powerful, inventive and noble as well as being distinctly danceable. His great recordings are here captured, remastered and preserved on one brilliant disc. Bill Lamey is to Scottish music what Michael Coleman was to Irish music--no higher accolade could be given!

TOMMY PEOPLES & PAUL BRADY　29003

The great acclaim and respect Tommy Peoples has earned derive not only from his great technical skill, but equally from the eloquence and power of his music. *"....This is an amazing album by two astonishing musicians....Peoples' headstrong fiddling is staunchly traditional in its no-nonsense melodic propulsion and rhythmic sturdiness."* --TOM BINGHAM, AUDIO *"....This is one disc with which I would defy anyone to find fault."* --BILL MEEK, THE IRISH TIMES

KELLY, O'BRIEN, SPROULE　29015

James Kelly(fiddle) and Paddy O'Brien (accordion) stand in the foreground of brilliant young Irish musicians. They here combine their talents with master guitarist Daithi Sproule to produce mighty performances of rarely heard tunes, many of them absolute gems. And Daithi adds some lovely vocals as well. *"....Their sound is powerful, sometimes wild and somewhat primitive. It is felt along the spine and in the feet, as well as heard with the ear."* --THERESA TIGHE, ST. LOUIS POST

FRANKIE GAVIN & ALEC FINN　29008

Frankie Gavin is one of the most respected and exciting musicians playing Irish music today. His wonderfuuly animated fiddling is the product of a pointedly personal style that has evolved out of bits and pieces of all that is best in Irish music. Alec Finn's bouzouki accompaniement here is brilliant beyond description. *"....The musicians associated with the group DeDanann offer us superb fiddling coupled with excellent backup. The music is alive with that unusual compulsion engendered by confidence, ease, and relaxation."* --BILL MEEK, THE IRISH TIMES

ANDY McGANN & PAUL BRADY　29009

Andy McGann is the master technician, an artist who has complete control over his instrument. Andy, whose fiddling is distinctive for its sweetness and clarity of tone, has the genius to summon at will unexpected flourishes of pure skill and imagination. *"....This record is the best answer to the question, 'What is Irish music?' It comes from the hands of one of the few true masters, with some of the finest guitar accompaniment you'll find."* --MIKE SAUNDERS, VICTORY MUSIC

LIZ CARROLL & TOMMY MAGUIRE　29010

Liz Carroll's amazing virtuosity has already earmarked this fine young musician as one of the great Irish fiddlers of our time. Tommy Maguire shares equal esteem for his great control and rolling, highly ornamented accordion playing. *"....Liz plays with grace and restraint while retaining the drive I love so well.... Tommy's a first rate box player....Together they perform some of the finest duet playing I've ever heard."* --MIKE SAUNDERS, VICTORY MUSIC

LIZ CARROLL - A Friend Indeed　29013

Although only 22 years old, Liz Carroll is already recognized as one of the great Irish fiddlers now playing. Her technique is nothing less than remarkable, her tone rich and strident. This album conveys all the dynamic energy and dramatic flair that distinguishes her playing. *"....One of the most enjoyable fiddle albums released in a long time....The full rich sound she gets out of her fiddle is at the same time graceful, powerful, and beautiful."* --COLLEGE MEDIA JOURNAL

THE PURE GENIUS OF JAMES MORRISON　33004

Only once in a very long while, in a time span measured in generations, does a musician of James Morrison's stature come along. He had the power, as they say--uncanny at the least, unbelievable at times, stunning was the sheer brilliance of his fiddling. Morrison's magnificent staccato bowing is without peer in all the history of recorded Irish music--his perfect articulation and phrasing are breathtaking. *"....the surprises and special phrasings that identify a true master."* --ROBERT GANZ, COME FOR TO SING

MICHAEL COLEMAN - Classic Recordings　33006

Featuring many of the master's finest recordings--the ones that have indured longest in the minds and hearts of his countless admirers. Included are three private recordings that have never been issued before. Artistry of the highest caliber.

THE LEGACY OF MICHAEL COLEMAN　33002

Michael Coleman was the most respected and influential Irish fiddlers of this century, and justifiably so; the genius of his combined technical expertise, consummate phrasing, exquisite tone, and brilliant tune settings has never been equalled. *"....An extraordinary technician....overwhelming testimony to his artistic creativity....on first listening, I found it impossible to resist replaying both sides twice."* --JOHN HARMER, RECORD SPECIAL *"....The precision, delicacy, fluency, and sheer bouyancy of his playing is bound to steal you away."* FOLK LIFE

THE WHEELS OF THE WORLD　33001

The milestone sampler of the great Irish recordings made in the 1920's, this album brings to life many of this century's greatest moments in Irish music performed by some of the most respected Irish musicians who ever lived--names like Patrick Touhey, Michael Coleman, James Morrison, etc. Extensive notes are included. *"....An invaluable historical record... a new and enlightening perspective"* --TOM McPHAIL, IRISH EVENING PRESS

PADDY KILLORAN'S BACK IN TOWN　33003

Only the recordings of Michael Coleman have been more disseminated and influential than those of Paddy Killoran. His beautiful style stresses brisk rhythms and very controlled rich tone. The duets with fiddling comrade Paddy Sweeny are some of the most superb Irish music ever recorded. *"....Both the solo fiddle items and the duets with Sweeny stand tc lay as spendid examples of traditional music."* --BILL MEEK, THE IRISH TIMES

JOE RYAN & EDDIE CLARKE　　　**CROSSROADS**　　　Green Linnet 1030

A fine album of fiddle and harmonica duets and some solos. Joe Ryan plays in the fiddle style of his native West Clare, strident and expressive, and very annimated. Eddie Clarke is an outstanding young harmonica player from Cavan who likewise employs great spirit and vitality in his music. Together they have made here a most enjoyable and commendable record.　$5.95

THE BEST OF THE BOTHY BAND   Green Linnet 3001
Covering the whole recorded span of the fabulous Bothy Band, this album is a mighty
piece of work. No other band ever came close to the Bothy's breathtaking sensualism,
and no other group ever offered such an incredible array of individual talent: Tommy
Peoples, Paddy Keenan, Matt Molloy, Kevin Burke, Donal Lunny, Triona and Michael
O Domhnaill!! Here are many of their finest moments: The Salamanca/Pretty Peg/Blackbird/
Maids Of Mitchelstown/Casadh An tSugain/Music In The Glen/Fionnghuala/Old Hag You Have
Killed Me/Do You Love An Apple/Rip The Calico/Death Of Queen Jane/Green Groves Of Erin.
$6.75

KATHLEEN COLLINS   29002

Kathleen Collins, an All-Ireland champion,
is a musician of consummate skill and taste,
always maintaining in her playing the finest
balance of expression and intensity. Her
fiddling is pointedly introspective.
"....Kathleen's strong rhythms and tasty
settings are a pleasure to listen to, and
the choice of tunes is quite fine....defin-
itely an album to own."
                    --LORI COLE, RECORD SPECIAL

ANDY McGANN & PADDY REYNOLDS   29004

A fiddle duet album by two of the finest
Irish musicians in the world. Close note-
for-note anticipation and dynamic energy
are the hallmarks of their performances.
"....Some of the finest Irish music now
being played....This recording captures
the two at their light-hearted best. Not
only is their spirit infectious, but their
virtuosity is dazzling."
                    --JEAN STEWART, SING OUT

BARDE   IMAGES   Flying Fish 217
Irish and French dance music and songs performed by this very popular Canadian group
which features fiddles, whistles, accordion, banjo, guitar, concertina, piano, and
Celtic harp. The standard of playing is not strong, but the emphasis seems to be on
entertainment, and that seems to be the groups strength. The program of selections
features a good balance of instrumentals and vocals. $6.50

JOHN VESEY   29006

John Vesey is still the man many regard as
the foremost living exponent of the art of
Sligo fiddling . Paul Brady supplies excellent guitar backup for John.
"....Vesey is noted for his lovely bowing
and light touch." --Marty Schwartz, KITE

JIMMY DOYLE & DAN O'LEARY   29007

Jimmy Doyle on accordion and Dan O'Leary
on fiddle, both steeped in fine old Kerry
stylings, capture perfectly the distinctive phrasings needed for these fine old
polkas and slides presented here.
"....It is charming, interesting music,
and quite different!"
                    --KERRY BLECH, FOLK CAPSULES

SVEN NYHUS - Norwegian Fiddling   21003

Sven Nyhus, the presiding master of traditional Norwegian fiddling, is a superb
technician on both the Hardinger and the
regular fiddle. The Hardinger fiddle has
four sympathetic strings which produce a
haunting drone harmony. Sven's full rich
tone and very strident rhythm remind one
of the finest primitive American fiddling.
This is about as strong and as evocative
a representation of Norwegian music as you
will ever hear.

THREE SWEDISH FIDDLERS   21001

An album of superb unaccompanied duet fiddling by three of Sweden's finest young musicians, each steeped in the hauntingly
beautiful body of music native to Dalarna
province--their performances evoke all the
potential mood and drama the tunes of that
region embody.
"....A musician wants to set people in motion, both inside and outside. Good music
gives life to fantasy, to emotion, and to
the legs....When Bjorn, Pers, and Kalle
play there is double hope, plus an essence,
a pulse, and exhuberant sensualism."
                    --MONICA AND CARL-AXEL DOMINIQUE

Philo Records
The Barn
No. Ferrisburg, VT 05473

FR 124 Pine Island "Live Inside"

One of Northern New England's favorite string bands, Pine Island has created more excitement in clubs and concert appearances than any other with their innate sense of traditional music, country, swing and even blues. This album, recorded live at the Chelsea House Folklore Center, has become a classic for Pine Island's many fans.

FR 152 Eaglebone Whistle

This unusual and eclectic group is from Austin, TX. They are not easily labelled as their repertoire draws on sea chanties, French ballads, bluegrass, hoedowns, cajun ballads and Irish traditional tunes. The thread that draws this band together is an extraordinary choice of diverse material, careful arrangements and very fine string work.

FR 101 The Campbell Family "Champion Fiddlers"

The Campbell Family Fiddlers are self-taught fiddle players and makers from the hills of Vermont. This album includes contest-style fiddling from Irish, Scottish and American traditions, played on fiddles with piano and guitar accompaniment.

FR 119 Rodney & Randy Miller "Castles in the Air"

This album of New England/"Northern" style fiddling features Rodney on violin, backed by Randy on piano, guitar, and melodion, with Peter O'Brien on harmonica. Northern style fiddling is an amalgam of Irish/Scottish/Cape Breton/Canadian styles, and is generally used as an accompaniment to New England contra dancing. "Highly recommended." PEOPLE IN MUSIC

FR 146 The Fly By Night String Band

Scott Ainslie, Bill Christophersen, Scott Kellogg and Kevin Krajick are joined in this fun album of their favorites by friend Matthew Amson to create a record of singular excitement. The group from New York has been playing together for years. Their repertoire is drawn from diverse sources including Gus Meade, Tommy Jarrell, Alfred Reed and Woody Guthrie. A fine album of string band music.

FR 132 Ron West "Vermont Fiddler"

Ron West has long been recognized as one of Vermont's leading old time fiddlers. An officer and charter member of the Northeast Fiddlers Association, Ron has been a guiding light in the organization as well as a highly sought after performer in his own right. His style is a fine example of this region's traditional fiddling.

PH 2022 Louis Beaudoin "La Famille Beaudoin"

This second album of the Beaudoins captures the excitement of a traditional holiday gathering bringing together all of Louis' musical family, including daughters Lisa and Louise, his wife Julie, his brothers Wilfred, Robert and Fred. Perhaps the highlight of this diverse and joyous LP is "La Grande Chaine" called by Fred in the original (French) style.

PH 2000 Louis Beaudoin

Louis Beaudoin and his family are truly the first family of French Canadian music. With his wife Julie, his brother Willy (guitar) and his five daughters (playing piano and clogging), Louis was recognized nationally as being perhaps the best exponent of this unique style of fiddling. His music is primarily composed of reels, jigs and waltzes derived from material that he learned from his father. This material in turn derived from Irish and Scottish material that was influential in the evolution of the "musique quebecoise". "A lovely record... his playing comes through nicely and is a pleasure to listen to..." ALAN JABBOUR

fiddling

FR 103 Clem Myers

One of the organizers of the Northeast Fiddlers Association, Clem has also been a many time winner of the regional fiddling championships. This album contains his most often requested selections, including two original compositions as well as a number of fiddle standards. Clem is accompanied by guitar, bass and piano.

FR 201 Jerry Robichaud "Maritime Dance Party"

This fine collection of tunes by Jerry Robichaud exemplifies the maritime style of fiddling. Unlike the more formal Cape Breton style, the maritime style is characterized by brisk tempo and a spirited bounce that makes it highly suitable for dancing. Jerry is perhaps the best exponent of this unique style of fiddling.

FR 122 The Northeast Fiddler's Association

"Oldtime Fiddling"

Tenth annual Old Time contest at Barre Auditorium, Vermont, this historic document is a collection of all the best of the regional fiddling in Northern New England and Eastern Canada. There is a wide diversity of fiddle styles, but the contest has strict rules about traditional material (with the exception of the Trick and Fancy division) making for a fine anthology of traditional styles without the usual contest cliches.

FR 144 The Double Decker Stringband

"Giddyap Napoleon"

The Double Decker Stringband sounds like an old 78 rpm record from Atlanta, GA or Bristol, VA, because they perform a kind of Southern Country music that was at its peak of popularity some 50 or 60 years ago. This music is less structured than its grandchild of today and yet it is highly evolved and fairly rips with character. It's reassuring to know that groups like this can bring us old time music from more than 60 years ago with an authority and vibrancy that will ensure a long life to a national heritage that's worth its weight in gold.

FR 203 Rodney and Randy Miller

"New England Chestnuts"

The growing popularity of contra dancing inspired this refined collection of contras designed for dancing. Rodney and Randy have been playing for New England dances for over ten years and are joined by friends on this, their second LP. The tunes on this record form an elite group of contras called chestnuts which have proven the most popular over the past two centuries.

FR 204 Rodney and Randy Miller

"More New England Chestnuts"

A continuation of their previous album, Rodney and Randy once again play the traditional favorites of New England contra dancers.

FR 140 The North Fork Rounders

"Gee, Ain't It Grand When You Hear that Band"

From Ohio, this fine string band drew their inspiration from the works of Uncle Dave Macon and the style of the Skillet Lickers. For this album, the band has expanded their vision of music to include ragtime, swing, dixie, early jazz, and even classical ("Fiddlin' Satie"), still maintaining the excitement and spontaneity of their roots.

PH 1023 Jay Ungar and Lyn Hardy

"Songs, Ballads and Fiddle Tunes"

Jay Ungar is an accomplished fiddler, mandolin player and guitarist who appears on many albums of folk and popular music. Jay is a former member of Cat Mother and the All Night Newsboys, The Putnam String County Band and the David Bromberg Band. Lyn has an extraordinary country voice and excels at strong rhythm guitar work. Together they create a potpourri of fine traditional music that is reminiscent of the many good time southern string bands which were so prevalent in earlier days. "An extraordinarily pleasing collection...lilting harmonies and intelligent, unconventional back-up..." RECORD WORLD

FR 136 Arm & Hammer String Band

"Stay on the Farm"

The Arm & Hammer String Band, comprised of Sid Blum, Joel Eckhaus, Pete Sutherland and Hilary Woodruff has been a staple of the Old Time Music scene in the Northeast for a good number of years, playing for dances, festivals and concert dates. They can be credited with really bringing southern old time music to New England, digesting it, playing it, mixing it up with New England traditions and creating their own exciting blend of southern and Northeastern traditions. Their repertoire runs from Uncle Dave Macon's "We're Up Against it Now" to Louis Beaudoin's "Les Guenilles".

FR 141 The Bluestein Family Album

"Sowin' on the Mountain"

A lively album of traditional American and international music with banjo, guitar, fiddle, mandolin, autoharp and vocals by the Bluestein family of Fresno, California. Included are fine renditions of songs by Malvina Reynolds, Woody Guthrie and many other traditional favorites. "...a fabulous album and one of the finer old time country items to be released in a while." DISC COLLECTOR NEWSLETTER

FR 200a Yankee Ingenuity
FR 200b Yankee Ingenuity

"Kitchen Junket Without Calls"
"Kitchen Junket With Calls"

This spirited collection of traditional New England Squares is performed by many-time contest winner Donna Hinds, accompanied by Tony Parkes who is well known for his piano playing and facility with calls. They are joined by friends on bass, banjo, mandolin, and other instruments. The tunes are selected for dancing and are 7 x 32 except for the polka and the waltz. The tempos vary from 120 - 128. This album is available both with and without the calls.

PH 2019 Tom Anderson & Aly Bain

"Shetland Fiddle Music: The Silver Bow"

"The Silver Bow", recorded in the Shetlands, is an excellent document of the music of the Islands, and includes extensive notes on the musicians and their music. The legendary Tom Anderson and his colleague Aly Bain (a member of the Boys of the Lough) play a wide variety of this distinctive form of fiddle music.

PH 1042 The Boys of the Lough

"The Piper's Broken Finger"
The Boys are joined here by champion piper Finlay MacNeill, whose unfortunate accident just prior to the recording of this album led to the naming of the title cut, Cathal McConnell's latest reel. Other songs include "Lady Anne Montgomery", "Heave and Go", "Colonel Robertson", and "The Lament for Limerick".

PH 1051 The Boys of the Lough

"Good Friends - Good Music"
In this fine album, the Boys pay tribute to their many traditional musician friends from both the US and the UK. They are joined by close friends Louis Beaudoin, Kenny Hall, Jay Ungar, and many more. The musicianship and playing has to be heard to be believed.

PH 1031 The Boys of the Lough

"Lochaber No More"
More from the Boys of the Lough, including "The Laird O'Drumblair", "The Blantyre Explosion", "The Trowie Burn", "Da Back Reel", and many more.

PH 1026 The Boys of the Lough

"Live at Passim"
The Boys of the Lough need no introduction to fans of traditional Irish music. They have been touring the states for several years, always performing to packed houses. The combination of whistles, pipes, guitar, boron, mandocello and the extraordinary fiddle of Aly Bain make for an exciting blend of Irish music.

PH 2005 John McGreevy & Seamus Cooley

John McGreevy and Seamus Cooley are two veteran Irish musicians living in the Chicago area. Their unique combination of concert flute and fiddle makes for a very rich and fluid sound that lends itself well to the reels, jigs, slow airs and hornpipes that comprise this collection. "A delight and a joy to all who love real traditional Irish airs." NORTHERN JUNKET

PH 2007 Jules Verret "La Famille Verret, Vol. I"

This extraordinary set includes an LP by Jules Verret, the patriarch of the Verret family and a fifty page book explaining all of the music and matching the traditional dance steps to the music. Detailed drawings are included, making the set invaluable for traditional dance instruction as well as for listening. The presentation is bilingual making it of strong interest to students of French culture and language. The fiddle style of M. Verret is unique in Quebec and bears a stamp of elegance that is reminiscent of early French music.

PH 42016 Jean Marie Verret

"La Famille Verret, Vol. II"
The second of the Verret Family albums of traditional French Canadian dance music, this album features Jean Marie Verret on fiddle accompanied by Lise Verret on piano. One side of the album is a five-part Caledonia, while the reels and waltzes that complete the record are indigenous to the Lac St. Jean region of Quebec and are played in the unique style of the legendary Joseph Bouchard, with whom Jean Marie studied.

FR 202 Sandy Bradley   "Pot Luck and Dance Tonight"

This fine album is a pot luck of favorite dance tunes done with spontaneity and attention to danceability. Sandy Bradley calls the dances, accompanied by the Gypsy Gyppo String Band, Tracy Schwarz, the Arm & Hammer String Band, and others. All the calls and dance instructions are enclosed. This makes for a fine evening of dancing at home or with friends.

FR 118 Marie Rhines   "The Reconciliation"

Marie is a classically trained violinist turned fiddler. On this album she plays jigs, reels, hoedowns and breakdowns with a sound that surpasses that of the traditional fiddle players. "It was a joy to share with the audience a reaction that shifted from respect through amazement to incredulity and finally to a thunderous ovation and relentless demand for more. The combination of the keen ear and technical facility of Marie Rhines assures a performance that is absolutely spellbinding." ROBERT J. LURTSEMA

PH 2001 Jean Carignan

Jean has been called the greatest fiddler alive in North America today. His interpretation of the traditional music of Ireland, Scotland, and French Canada is unequalled in its sensitivity and discipline. "...the record is good, not only as an example of extraordinary fiddle playing, but as a well-recorded document of musical styles and techniques that will probably not survive beyond Jean Carignan...no one in the world can play with the precision and flair of Carignan..." THE MONTREAL GAZETTE

PH 2012 Jean Carignan

"Hommage à Joseph Allard"

On this album Jean Carignan pays tribute to Joseph Allard, the legendary French Canadian fiddler whom he met as a child and studied with for many years. He is accompanied by piano on this collection of reels, quadrilles, and other fiddle tunes. "Quite simply the finest traditional Quebecois music" THE MONTREAL GAZETTE

PH 2018 Jean Carignan   "The Music of Coleman, Morrison & Skinner"

In this third album by Jean Carignan, he explores the music of the Irish and Scottish greats that were so influential in the formation of his own country's music. His flair and technique have earned him the reputation of being the world's greatest living fiddler. "...in his hands, the violin is a universal folk instrument with a creative vitality, a dynamic expression of its own...shaped by Jean's own lively, inventive intelligence." YEHUDI MENUHIN

"But there are lots of tunes, like a lot of the Irish reels that have too complicated a melody and not enough beat. They're not very good for dancing even though they're great tunes to listen to. Also sometimes a tune isn't good for dancing if it's written in a key that's too low, where most of the notes are played on the lower two strings, the G and the D. In that low range the tune gets covered up by all the other sounds in the hall: the piano, the dancer's feet and all. So with a tune like that I'll change it to a higher key, so it's played mostly on the higher two strings. Then the tune can be heard by the dancers."

— Rod Miller
New England dance fiddler
(A Time to Dance)

PH 41028 The National Folk Festival

"Good Time Music"

This album is an anthology of the best of the 1972, 1973 and 1974 National Folk Festivals held in Vienna, VA. One side is devoted to the mainstream country music tradition, with an emphasis on string bands, while the other is a sampling of some of the less well-known types of traditional bands around the country, particularly dance bands. Featured performers include The Highwoods String Band, The Louisiana Aces, The Wild Magnolias, Louis Beaudoin, The Balfa Brothers, and others. "A great cross-section, and the music is a delight to listen to." THE MONTREAL GAZETTE

ROOSTER RECORDS

RFD 2 Bethel, Vermont 05032
802-234-5094

101 - The Corn Dodgers - "Cotton Eyed Joe" An album of Old Time Southern music for listening, dancing, and playing along: George Ainley (fiddle), Ahmet Baycu (banjo), and William Wright (guitar). The album also features several friends, and many "live" cuts. *Wagoner; Ida Red; Lynchburg Town; Watermelon On The Vine; Goin Down The River; Citico; Prettiest Gal In The County; Four Cent Cotton; Sugar In The Gourd; Richmond Cotillion; Polly Wolly Doodle; Cotton Eyed Joe.*

102 - The Works of Jon Cooper - An eclectic view of an exciting musician from Portland, Maine. Jon plays many styles on the fiddle, sings, and plays dobro. The record includes tunes from Canada, Ireland, Europe, New England, and the South. Many friends add to the music on this album. *Real De Montreal, Blarney Pilgram, Corrina, Pravo Horo, Lark In The Morning, On The Steppes of Manchuria, Bonaparte Crossing The Rhine, French Medley (Woodchopper's, New Bedford, and Walker St. reels), Blind Fiddler, Eleno Mome, The Gray St. Blues, Won't Someone Give The Fiddler A Dram?*

103 - Wild Mountain Thyme - "Thyme and Thyme Again" - A five-piece string band from Maine, playing old-time and bluegrass favorites. Many vocals and several jazz originals. With Doreen Conboy, Joe Barth, Jon Cooper, Creighton Lindsay, and Mike Burd. *Growlin' People, Darlin' Corey, French Medley (Reel de Montreal, Bay of Fundy, Big John McNeil), Pistol Packin Mama, Sasquatch, Pukea-Likea-Ua, Paddy On The Turnpike, Old Cow Hand, Cheek and Toe to Toe, Who's That Knockin' At My Window, Fiddler's Dream, Old Black Dog, Little Feet, Dandelion Wine.*

104 - Tom MacKenzie - "Finally Tuned" - Tom plays hammered-dulcimer, banjo, and sings. This LP includes many favorite New England dance tunes, Old Time Southern songs, bluegrass, and originals. With Pete Sutherland (fiddle), Robert Resnick (penny whistle, bones, and guitar), and Chris Jones (guitar). *Baker's March, Little Dutch Girl, Possum On The Rail, Rachel, Rocky Mountain Goat, Sugar Hill, Half Creek, Macalmoyle's Reel, Gal I Left Behind, Fanny Power, In The Hall Of The Mountain King, Frosty Morning, Cattle In The Crops, Keep Up With The Jones', Eskimo Reel, Ice On The Pond, Tom and Jerry, Jerusalem Ridge, John Brown's March, Road To The Isles.*

105 - Ben Guillemette - Ben is a well-known fiddler from Sanford, Maine. He has won many first prizes in major Old-Time fiddler competition in over thirty years of playing. The album includes French Canadian and Irish classics, New England dance tunes, polkas, waltzes, and swing vocals. With Toots Bouthot (vocals and guitar), Dick Monroe (accordian and vocals), Joe Girard (piano). *Shelbourne Reel, York County Hornpipe, Invitation To The Blues, White Leaf and Cobbler's Reel, Silver and Gold Waltz, Naomi's Jig, Spud Island Breakdown, Dundee Hornpipe, Tarbolton Medley, Accordian Polkas, Tired Of Living, Rudy's Reel, Canadian Waltz, Front Door, Grant Lamb Hornpipe, Don Messer's Breakdown.*

113 - Hard Driving! (released Fall, 1981). "This album is not recommended for those who are easily excited nor for those individuals in search of the correct words to old standards. But, if you like hard-driving Bluegrass that will knock your socks off - This is for you!" - Geoff Stelling's Hard Times Bluegrass Band. With Geoff Stelling (banjo), Gary Carr (guitar), Tommy Rozum (mandolin and fiddle), and Randy Hupp (bass). *Big River, Blue Night, I Want To Hide, Sled Ride, Big Boss Man, Pig In A Pen, Ruby, Arab Bounce, Deep River, Rabbit In A Log, Pike County, Nine Pound Hammer, I Wonder Where You Are Tonight, Cross-Eyed Fiddler.*

Sandy Bradley and The Small Wonder String Band Record Foolish Questions

Sandy Bradley, nationally known dance caller, and dynamic singer and guitar player is doing her first album with Jere and Greg Canote. Individually they are extraordinary musicians - together they are The Small Wonder String Band, and their album "Foolish Questions" is a great collection of old-timey music, featuring lots of harmony, and hot fiddlin'. Sandy also has performed and recorded with the Gypsy Gyppo String Band, and has two albums with Rod and Randy Miller, and the New England Chestnuts. This is her first album on the Rooster label.

Swallowtail's Collective Approach To Music Making

Swallowtail, a six-member contradance band from Massachusetts and New Hampshire, has been performing throughout New England since 1978, and last year completed a very successful cross-country concert tour. The group traveled from New York City to Seattle, and performed on the highly acclaimed National Public Radio program "Prairie Home Companion".

Their music features a wealth of instrumental textures. Oboe and virginal (a small harpsichord), provide the most unconventional colors, but the variety of traditional instruments alone provide many opportunities for experimenting with textures and sound. Their musical roots are solidly implanted in the New England contradance tradition, but they just don't sound like any other contradance group. That may be due in part to the fact that Swallowtail relys on the efforts of all of the members to achieve a finished sound. They are a collective, and in their playing, as well as in their arrangements, they have rediscovered that wonderful truth that the whole can be greater than the sum of its parts.

The Delta Sisters - Music from the Old Timey Hotel

The Story of the Delta Sisters and The Old Timey Hotel

Once upon a time, Frannie lived in her car and Jeannie lived on the road. They met at Sweetsmill while cutting up chickens for a big feast. They became good friends, and soon after, Frannie built a house in the woods behind Peter's house in East Caspar, California. It is a quiet house with no phone and only trees for distraction. This house became known as the Old Timey Hotel, a refuge for the homeless or "on the road" musicians, as well as a honeymoon cottage, a birthing center, and most of all, a fantastic place to make music. The old redwood walls seem to encourage it, and the "music police" are far away. The hours of music that have filled this house are uncountable, but are audible in the Delta Sister's music, which is influenced and fed by the many musical friends who have passed through the Old Timey Hotel. The thing that unifies these influences is a unique vocal and harmonic blend.

There is a Louisiana branch of the Old Timey Hotel out on a prairie near Chataigner, better known as the Buvette. This 150-year old cedar and cyprus house was once a store, later a place to hide prohibition liquor, an animal barn, and more recently. a place for Jeannie and Ken to live while absorbing Cajun culture. Many friends have passed through to partake of cayenne pepper and French music.

Any house that cannot be locked, that can be warmed with wood and filled with music, doors open to those who share, could be an Old Timey Hotel.

Jeannie McLerie and Frannie Leopold are The Delta Sisters. Along with some very talented friends, Jody Stecher, Eric Thompson, Gene Parsons, Will Spries, AJ Soares, Sue Draheim, Susie Rothfield, Jim Noyes, Gary Peterson, and Jeanie's husband Ken Keppeler, they have put together an album, which, according to one reviewer, has so much enthusiasm and friendliness radiating from their voices that it would be a shame to change one note. We agree.

111 - The Delta Sisters - "Music From the Old Timey Hotel" (released August, 1981). This album features Jeanie McLerie (of the Harmony Sisters) and Frannie Leopole singing and playing original cajun tunes, songs by the Boswell Sisters, the Delmore Brothers, and other country greats.

Back-up musicians include: Jody Stecher, Eric Thompson, Susie Rothfield, Sue Draheim, Will Spires, Gene Parsons, A.J. Soares, Ken Keppeler, Jim Noyes and Gary Peterson. *Texas Girl; Port Arthur Blues; Lovebridge Waltz; South; Tourne, Tourne, Bebe Creole; Don't You See That Train; Blues me Prend; Blue Railroad Train; La Vie est Bonne; Campanas del Ovido; If It Ain't Love.*

108 - The Ambassadors - A four-piece band from Maine, whose material includes traditional music from around the world, blues, swing, classic jazz, and originals. They all sing, with Beth Borgerhoff playing piano accordian, piano, triangle; Jon Cooper, fiddle, dobro; Creighton Lindsay, guitar, tenor banjo; Bau Graves, bass, 1 and 3 button accordians, ukelele. This album was recorded "live" at three separate concerts. *Medley (Cobbler's, Sherbrooke, St. Anne's, and Gaspe Reels), He's A Real Gone Guy, De Rodillas Quisiera Mirarte, Acorn Stomp and Pike's Peak, Honky Mammas, Too Busy, Belasicko Oro, Mary Warner Blues, Long Old Road, Port Arthur Blues, Salty Boogie.*

106 - The Corn Dodgers - "Nobody's Business" - This three-man group plays some of the most exciting music since the likes of such 1920's Georgia bands as The Skillet Lickers, The Georgia Yellow Hammers, and Johnson's Clodhoppers. *Nobody's Business, Good Gal, Riley's Hen House Door, Lonesome Road Blues, Goodbye Booze, Jenny On The Railroad, Red Hot Breakdown, Oh My Little Darling, I Ain't No Better Now, Goodbye Liza Jane, Birmingham, Paddy On The Handcar.*

109 - A Christmas Present - An instrumental LP of traditional Christmas tunes played in an old-time style by Jim Reiman and William Wright. The instrumentation is varied, with guitars, fiddles, mandolins and percussion. *Good King Wenceslaus, It Came Upon A Midnight Clear, Rudolph and Frosty, O Tannenbaum, God Rest Ye Merry Gentlemen, Oh Holy Night, Jingle Bells, Angels We Have Heard On High, We Wish You A Merry Christmas, We Three Kings, Deck The Halls, Joy To The World, Wassail Song.*

A Christmas Present

ALCAZAR PRODUCTIONS, INC.
Box 429
Waterbury
Vermont 05676

DE DANANN: Song For Ireland (SUH 1130) We all did a double take when we heard that Sugar Hill, a bluegrass label, was bringing out the new De Danann record. But they did, and Frankie Gavin, Alec Finn, Johnny (Ringo) McDonagh, Martin O'Connor, and Brendan Reagan have produced another fine album of the best in Irish traditional music. This album is evidence of a wonderfully close knit ensemble (and brilliant individual virtuosity) which has continued to refine its style with each album. They have continued to present selections with a subtle finesse. Their other albums, equally recommended, are: *De Danann* (Boot 4018), *The Mist Covered Mountain* (SH 79005), *Selected Jigs, Reels and Songs* (SH 79001) and *The Star Spangled Molly* (SH 79018). ACS

ARM & HAMMER STRING BAND: Stay On The Farm A & H 01c (cassette only) $7.00 Originally released in 1978 (FR 136) and unavailable for quite some time, we at Alcazar welcome back this title, as you might if you missed it the first time around, or if you never even had that opportunity. Although now only available as a cassette, the duplication was done Real Time on TDK AD60's (dolby "B") and it is a real bargain. The band members are: Sid Blum, Joel Eckhaus, Pete Sutherland, and Hilary Woodruff, all on an assortment of guitars, banjos, ukuleles, fiddles, a piano, bass, and vocals, playing Old Timey music. The song selection includes "Chinese Breakdown", "We're Up Against It Now", "Hale's Rag", "Shady Grove", "Vermont Medley", and nine other cuts. The original liner notes are included.

CRITTON HOLLOW STRINGBAND: Poor Boy YAH 108327 and Sweet Home YAH 002 Located about 10 miles from Paw Paw, West Virginia is a cut between North and Spring Gap Mountains called Critton Hollow. Since 1975, Critton Hollow has been the home base of an energetic stringband of the same name. They label their music folk, country (consider all the countries American music comes from) and traditional. Their mission in life is to help keep traditional music alive and kicking by bringing it to the people. Their two records convey this enthusiasm and love for the music admirably. Sing Out Magazine said "...for those who worry that this music is dying, listen to Critton Hollow and take heart." *POOR BOY* was released in 1978, and *SWEET HOME* in 1983. The latter includes the fine string bass, banjo and vocals of Joe Fallon, formerly of the Backwoods Band (Jes Fine, RDR 0128).

GRANT STREET STRING BAND (BON 111) Laurie Lewis, fiddle; Beth Weil, bass; Greg Townsend, guitar; Steve Krouse, banjo; Tom Bekeny, mandolin. This group hails from San Francisco, which is a long way from Kentucky, and this is their first album, but these folks have done their homework, and such nice female harmonies! It is a bluegrass album, but it is not the usual, hard-driving sound we've become accustomed to. In fact, many of the cuts here feature Laurie and Beth, which is unusual for bluegrass groups. But I don't mean to disparage the boys; they all play well, and they are all good musicians. That they include a healthy dose of songs by Hank Williams, Jimmie Rodgers and Bill Monroe shows also that they know their roots. JP

Fiddle

TOM ANDERSON:
Ringing Strings TOP 429

BAKER & FORRESTER
Red Apple Rag CTY 784
STEPHEN BALDWIN:
English Village Fiddler LER 2068
JAMES BRYAN:
Look Out Blues RDR 0175
HARRY CHOATES:
Fiddle King Of Cajun Swing ARH
5027
ROBIN DRANSFIELD:
Lord Of All I Behold LER 2026
LEONARD FINSETH:
Hills Of Old Wisconsin BNJ 1842
**CANRAY FONTENOT & THE
CARRIERE BROTHERS:**
Cajun Fiddle Styles, Vol. II, The
Creole Tradition ARH 5031
SKIP GORMAN:
New Englander's Choice FL 95
FIDDLING DOC ROBERTS:
Old Time Tunes CTY 412
SCHRYER TRIPLETS:
Pierre, Daniel, Louis... BOOT 7233

BUDDY SPICHER:
Fiddle Classics, Vol. I FF 278
DAVE SWARBRICK:
Flittin' SPN 101
VARIOUS:
Old Time Fiddlers, Vol. I VETCO 104
Old Time Fiddlers, Vol. II VETCO
106
Ukranian-American Fiddle & Dance
Music, Vol. I FLY 9014
Ukranian-American Fiddle & Dance
Music, Vol. II FLY 9015

Stringbands, Old Timey

ARM & HAMMER STRING BAND:
(formerly FR 136) A&H 01c $7
BAKER & FORRESTER:
Red Apple Rag CTY 784
**SANDY BRADLEY & THE SMALL
WONDER STRING BAND:**
Foolish Questions ROOS 118 (c)
COON CREEK GIRLS:
CTY 712
COUNTRY HAM:
VETCO 512
My Old Paint Mare VETCO 517
Old Time Mountain Music VETCO
510
Where Mountain Laurel Blooms
VETCO 515
CRITTON HOLLOW STRINGBAND:
Poor Boy YAH 108327
Sweet Home YAH 002

FALLS CITY RAMBLERS:
Ain't Nothin' In Ramblin' VETCO
504
GOLDEN EAGLE STRING BAND:
Body, Boots & Britches FW 32317
**JOSH GRAVES WITH BOBBY
SMITH & SHILOH:**
VETCO 3025
HOTMUD FAMILY:
...Til We Meet Here Again Or Above
VETCO 501
DAKOTA DAVE HULL:
Hull's Victory FF 294
HUTCHISON BROTHERS:
VETCO 505
JOHNSON MOUNTAIN BOYS:
Working Close RDR 0185
UNCLE DAVE MACON:
Volume II VETCO 105

JOE VENUTI:
Best Of CR203
Hooray For Joe CR 153
The Joe Venuti Blue Four CR 134
JOE VENUTI & EARL HINES:
Hot Sonatas CR 145
JOE VENUTI & EDDIE LANG:
Stringing the Blues 1927-32 CSP 224
JOE VENUTI & ZOOT SIMS:
Joe Venuti & Zoot Sims CR 1212

PENNELL.
PLAYING IN THE WINE GARDENS.

THE WORLD'S GREATEST BLUEGRASS BANDS

2-LP-set: CMH-5900
2-8-TRACK-set: CMH-8-5900
2-CASSETTE-set: CMH-C-5900
32 great NEW performances by the greatest names in Bluegrass Music: FANTASTIC VALUE!
OSBORNE BROTHERS: Georgia Mules And Country Boys/Bent, Broken And Blue/MAC WISEMAN: Wreck Of The Old 97/Rainy Day People/I Wonder Where You Are Tonight/LESTER FLATT: Dixie Flyer/Goin' Up Cripple Creek/Good Times Are Past And Gone/RENO & HARRELL: Long Gone/I Want To Go Back To The Mountains/B. G. Chase/CARL STORY: Buck Creek/I'm Rollin' On/Shout And Shine/BENNY MARTIN: Wabash Cannonball/Muleskinner Blues/Who's Gonna Hold You When I'm Gone/Ragtime Annie (with ARTHUR SMITH) Back Up And Push/JOSH GRAVES: Little Maggie Crossin' The Rockies (with BOBBY SMITH)/STONEMANS: Soldiers Joy/Watermelon On The Vine/GRANDPA JONES: Rosalee/ARTHUR SMITH: Conversation With A Mule/JOE MAPHIS: Orange Blossom Special/SMITH BROS.: Little Footprints In The Snow/CROSSROADS: Remembering JONES BROS.: Billy Boy/Jessie James/2ND GENERATION: Goin' Home In The Rain/RALPH SMITH: Bury Me Beneath The Willow

THE ORIGINAL BLUEGRASS (& Country Swing) SPECTACULAR!

2-LP-set: CMH-5902
2-8-TRACK-set: CMH-8-5902 /
2-CASSETTE-set: CMH-C-5902
32 hot new Bluegrass and Country Swing performances!
OSBORNE BROTHERS: Don't Let Smokey Mountain Smoke Get In Your Eyes/JIM & JESSE: Swing Low, Sweet Chariot/The Girl I Left Behind Me Great Speckled Bird/MERLE TRAVIS: John Henry/ There Ain't A Cow In Texas/Goodbye My Bluebelle/Westphalia Waltz/La Marcha De Los Mexicanos/MAC WISEMAN: I Wonder How The Old Folks Are At Home/LESTER FLATT: Will The Circle Be Unbroken/GRANDPA JONES: I Gave My Love A Cherry/Autoharp Concerto/JOHNNY GIMBLE & THE TEXAS SWING PIONEERS: Just Because/Fort Worth Hambone Blues/BLUE-GRASS CARDINALS: Pretty Red Wing/Just A Little Talk With Jesus/Don't Come Running NASHVILLE GRASS: Mother Maybelle (with JOHNNY CASH)/JOSH GRAVES: Little Home In West Virginia/BENNY MARTIN: Golden Slippers Payday In The Army/DON RENO: Cincinnati Rag BUDDY SPICHER: I'll Be All Smiles Tonight Life In The Finland Woods (with BENNY MARTIN)/CARL BUTLER: Motel Song/JOE MAPHIS & ROSE LEE: I'm Gonna Wear The Pants FELICE & BOUDLEAUX: I Can Hear Kentucky Calling Me/EDDIE ADCOCK & MARTHA: Love's Gonna Get You/HEIGHTS OF GRASS: Bile 'Em Cabbage Down/PINNACLE BOYS: Wheels/WYNN OSBORNE: Farewell Blues.

THE WORLD'S GREATEST BLUEGRASS BANDS #2

2-LP-set: CMH-5901
2-8-TRACK-set: CMH-8-5901/2-CASSETTE-set: CMH-C-5901
32 more great new recordings by your favorite Bluegrass artists!
OSBORNE BROTHERS: Cabin In Caroline/Jesse James/Don't That Road Look Rough and Rocky OSBORNE BROS. & MAC WISEMAN: Little White Church/Mother Maybelle/LESTER FLATT: We Don't Care What Mama Allow/Drive Time/Dusty Miller (with PAUL WARREN)/MERLE TRAVIS & JOE MAPHIS: Black Mountain Rag/Freight Train Li'l Liza Jane/GRANDPA JONES: Down The Old Plank Road/I Don't Love Nobody/Over The Waterfall/Nellie Bly/THE BLUEGRASS CARDINALS: The Old Man In The Park/Darlin' Corey/I Wonder Where You Are Tonight/BENNY MARTIN: Double Eagle Swing/I Can Hear The Hallelujahs In The Air/JOE MAPHIS: My Baby's Doin' Alright/Fiddle Pickin'/JOSH GRAVES: Brand New Carroll County Blues/Shiloh March (with BOBBY SMITH) DON RENO: Ridgerunner/Follow Me Boogie (with ARTHUR SMITH)/CHUBBY WISE: Lee Highway Blues/CARL STORY: My Lord Keeps A Record PINNACLE BOYS: Sittin' On Top Of The World EDDIE ADCOCK & MARTHA: Freewheelin' Boogie Bound To Ride/JIM SILVERS: My, My, My

PAUL WARREN with Lester Flatt & The Nashville Grass
America's Greatest Breakdown Fiddle Player

LP: CMH-6237
8-TRACK: CMH-8-6237/CASS: CMH-C-6237
Paul Warren was the stalwart fiddler for Flatt & Scruggs' Foggy Mountain Boys and Lester Flatt's Nashville Grass for a total of nearly twenty-three years. This album, assembled from tapes of radio shows and personal appearances is the only full album of Paul's spirited and exciting breakdown fiddling.
Durham's Reel/Indian Creek/Katy Hill/ 8th Of January/Twinkle, Little Star/Pretty Polly Ann/ Denver Belle/Listen To The Mockingbird/ Stony Fork/Liberty/Leather Britches/Sally Johnson/Dusty Miller/Hop Light Ladies/New Five Cents/Grey Eagle/Sally Goodin'/Tennessee Wagoner/Hoedown In Hickman County/ Black Eyed Suzy.

BUDDY SPICHER & BENNY MARTIN
The Great American Fiddle Collection

2-LP-set: CMH-9025
8-TRACK: CMH-8-9025/CASS: CMH-C-9025
The variety and vitality of American fiddling is showcased in this album by two of the finest practitioners of the art — Buddy Spicher & Benny Martin. Old-time breakdowns, hornpipes & waltzes, full-throttle bluegrass stompers, hot western swing sizzlers and soulful country classics — it's all here in one of the finest, most distinctive fiddle albums ever produced!
Liberty/Sweet Bunch Of Daisies/Hornpipe Medley If I Should Wander Back Tonight/Nashville Girls Georgiana Moon/San Antonio Rose/Bitter Creek I'll Be All Smiles Tonight/Lee Highway Blues Old Joe Coon/Down In Union County/Silver Bell & Red Wing/Wabash Cannonball/Forked Deer Tennessee Waltz/Secret Love/Put Your Little Foot/Sunny Side Of The Mountain/Down Yonder Someone Took My Place With You/Life In The Finland Woods/Soldier's Joy/Love Letters In The Sand/Over The Rainbow

BENNY MARTIN
The Fiddle Collection

2-LP-set: CMH-9006
8-TRACK: CMH-8-9006/CASS: CMH-C-9006
Country Music Magazine, America's number one country publication, calls him the 'Greatest Unknown Fiddle Player In The World.' Benny's artistry has played a major role in the shaping of bluegrass fiddling. Johnny Gimble, Josh Graves, Vic Jordan and many other fine pickers have joined Benny on the 25 songs in this album set.
Muleskinner Blues/Sweet Bunch Of Daisies/Alabama Jubilee/Home, Sweet Home/Little Footprints In The Snow/Georgiana Moon/Back Up And Push/Flint Hill Special/Blue Moon Of Kentucky/Bile 'Em Cabbage Down/Salty Dog/The Fiddler's Dream/Dueling Fiddles (with Johnny Gimble)/Somewhere My Love/ Black Mountain Rag/Under The Double Eagle/How Will I Explain About You/Beautiful Dreamer/Foggy Mountain Breakdown/Ragtime Annie/Fire On The Mountain/Bury Me Beneath The Willow/Cotton-Eyed Joe/Sunny Side Of The Mountain/Night Train To Memphis

BENNY MARTIN
Big Daddy of the Fiddle & Bow

2-LP-Set: CMH-9019
8-TRACK: CMH-8-9019/CASS: CMH-C-9019
A powerhouse album from one of the greatest fiddle players of all time! Benny is joined by his friends JOHN HARTFORD and BOBBY OSBORNE for some incredibly dynamic music. Guaranteed to make you sit up and listen!
The Star Spangled Banner/I'll Go Steppin' Too Nobody's Darlin' But Mine/Benny's Waltz Feelin' Good/East Nashville Robbery/Will The Circle Be Unbroken/Beneath The Old Rugged Cross/1814/Twinkle, Twinkle Little Star Cruisin' On The Blue Danube/Dim Lights, Thick Smoke/When I Grow Too Old To Dream/Fiddler's Birthday Party/Golden Slippers/Whispering Hope/Payday In The Army/Canaan Land/God Bless America

Arhoolie Records
10341 San Pablo Ave.
El Cerrito, Ca. 94530

OT-116 WESTERN SWING Vol. 2

Tune Wranglers: Up Jumped The Devil; **Jimmie Revard:** Blues In The Bottle ★ My Little Girl I Love You; **W. Lee O'Daniel:** Don't Let The Deal Go Down; **Milton Brown:** Hesitation Blues ★ Garbage Man Blues; **Light Crust Doughboys:** Gin Mill Blues ★ Weary blues; **Adolph Hofner:** Brown Eyed Sweet; **Cliff Bruner:** Milk Cow Blues ★ Tequila Rag; **Ramblin' Rangers:** Gettin' Tired; **Washboard Wonders:** Feather Your Nest; **Bob Wills:** Liza Pull Down the Shades.

OT-117 WESTERN SWING Vol. 3

Bob Wills: What's The Matter With The Mill ★ I Wonder If You Feel The Way I Do ★ Beaumont Rag; **Brown's Brownies:** Louise, Louise Blues; **Modern Mountaineers:** Everybody's Truckin' ★ Pipe Liner's Blues; **Adolph Hofner:** Alamo Rag ★ Sage Brush Shuffle; **Spade Cooley:** Oklahoma Stomp; **Jimmie Revard:** Fox and Hounds; **Bar-X Cowboys:** I'm Just An Outcast; **Shelly Lee Alley:** Women, Women, Women; **Hank Penny:** Peach Tree Shuffle; **Nite Owls:** Married Man Blues.

OT-121 WESTERN SWING Vol. 6
(From the 1940s to the 50s)

Johnnie Tyler: Oakie Boogie ★ Troubles On My Mind ★ **Sleepy Short & Lester Woytek:** Melting Pot Polka ★ **Luke Wills:** Never Turn Your Back To A Woman ★ **Bob Wills** Two-Step ★ **Buck Roberts & Johnny Gimble:** Don't You Darken My Door Anymore ★ **Bob Wills:** Silver Lake Blues ★ **Johnnie Lee Wills:** Boogie Woogie Highball ★ **Farr Brothers:** Farr-Away Blues ★ **T Texas Tyler:** My Bucket's Got A Hole In It ★ **Merle Lindsey:** Safety Pin Rag ★ **Don Churchill:** One Year Ago Tonight ★ **Lone Star Playboys:** Playboy Swing ★ **Buddy Duhon & Harry Choates:** Old Cow Blues.

OT-100 THE STRING BANDS

The Spooney Five: Chinese Rag ★ **Moatsville String Ticklers:** Moatsville Blues ★ **Charlie Poole:** If the River Was Whiskey ★ Hungry Hash House ★ **Scottdale string Band:** Japanese Breakdown ★ **Hackberry Ramblers:** Crowley Waltz ★ Tickle Her ★ **Allen Brothers:** Allen Brothers Rag ★ **Mississippi Mud steppers:** Jackson Stomp ★ **Gid Tanner & His Skillet Lickers:** Hawkins' Rag ★ **Grayson & Whitter:** Train 45 ★ **Hershel Brown & His Washboard Band:** Down Yonder ★ Nobody Loves Me ★ **Arthur Smith Trio:** Dickson County Blues ★ **Joseph Falcon with Clemo & Ophy Breaux:** Osson ★ **Roane County Ramblers:** Home Town Blues.

5020 ADOLPH HOFNER
"South Texas Swing"
(His Early Recordings 1935-1955)

South Texas Swing ★ Maria Elina ★ Does My Baby Love Me, Yes Sir! ★ Sam, The Old Accordion Man ★ Mistakes ★ Why Should I Cry Over You? ★ I'll Keep My Old Guitar ★ Jessie Polka ★ Shiner Song ★ I Never Felt So Blue ★ Longhorn Stomp ★ Happy Go Lucky Polka ★ Radio Broadcast.

OT-119 WESTERN SWING VOL. 4
(From The 1930's)

Tune Wranglers: My Sweet Thing ★ It Don't Mean A Thing ★ **Modern Mountaineers:** Gettin' That Lowdown Swing ★ You Got To Know How To Truck And Swing ★ **Jimmie Revard:** Tulsa Waltz ★ **Hank Penny:** Mississippi Muddle ★ It Ain't Gonna Rain No Mo' ★ **Claude Casey:** Pine State Honky Tonk ★ **W. Lo O'Daniel:** Lonesome Road Blues ★ **Washboard Wonders:** It Ain't Right ★ **Crystal Springs Ramblers:** Tired of Me ★ Down In Arkansas ★ **Shelly Lee Alley:** Try It Once Again ★ **Ted Daffan:** Blue Steel Blues ★ Worried Mind ★ **Milton Brown:** Baby Keep Stealin'.

OT-120 WESTERN SWING VOL. 5
(From The 1930's)

Tune Wranglers: I Believe In you ★ **Light Crust Doughboys:** Tom Cat Rag ★ Blue Guitars ★ **Buddy Jones:** Settle Down Blues ★ Mean Old Lonesome Blues ★ **Farr Brothers:** Cajon Stomp ★ Kilocycle Stomp ★ **Milton Brown:** I'll Be Glad When You're Dead, You Rascal You ★ Stay On The Right Sister ★ **Universal Cowboys:** Hot Mama Stomp ★ **Nite Owls:** El Rancho Grande ★ **Bill Boyd:** Thousand Miles Blues ★ **Jimmie Davis:** Honky Tonk Blues ★ High Geared Daddy ★ **Bob Skyles:** Hot Tamalee Pete ★ **Ocie Stockard:** Bass Man Jive.

OT-122 WESTERN SWING Vol. 7
(The 1950s)

Maddox Brothers & Rose: Okie Boogie ★ **Big Jim DeNoone:** E Ramble ★ **Herb Remington:** Swinging Strings ★ **Noel Boggs:** Stealin' Home ★ **Hoyle Nix:** Little Betty Brown ★ **Carroll County Boys:** Carroll County Blues ★ **Jimmy Bryant & Speedy West:** Bryant's Shuffle ★ **Art Gunn:** Boogie Woogie Blues ★ Last Tear ★ **Buster Doss:** Graveyard Boogie ★ **Jack Rhodes with Al Petty:** Al's Steel Guitar Wobble ★ **Tex Williams:** Williams Rag ★ **Ole Rasmussen:** Charleston Alley ★ New Star Rag.

OT-101 THE STRING BANDS — Vol. 2

A.C. (Eck) Robertson: Sally Gooden ★ **Earl Johnson's Clodhoppers:** All Night Long ★ **Scottdale String Band:** Carbolic Rag ★ **Carolina Taar Heels:** Lay Down Baby, Take Your Rest ★ **Hackberry Ramblers:** Hackberry Trot ★ **Byrd Moore's Hot Shots:** Three Men Went A Huntin' ★ **Darby & Tarlton:** Alto Waltz ★ **The Spooney Five:** My Little Girl ★ **Bayless Rose:** Jamestown Exhibition ★ **Ashley's Melody Men:** Bath House Blues ★ **Buster Carter & Preston Young:** I'll Roll In My Sweet Baby's Arms ★ **Riley Puckett:** Darkie's Wail ★ **Uncle Bud Landress:** Rubber Dolly Rag ★ **Three Stripped Gears:** Black Bottom Strut ★ **Little Joe Arwood:** Cue Ball Blues ★ **Nathan Abshire:** Cannon Ball Special.

9007 TEXAS-MEXICAN BORDER MUSIC Volume 5
THE STRING BANDS —
End of a Tradition

Orquesta Colonial: Cielito Lindo ★ **Mariachi Coculense Rodriguez:** La Cuatro Milpas ★ **Trovadores Tamaulipecos:** Tamaulipeco ★ **Trio Alegre:** Peor Es Nada ★ El Poder Del Amor ★ **Mariachi Acosta:** Ojitos Chinos Y Negros ★ **Santiago Morales:** La Respingona ★ **Orquesta Fronteriza:** Adios Amor Mio ★ **El Ciego Melquiades:** Panchita ★ **Cuarteto Monterrey:** Mancornadora De Mi Corazon ★ **Los Alegres:** Marosovia ★ **Medina River Boys:** Andale, Vamos Platicando ★ **Guerrero Y Garcia:** Buscare Quien Me Consuele ★ **Andres Huesca:** El Jarabe Veracruzano ★ **Lydia Mendoza:** Panchita ★ Se Murio La Cucaracha.

9018 TEXAS-MEXICAN BORDER MUSIC Vol. 11: EL CIEGO MELQUIADES
(The Blind Fiddler)

Aqui Esta Tu Amor ★ A Mi Amor ★ Muchacha Modernas ★ Quisiera Llorar ★ Viva Laredo ★ Impossible ★. Cholulu ★ Concha ★ Isabel ★ Jalisco Nunca ★ Los Aeroplanos ★ Andrea ★ Te Espero Afuera ★ La Viudita ★ Manuelita.

3009 Music of Mexico
Vol. 2 SONES HUASTECOS
"Los Caporales De Panuco"
Recorded In Tampico
(Features Fiddle And Falsetto Vocals)

El Gustito ★ La Pasion ★ La Gata ★ Las Tres Huastecas ★ El Lunarcito ★ El Llorar ★ Las Flores ★ El Huerfanito ★ El Aguanieve ★ El Tejoncito ★ El Toro Requeson ★ El Toro Sacamandu.

9025 HOT SWING FIDDLE CLASSICS
1936-1943
(Stuff Smith, Emilio Caceres, &
Svend Asmussen)

I Hope Gabriel Likes My Music ★ I'm Putting All My Eggs In One Basket ★ After You've Gone ★ Robins And Roses ★ I Got A Heavy Date ★ I Got Rhythm ★ Humoresque In Swing Time ★ Jig In G ★ Running Wild ★ Honeysuckle Rose ★ Melancholy Baby ★ It Don't Mean A Thing ★ My Blue Heaven ★ Some Of These Days.

3006 KLEZMORIM "East Side Wedding"
(Yiddish instrumental and vocal music of
the lower East Side with Fiddles, Flute,
Clarinets, Accordion, Bass, Mandolin, etc.)

Yoshke, Yoshke ★ Di Grine Kuzine ★ Doina (instr.) ★ Fidl Volach ★ Dem Ganefs Yiches ★ Kacerac ★ Thalassa ★ Sherele ★ Trello Hasaposerviko ★ Cintec De Dragoste/Hora Lui Damian ★ Finf-un-Tsvantsiger ★ Sirba/Hora.

4009 ANY OLD TIME
"String Band"
(Five Woman Band Playing And Singing)

Let Me Fall ★ Dear Companion ★ Turkey Buzzard/Chinquapin Hunting ★ I Wish I'd Stayed In The Wagonyard ★ Ma Cher Bebe Creole ★ Dixieland One Step ★ Home In Pasadena ★ C-U-B-A ★ Free Little Bird ★ I've Got What It Takes ★ I Bid You Goodnight.

5010 THE LOUISIANA HONEYDRIPPERS — "Bayou Bluegrass"

Calinda ★ Run, Boy, Run ★ Liza Jane ★ My Last Dollar Is Gone ★ Old Dan Tucker ★ The Lakes of Ponchartrain ★ Rabbit, Where's Your Mammy? ★ Underneath the Weeping Willow ★ Chicken Pie ★ Kissin' Cousins ★ Woodchuck in the Deadnin' ★ Pore Man ★ Whoah, Mule, Whoah ★ Great Big Billy Goat ★ Raisin' A Rukus ★ Bill Cheatum ★ The Fisher's Hornpipe. (Originally issued as Folklyric LP 122)

5011 SNUFFY JENKINS — "Carolina Bluegrass"
Featuring Homer 'Pappy'' Sherrill on fiddle)

Watermelon Hangin' On Vine ★ Step It Up and Go ★ Possum Up A Gum Stump ★ Spanish Fandango ★ Long Journey Home ★ Charmin' Betsy ★ Dixie, There's No Place Like Home ★ Television ★ Big Eared Mule ★ The Covered Wagon Rolled Right Along ★ Boggy Road To Texas ★ Twinkle, Twinkle, Little Star ★ Miller's Reel ★ Gonna Catch That Train An' Ride ★ Born In Hard Luck ★ The Sweetest Gift, A Mother's Smile ★ Long Time Gone ★ Snuffy's Talking Blues. (Originally issued as Folklyric LP 123)

5019 DEWEY BALFA—MARC SAVOY— D.L. MENARD: LOUISIANA CAJUN MUSIC

"Under the Oak Tree" (vocals with fiddles, accor dion, guitar & string bass) Jolie Blonde de Bayou ★ Petite Fille de la Campagne ★ En Bas d'un beau chene vert ★ Port Arthur Blues ★ J'ai fait un gros erreur ★ J'etais au bal ★ Mardi Gras Jig ★ La Porte dans arriere ★ J'ai passe devant ta porte ★ Cajun Reel ★ Je peux pas t'oublier ★ Mon bon vieux mari ★ Lake Arthur Stomp.

5009 FOLKSONGS OF THE LOUISIANA ACADIANS

(Various Cajun groups — recorded and collected in Mamou, La. by Dr. Harry Oster — an award winning album originally issued as Folklyric LP' A-4) Grand Texas ★ Colinda ★ Tu Peux Cogner Mais Tu Peux Pas Rentrer ★ La Patate Chaude ★ Je Charche Tout Partout ★ T'es Petite, Mais T'es Mignone ★ La Danse De La Limonade ★ La

5005 JOSEPH FALCON
"Louisiana Cajun Music"
(Recorded at a dance in Scott, La.)

Les Flambes D'Enfer ★ Le Tortillage ★ Lacassine Special ★ Allons A Lafayette ★ Osson Two Step ★ Hip Et Taiaut ★ Creole Stomp ★ Allons Danser Colinda.

5004 CAJUN FAIS DO-DO

Nathan Abshire: Cajun Two Step ★ Gabrielle Waltz ★ Grey Night Special ★ Ma Negresse ★ Bayou Pon Pon ★ Old Folks Polka ★ Calcasieu Waltz ★ Le Temps A Pres Finis; **Breaux Brothers:** Hey Ma ★ Crowley Two Step ★ Le Branch De Muriee; **Landreneau Band:** In A Pile Of Hay ★ Chere Mom ★ Grand Mamou; **Isom J. Fontenot:** Medelainne ★ La Valse De La Misere ★ Crowley Two Step ★ La Betaille.

1070 "BOISEC" ARDOIN "La Musique Creole"

("Boisec" Ardoin - accordion and vocals; Canray Fontenot - fiddle and vocals) Home Sweet Home ★ Laccasine Breakdown ★ Les Barres de la Prison ★ Chere Ici, Chere La Bas ★ Opelousas Waltz ★ Canray's One Step ★ Petite et la Grosse **(Canray Fontenot with the Ardoin Brothers)** Ses Parents Ne Veulent Plus Le Voir ★ Joe Pitre A Deux Femmes ★ Le Boss ★ Jupe Courte ★ Jolie Catin.

OT-106 J.E. MAINER'S MOUNTAINEERS Vol. 1

Don't Get Trouble In Your Mind ★ Answer To Greenback Dollar ★ Sparkling Blue Eyes ★ Kiss Me Cindy ★ Why Do You Bob Your Hair Girls ★ We Will Miss Him ★ Just Over In The Gloryland ★ Seven And A half ★ Searching For A Pair Of Blue Eyes ★ Write A Letter To Mother ★ Sparkling Blue Eyes No. 2 ★ A Change All Around ★ Maple On The Hill No. 2 ★ Let Her Go God Bless Her.

OT-107 J.E. MAINER'S MOUNTAINEERS Vol. 2

Concord Rag ★ In A Little Village Churchyard ★ Country Blues ★ Drunkard's Hiccoughs ★ New Lost Train Blues ★ Fatal Wreck Of The Bus ★ Don't Go Out ★ Going Back West In The Fall ★ I Once Loved A Young Man ★ Train No. 11 ★ Broken Hearted Blues ★ Blue Ridge Mountain Blues ★ Back To Johnson City ★ When I Reach My Home Eternal.

9014 UKRAINIAN-AMERICAN FIDDLE & DANCE MUSIC 1926-1934 Vo. 1

Pawlo Humeniuk: Kolomyika Druzky ★ Kolomyika Druszby ★ Ukrainske Wesilie Parts 1 & 2 ★ Hraj, Abo Hroszi Widdaj ★ Oberek Z Pod Babiej Gory ★ **Theodor Swystun:** Yak Poidu Z Kinmy Na Nicz ★ Diwocza Widowa ★ **Ukrainska Selska Orchestra:** Newylnik Waltz ★ Mishszanska Kolomyika ★ **Josef Pizio** (seen on cover): Hutzulka Halycz ★ **Michael Thomas:** Pidhirska Kolomyika ★ **Trembita Orchestra:** Ebba Polka.

9015 UKRAINIAN-AMERICAN FIDDLE AND DANCE MUSIC 1926-1934 Volume 2

Pawlo Humeniuk: Oj, Pidu Ja Szicher Wicher ★ Kozak-Trepak, Tanec ★ Chrestyny Parts 1 & 2 ★ Kolo Haju, Prochodzaju ★ Hop Walc ★ **John Grychak:** Koketka Polka ★ **Ukrainska Selska Orchestra:** Ruta Kolomyika ★ **Orchestra Bratia Holutiaky-Kuziany:** Dribnyj Tanec ★ Wessla Muzyka ★ **Josef Davidenko:** Kozak ★ **Theodor Swystun:** Kozacka Szumka ★ **Josef Pizio** (seen on the cover): Nadwirna Kolomyika ★ **Samuel Pilip:** Lemkiwska Traiska.

9026 POLISH-AMERICAN DANCE MUSIC "The Early Recordings: 1927-1933"

Zbojinicy W Karcmie ★ Cialy Do Baksy ★ Pawel Walc ★ Wesele W Ogrodzie ★ Na Wierzchu Giewonta ★ Tam Pod Kragowem Na Bloniu ★ Zielony Mosteczek ★ Orgowiny Wesela ★ Koscieliska ★ Wianek Majowy ★ Kujawiak Babki ★ Krakowiaki Z Bochni ★ Oberek Od Przymysla ★ Leci Zajac Do Lasu. (Various Bands and Groups)

5001 THE HODGES BROTHERS
(Vocals with Fiddle, guitar, Mandolin, Bass)

Mississippi Baby ★ The Leaves Is Falling On The Ground ★ Fifty Years Waltz ★ It Won't Be Long ★ Bile Dem Cabbage Down ★ On The Banks Of The Ohio ★ Hooknose In Town ★ Carroll County Blues ★ Watermelon Hangin' On The Vine ★ Little Church House On The Hill ★ Charmin' Betsy ★ Never Alone Waltz ★ Bogue Chitto Fling Ding ★ Six White Horses ★ Ida Red.

5002 J.E. MAINER'S MOUNTAINEERS
(Vocals with Fiddle, Banjo, Guitar, Mandolin, and Bass)

"The legendary Family from the Blueridge Mountains." Mississippi Sawyers ★ Ramshackle Shack ★ Run Mountain ★ Short Life of Trouble ★ If I Lose Let Me Lose ★ Greenback Dollar ★ Seven And A Half ★ Sally Goodin ★ Maple On The Hill ★ Home In Louisiana ★ Wild Bill Jones ★ Shake My Mother's Hand For Me ★ I'm Just Here To Get My Baby Out Of Jail ★ Mama Don't Allow.

ANDY'S FRONT HALL

FOLK MUSIC BY MAIL
RD 1 WORMER ROAD, VOORHEESVILLE NY 12186

SELECTED RECORDINGS

American:
VASSAR CLEMENTS "Crossing the Catskills"
Rounder 0016
VASSAR CLEMENTS "The Bluegrass Session"
Flying Fish 038
KENNY BAKER "Kenny Baker Plays Bill Monroe"
County 761
AMERICAN FIDDLE TUNES, edited by Alan Jabbour.
Library of Congress L62. Anthology; recorded in the field.
NEW ENGLAND TRADITION FIDDLING 1926-1975: An Anthology of recordings. Featuring jigs, reels, hornpipes, waltzes and a march—reissues of commercial recordings, library of congress recordings and new recordings. With booklet JEMF 105.
J.P & ANNADENE FRALEY "Wild Rose of the Mountain"
Rounder 0037

Instruction:
TRACY SCHWARZ "Learn to Fiddle Country Style"
Folkways 8359
PETER FELDMAN "How to Play the Country Fiddle" Vol. 1, Vol. 2, Vol. 3. Everything a beginner needs to learn old-time country fiddling. Each record comes with a booklet.
Sonyatone (1) 101; (2) 102; (3) 103
DEWEY BALFA & TRACY SCHWARZ "Traditional Cajun Fiddle" Folkways 8361

Irish:
MICHAEL COLEMAN "The Classic Recordings Of"
Shanachie 33006
JAMES MORRISON "The Pure Genius Of"
Shanachie 33004
KEVIN BURKE "If the Cap Fits" Mulligan 021
PADRAIG O'KEEFE, DENIS MURPHY, JULIA CLIFFORD "Kerry Fiddles" Topic 309
EUGENE O'DONNELL "Slow Airs and Set Dances" with Mick Moloney. Green Linnet 1015
BRENDAN MULVIHILL "The Flax in Bloom" Traditional Irish Music. Green Linnet 1020
MARTIN MULVIHILL with Mick Maloney "Traditional Irish Fiddling from County Limerick. Green Linnet 1012

Shetland:
TOM ANDERSON, ALY BAIN "The Silver Bow" Philo 2019

Sweden:
ERIC SAHLSTROM, GOSTA SANDSTROM "Fiddle Music from Uppland" Philo 2017
THE DANCING BOW An Anthology of Swedish Fiddle Music. Sonet 201 (2 lps)

Scottish/Cape Breton:
WINSTON "SCOTTY" FITZGERALD (1) Celtic 17; (2) Celtic 40; (3)Celtic 44
GRAHAM TOWNSEND Classics of Irish, Scottish and French-Canadian Fiddling. Rounder 7007
JOE CORMIER "The Dances Down Home" Rounder 7004
JERRY HOLLAND Cape Breton Fiddler. Rounder 7008
WINNIE CHAFE "Highland Melodies of Cape Breton" Rounder 7012
CAPE BRETON SCOTTISH FIDDLE Anthology. Topic 353 (Vol. 1) Topic 354 (Vol. 2)
JAMES F. DICKIE "Delights—In the Style of Scott Skinner" Topic 279
CAPE BRETON SYMPHONY Anthology—Various Fiddlers. Glencoe 001
JEAN CARIGNAN
   "Old-Time Fiddle Tunes" Folkways 3531
   "Jean Carignan" Philo 2001

"Rend Hommage a Joseph Allard" Philo 2012
"Gaelic Music" Philo 2018
LOUIS BEAUDOIN
   "Louis Beaudoin" Philo 2000
   "The Beaudoin Family" Philo 2022

FHR-018

TRADITIONAL MUSIC OF IRELAND AND SHETLAND

How To Change A Flat Tire. This is the second album by the Tires on the Front Hall label. This time the band is four members featuring fiddle, concertina, mandolin, banjo, recorder and whistles. An all-instrumental album of the tunes of Ireland and Shetland.
TITLES: Langstrom's Pony, The Ballykeal Jig, The Pipe on the Hob, Sister Jean, Kiss Her and Clap Her, Gibbie Grey's, Andrew Polson's Farewell to Williamstown, Peter's Jig, Martin's New Haircut, Paddy Fahy's, Green Grow the Rushes, Farewell to Peggy, Richard Dwyer's, Jack in the Fog, The Gammaho, Martin Talty's, A Pinch of Snuff, The Yorkshire Lasses, Father Burke, The Whinny Hills of Leitrim, Elizabeth Kelly's Delight, Foxy Mary, Art O'Keefe's, The Scartagien Jig, Da Muckle Reel O'Finnigirt, Jeannie Choke Da Bairn, Wha'll Dance Wi' Wattie?, Square Da Mizzen, Da Black Hat, Paddy McFadden, Behind the Bush in Parkhanna, The Highlander.

FHR-05

SATURDAY NIGHT IN THE PROVINCES

Fennig's All-Star String Band featuring Bill Spence on Hammered Dulcimer, Tom McCreesh on fiddle and Toby Fink on piano. This sequel to the critically acclaimed **The Hammered Dulcimer (FHR-01)** is a selection of new and old tunes from America and the British Isles played in a style unique among contemporary string bands.
Folk Review (England): "Let it be said that Bill Spence is a fine dulcimer player and Tom McCreesh an equally fine fiddler. The distinctive quality of the hammered dulcimer contributes an unusual and fascinating timbre to the ensemble— almost a new dimension to the folk band sound, which has yet to be fully exploited."
TITLES: Jaybird, Cherokee Shuffle, Young Jane, Down the Brae, Remember Me, Star of Munster, Tom's Reel, Georgia Railroad, Margaret's Waltz, The Wedding Day, Swinging on a Gate, Tobin's Favorite, Swallow Tail Jig, Off She Goes, I Think of You, Morgan Megan, Gallopede, Rufty Tufty, The Rose Tree, Greenfields of America, Staten Island, Off to California, Harrison's I, Star of the Country Down.

FHR-03

SWINGING ON A GATE

Dudley Laufman and the Canterbury Country Dance Orchestra. Jigs, reels, waltzes and Morris tunes played on accordion, flute, fiddle, piano, banjo and guitar. New old-time country dance music in a unique New Hampshire manner.
Folk Scene Magazine: "This is an album for limberjack owners, spoon players, clog dancers or anybody who wants some infectious, foot-tapping music around for instant spirit raising."
TITLES: Symondsbury Mummers March, Lassie's Fancy, Dover Pier, Johnny's Gone to France, Rosebud Reel, The False Bride, Kitty McGee, Spanish Jig, Mouse in the Cupboard, Still They Say She's Kind of Pretty, All Around My Hat, Fieldtown Processional, Ring O'Bells, Swinging on a Gate, Zepher and Flora.

FHR-017

DANCE LIKE A WAVE OF THE SEA
Walt Michael, Tom McCreesh and Harley Campbell

Kite: "There are a number of eclectic groups today who handle different traditions like bluegrass and old-timey, but this album has to rate at the very top nationally for superior production, superior talent and superior music selection. From Michael's hammered dulcimer work to foot-stomping breakdowns (including the superb Tony Trischka on banjo) to a beautiful Bruce Phillips ballad, this lp is almost uniformly excellent."—Marty Schwartz
TITLES: Prince William's Medley, The Kentucky Waltz, The Black Nag, Icy Mountain, Little Sadie, Breakin' Up Christmas, High on a Mountain, Southwind, Goin' Away, Spring in the Valley, Little Rabbit, Sally Johnson, The Old, Old House, Sittin' on Top of the World, The Cuckoo's Nest, The Star of the County Down, The Fiddler of Dooney, Sons of Jubal.

THE HAMMERED DULCIMER FHR-01

Bill Spence with Fennig's All-Star String Band. The definitive hammered dulcimer recording, featuring 29 great country dance tunes with fiddle, banjo and piano. Includes "Gaspe Reel," the theme from the PBS-TV show "Crockett's Victory Garden."
"Recording of Special Merit...A charming album with a fey and sprightly spirit hopping around above a solid grassroots footing. The whole album is good stereo; it is beautifully engineered, an almost unheard of quality in a disc from a low-budget folkie label."—**Stereo Review Magazine**
TITLES: The Boys of Wexford, Scotland the Brave, Come Dance and Sing, Ragtime Annie, Sandy River Belle, The Black Nag, Childgrove, Smash the Windows, Coleraine, Haste to the Wedding, The Flowers of Edinburgh, Temperance Reel, Times are Gettin' Hard, Gaspe Reel, Fiddle Head Reel, Don Tremaine's Reel, Dubuque, Galway Hornpipe, Rights of Man, Harvest Home, Fisherman's Favorite, Colored Aristocracy, Over the Waterfall, Prince William, Huntsman's Chorus, Golden Slippers, Old Joe Clark, Mississippi Sawyer, Cabri Waltz, Midnight on the Water.

FHR-010

THE HAMMERED DULCIMER STRIKES AGAIN

Bill Spence with George Wilson and Toby Fink. The third album of hammered dulcimer music, this time all instrumental with several solo dulcimer cuts and a guest performance by Tom McCreesh.
Come For To Sing: "Bill Spence is probably the best known hammered dulcimer player around today and is responsible for both the resurrection of the instrument and the increasing popularity of contra dancing."
TITLES: Walpole Cottage, The Three Sea Captains, Old Man Dillon, Johnny the Blacksmith, Sort of Silver Bells, McCusker's Delight, Bill Cheatum, Liberty, St. Adele's Reel, Woodchopper's Reel, You Married My Daughter But You Didn't, Planxty Erwin, Little Judique Reel, Parry Sound Reel, Mudgey Waltz, Margravine's Waltz, Spring in the Valley, Church Street, St. Mary's, Hannah's Medley, The Tempest, Double Lead Through, Hobart's Transformation.

june appal recordings
box 743
whitesburg, kentucky
41858

JA030—ROAD TO HOME Marion Sumner has earned the title "Fiddle King Of The South." His years on the road with Opry stars such as Johnny and Jack, Kitty Wells, Roy Acuff, Jim and Jesse and Don Gibson have made him a legend among fellow musicians. Selections on Marion's first solo album include *Dragging The Bow; Beaumont Rag; Georgiana Moon* and *Up a Lazy River.*

JA033—LAST CHANCE The Home Folks The 'old mountain sound' from Scott County, Virginia, describes the sound of The Home Folks. The Home Folks are Beachard Smith, singer and fiddler; Paul Davis, lead guitarist; Will Keys, banjoist; and Tom Bledsoe, vocalist and rhythm guitarist. Together, they produce a relaxed, freewheeling music that reflects the many different influences they have absorbed over the years. Songs on the album include *Step Light Ladies; Eighth of January; Poor Ellen Smith; Silver Bells* and *Sycamore Shoals.* FROM THE APPAL SEED FIELD RECORDING PROJECT with an informational insert.

JA029—JUBILEE Guy Carawan A refreshing collection of Irish and American fiddle tunes as well as some beautiful ballads, old and new. Featured are Guy and Candie Carawan's vocals, hammered dulcimer, fiddle, tin whistle, banjo, Jew's Harp and guitar. Selections include *Haste To The Wedding; Daddy, What's A Train?; Whiskey Before Breakfast; When the Fiddler Has Played His Last Tune For The Night.*

JA003—HOW CAN I KEEP FROM SINGING? John McCutcheon & Friends John McCutcheon's debut album demonstrates his tremendous range of musical abilities. This album presents an outstanding variety of material shifting easily between fiddle, banjo, hammered dulcimer, guitar, autoharp, and dulcimer. Selections include *The Devil and The Farmer's Wife; Bluebird Song; Froggie Went A-Courtin'; Down Came An Angel; Hammered Dulcimer Medley* and many others. Album contains booklet with lyrics.

JA028—FROM EARTH TO HEAVEN Wry Straw This debut album by the popular and versatile string band from Scott County, Virginia, features a wide range of oldtime music. John McCutcheon, Rich Kirby and Tom Bledsoe combine hammered dulcimer, fiddle, banjo, guitar, mandolin and autoharp in selections including *Hot Corn, Cold Corn; I Get The Blues; Rye Cove; Dill Pickle Rag; Land Beyond The Blue.*

JA007—Deep In Tradition—*Tommy Hunter* "Tommy Hunter is a fiddler whose style is closest to the relaxed Kentucky sound of J.P. Fraley, although Hunter hails from North Carolina. His fiddling seems simple, each note ringing crisp and clear, unadorned by vibrato, although occasionally ornamented with a beautifully executed trill. Hunter is the kind of fiddler who is easily underestimated.... His primary concern is to relate the melodic contours of a tune, and in this way he is closer in style to traditional Irish musicians than Appalachian fiddlers. However, unlike the Irish, Hunter uses ornament sparingly.... Appropriately understated guitar accompaniment is provided by John McCutcheon. If this were a Rounder release, you'd already own it. Get this one."

Richard Carlin
IN THE TRADITION

JA015—PLANK ROAD Plank Road String Band The current renaissance of oldtime Southern string band music has yielded a great many fine young groups cranking out infectious fiddle and banjo music, much to the delight of people all over the world. The Plank Road String Band from Lexington, Virginia have performed from fiddle conventions to court houses to Europe to the White House. The group has made a name for themselves and their unique, driving combination of twin fiddle, banjo, guitar, and cello.

JA030—Road To Home—*Marion Sumner* "... and it's great, nothing short of great, some of the best fiddling I've heard.... **Road To Home** is Marion's first solo album. Considering he's been playing for almost fifty years, all I can say is... I hope we don't have to wait this long for his next one."

KRBD NEWSLETTER
Ketchikan, Alaska

JA023- SYCAMORE TEA Dutch Cove Old Time String Band The much heralded instrumental album by this award-winning North Carolina string band. The perfect accompaniment for clog dancing. Dutch Cove plays polkas, hornpipes, jigs, reels and waltzes. Quay Smather's family band draws from the vast repertoire of the Smather's fiddling tradition. The 22 songs include *Sugar In The Gourd; Fisher's Hornpipe; Spotted Pony* and *Fire on the Mountain.* The album comes with a booklet of lyrics.

DownHome MUSIC, INC.

Free Reed 028 OLD SWAN BAND
Old Swan Brand (Recorded 3 years ago
this album has finally been issued - a
selection of English country dance
music and traditional and music hall
styled songs performed by excellent
young band which features the
marvelous melodeon work of Rod
Stradling - with tambourine, mouth
organ, fiddle, whistles, banjo, etc)
.... $12.98

Thule 116 SHETLAND FIDDLERS ON
STAGE (We've finally been able to get
copies of this record featuring a large
group of fiddlers from the Shetland
Islands led by noted fiddler Tom
Anderson) $12.98

Celtic Music CM006 BRIAN MILLER &
CHARLIE SOANE : The Favorite Dram
(Another splendid discovery from
Scotland - Miller is a superb singer
and strong guitar player and Soane is a
very fine fiddle player who draws on a
variety of traditions in his playing -
the material is a mixture of tried &
true pieces along with lesser known
items - a truly impressive debut album)
.... $9.98

Arfolk 210 GERANIUM
(Splendid group perfoprming
traditional songs and tunes from Alsace
-the German border regions of France -
some songs sung in French and some in
German - with violin, accordeon, flute
, guitar, concertina, psaltery,
dulcimer, jaw harp, etc) $10.98

Rambler 105 HOT AS I AM - WESTERN
SWING, 1935-1941 (Another supertb
collection from this fine label
featuring a great selection of hot
music by The Light Crust Doughboys,
Cliff bruner's Texas Wanderers, The
Tune wranglers, The Modern
Mountaineers, Milton Bown & His
Brownies, and more - with excellent
sound, discographical details and
extensive notes based on first hand
interviews with surviving band mambers)
.... $6.98

Longhorn 011 BOB WILLS, TOMMY
DUNCAN & THE TEXAS PLAYBOYS
31st Street Blues (15 cuts from mid
40s radio transcriptions - never
issued on record before and featuring a
hot band including Joe Holley, Noel
Boggs, Junior Barnard, Alex Brashear,
Jessie Ashlock, Milard Kelso and
others - features several songs not
recorded elsewhere by Bob - a must for
lovers of the music of this great
artist) $6.98

Inner City 1104 DJANGO REINHARDT :
Volume 1 (Two L.P. set featuring 28
classic recordings from 1936 & 1937 by
this great pioneer jazz guitarist with
The Quintet Of The Hot Club Of France
with Stephane Grapelli - great sides
originally reissued on French Pathe as
wEll as some other labels - excellent
sound and notes) $11.98

Blue Sound 3002 STEPHANE GRAPPELLI '80
(Another album by the ever prolific
Grappeli - 12 original tunes - with
rhythm section) $11.98

GEMS OF IRISH & CAPE BRETON FIDDLING-
Cathie Whitesides

In 1970 Cathie discovered Irish music and through that the music of Scotland and Cape
Breton. Learning from older traditional players and private tapes of Cape Breton
players, she has mastered the art in a way equaled by few players in this generation.
She says, "The tunes on this lp are favorites of mine, each one remarkable in some way
whether it be an odd setting, the sort of melody that talks back to you, a little-
played tune of interest, or one that recreates the presence of the fine player I
learned it from." INSTRUMENTS: Fiddle/guitar/tenor banjo/piano/accordian/harmonium.

*TUNES: Mrs. Menzie of Culdares, Welcome Whiskey Back Again, Captain Keeler, Gallow-
glass, My Cabin Home, Farewell to Erin, Callahan's, The Limestone Rock, Strathspey,
MacKinnon's Brook, Three Old-Time Wedding Reels, Blue Bonnets Over the Border,
Farewell to Whiskey, Memories of Ronald Beaton, Mr. Moore, The Earl of Hynford's
Reel, The King of the Clans, Christmas Eve, The Thatched Cabin, The Waltz and the
Jig, Christy Campbell. KM 231 LP . . . $6.95*

SWARBRICK - Dave Swarbrick, of the Fairport Convention, here steps out on his own
to do an lp of English string band music featuring his incredible fiddle.
*TITLES: The Heilanman/Drowsey Maggie, Carthy's March, The White Cockade/Doc
Boyds Jig/Durham Rangers, My Singing Bird, The Nightingale, Once I Loved a
Maiden Fair, The Killarney Boys of Pleasure, Lady in the Boat/Rosin the Bow/
Timour the Tartar, Byker Hill, The Ace and Deuce of Pipering, Hole in the Wall,
Ben Dorian, Hullichans/Chorous Jig, The 79th Farewell to Gibraltar, Arthur Mc
Bride/Snug in the Blanket KM 337 LP . . . $6.95*

Barring - A technique whereby one finger is used to fret two or more strings simultaneously. For example, in the Irish fiddle tune "Drowsy Maggie," the index finger can cover both the E note on the D string and the B note on the A string to start the tune.

Bass Bar - A long, tapered piece of wood which is glued to the underside of the belly (inside the violin) under the G string.

Belly/top/soundboard - The rounded upper surface of the fiddle with the F holes, made of spruce. *(See chapter on "Buying a Fiddle")*

Bluegrass - As the popularity of traditional string bands faded out in the late 1930s, a new style of performance oriented music developed, typified by the high lonesome singing of Bill Monroe combined with the innovative banjo playing of Earl Scruggs. Fiddle and other instrumental parts became improvisational and flashier than in previous times. Bill's "Blue Grass Boys" made their first recordings in 1941, and were joined by the 19 year old Scruggs in 1945. The name has stuck.

Bridge - Carved piece of maple which stands centered between the innermost notches on the F holes and which supports the strings. *(See chapter on "Obtaining a Fiddle")*

Call - In country dancing, the instructions of the dance caller during the dance.

Chinrest - The cupped piece attached by clamps to the body of the fiddle in which the chin rests while playing.

Chord - Two or more tones played simultaneously.

Chunk/chop - A percussive sound made by striking strings sharply with the bow. This technique is often used by bluegrass fiddlers to mark time between solos.

Clawhammer - "Old time" or mountain style banjo playing which predates bluegrass picking, and is still used in old time string bands and for square dances. The back of the finger nail of the leading finger strikes the string followed by a plucking of the string by the fleshy part of the thumb. This is sometimes described as "frailing," "knocking," or "rapping" a banjo.

Clogging - The term originally comes from the British Isles and is commonly used in the United States to describe team dancing in square dance-like figures to fast fiddle tunes. The style is derived from and related to "buck dancing," and "flat foot" solo dancing.

Contra dancing - A type of American country dancing most popular in New England, similar to square dancing, with mostly French origins. Most dances are in "longways sets," similar to the Virginia reel, but with more complicated figures.

Country dancing - Includes contra dancing, square and round dancing, the Virginia reel, and any sort of country type figures which are designated by a caller to live music.

Crooked tunes - A term used to describe tunes in which one part is longer than another or where there are extra measures or missing measures and beats.

Cross tuning - Normally, fiddles are tunes G–D–A–E, but by retuning the strings, different fingerings and sounds are possible. For example, A–E–A–E is often used for southern U.S. tunes in the key of A. Benny Thomasson, in the tune "Midnight on the Water" composed by his father and uncle, used D–A–D–D which is sometimes known as "Black Mountain tuning." C#–A–E–A tuning is often used for Texas tunes such as "Bumblebee in the Gourd Vine" and "Lost Indian." Many other tunings are possible, and are used in various American and European fiddle traditions.

Double stop - Two strings bowed simultaneously, and either one, two, or neither fingered.

Drone - A continuous tone which accompanies other melody notes. This effect can be created by playing two adjacent strings simultaneously — the note played on one string remains constant (the drone), while different notes are fingered on the other.

Ebony - A very hard and dark wood imported from Africa which is strong and resistant to wear.

F hole - The "f" shaped holes in the top of the violin. *(See the chapter on "Buying a Fiddle")*

Fine tuners - Small screw-type adjustable mechanisms attached to the tail piece which can be used to tighten or loosen the strings.

Fingerboard - The long piece of ebony under the strings which is attached to the neck. *(See chapter on "Buying a Fiddle)*

Flatfoot - A type of solo dancing similar to clogging which is done to fast southern fiddle tunes, and where the feet are not brought above the knees while dancing.

Fret - Either the process of stopping a note at a particular place on a fingerboard with a finger, as in "to fret" a string, or a term used to refer to the piece of metal fret wire set into the fingerboard of an instrument.

Frog - The black rectangular piece of wood that slides against the bow and serves to anchor the bow hair.

Hoedown - Refers to a fast fiddle tune in 2/4 time and is sometimes called a breakdown or reel. The term is also used to describe a dance at which fiddle music is played.

Hornpipe - The word is derived from an early double reed type instrument made from animal horn. The term is sometimes used to describe a type of solo dancing common to sailors in the mid-18th century. The term more commonly refers to a style of tune. Even-rhythmed hornpipes are similar in style to reels and are played faster than uneven-rhythmed hornpipes which came to have dotted rhythms as a 19th century innovation.

Jam/jamming - An informal playing session with a group of musicians, where the music is more typically improvised rather than worked out ahead of time.

Jig - The term refers either to a type of Celtic dancing or a tune which might be played for someone dancing a jig. Shakespeare uses the expression to 'jigg off a tune' in the Play *Love's Labour's Lost.'* There are three main types of jigs: single jig in 6/8 time such as "The Road to Lisdunvarna," double jig in 6/8 time such as "The Irish Washerwoman," and "slip" jigs in 9/8 time such as "The Rocky Road to Dublin."

Lick - A player's term for a rhythmic or melodic ornament used to embellish a tune.

Modal tunes - The term is used to describe tunes from various traditions which use scales that are neither major nor minor. Examples may be found in southern Appalachian tunes such as "Cluck Old Hen," and "Shady Grove."

Mute - A wood, metal, or plastic device which clamps onto the bridge of a fiddle to reduce its volume.

Nut - A small notched piece of ebony at the end of the finger board which supports the strings.

Old timey - The term refers to a pre-bluegrass stringband style, with country dance rhythms and which includes music from vaudeville, minstrel shows, British Isles folk traditions, and early 78 rpm country recordings.

Pegs - The tapered pieces of hardwood, usually ebony, which fit into the pegbox, and are used for tuning the strings.

Pegbox - The hollowed out portion of the neck of the fiddle in which the strings are attached to the pegs.

Peghead - The portion of the fiddle neck which bears the scroll and pegs.

Pernambuco - A South American wood used for fine bows.

Planxty - In Ireland, a tune composed for a patron which sometimes has a phrase syllabically like the patron's name.

Positions - Most fiddlers play in "first position" with the hand remaining close to the pegbox while playing. To obtain higher notes, the player moves her hand up the fingerboard toward the bridge. When the first finger plays what the third finger ordinarily plays, this is called third position, for example.

B.Sullivan.

Purfling - Very thin strips of wood which are inset into the edges of the fiddle on both belly and back.

Reel - A dance of longways sets of couples, or the accompanying music which is usually in 2/4 time.

Rosin - The resin which is rubbed onto the bow hairs so that they grip and therefore vibrate the strings when drawn across them.

Roundpeak - A term used to describe a highly rhythmic style of North Carolina fiddling typified by the playing of Tommy Jarrel.

Schottische - A tune similar to a Strathspey but closer to a 2/2 meter and played faster.

Scroll - The end of the fiddle neck which is carved into a spiral shape. *(See the chapter on "Buying a Fiddle")*

Set - A group of couples assembled for dancing. The term also describes the assortment of tunes played by the band or performer.

Shoulder rest - Some players of both classical violin and fiddle music find that a shoulder rest helps them support the fiddle under their chins. Some rests are semi-rigid and clamp onto the fiddle. Others are soft fabric covered sponges that attach with rubber bands. Some people make their own shoulder rests by folding up wash clothes or other materials to the desired thickness.

B SOLLIVAN

Shuffle - A rhythmical bowing pattern. The most common country shuffle sounds like daaa-dada-daaa-dada-daaa, etc. (Nashville shuffle) There are many other possible rhythms that can be shuffled. The most complex shuffle patterns occur in traditional southern U.S. style fiddling, and in bluegrass.

Sides/ribs/upper, middle, and lower bouts - *(See chapter on "Buying a Fiddle")*

Sligo - Refers to a highly ornamental Irish fiddle style typified by the playing of Michael Coleman, which originated in the Sligo area of Ireland.

Slur/slurring - Playing two or more notes in one bow direction, rather than changing the bow direction for each note.

Soundpost - A round dowel-like piece of spruce inside the fiddle which transmits the vibrations from the belly to the back and also helps provide support under the bridge. *(See chapter on "Buying a Fiddle")*

Standard pitch - Refers to a tone of standard frequency as determined by international agreement, e.g. A = 440 Hz. (cycles per second).

Strathspey - A slow reel originating in Scotland, and played in 4/4 time with characteristic halved and dotted notes described as the "Scots snap."

Strings - These may be made of animal gut, metal, or synthetic materials. *(See chapter on "Buying a Fiddle")*

Tail Button - The black round peg at the bottom of the fiddle to which the tail gut is attached.

Tail gut - A strand of gut or nylon which wraps around the tail button and is attached to the tail piece.

Tailpiece/string holder - The triangular shaped piece of wood or metal to which the strings are attached.

Texas style fiddling - Refers to a contest style of fiddling with its roots in Texas, and is typified by the playing of Benny Thomasson, with highly developed melody variations, and jazz-like backup from the accompanying instruments.

Vibrato - The pulsating sound made by rolling or vibrating the finger back and forth in one position on the fingerboard.

Subject Index

Band Index

Adolf Hofner and his San Antonians 100, 120
Albion Country Band 105
Alladin Laddies 101
Allen Brothers 120
Ambassadors 116
American Swedish Spelmans Trio 103
Any Old Time String Band 88, 120
Applejack 102
Ardoin Brothers 121
Arkansas Sheiks String Band 89
Arm and Hammer String Band 32, 102, 112, 114, 117, 118
Arthur Smith Trio 120
Ashley's Melody Men 120

Backwoods Band 94
Baker and Forrester 118
Balfa Freres 107
Banjo Dan and the Midnight Plow Boys 35
Bar X Cowboys 100, 120
Barde 110
Beatons of Mabou 104
Bill Boyd and His Cowboy Ramblers 99, 120
Bill Monroe and His Bluegrass Boys 105
Binkley Brothers 90
Blue Ridge Mountaineers 92
Blue Ridge Playboys 101
Blue Sky Boys 90
Blue Velvet Band 105
Bluegrass Cardinals 119
Blues Project 105
Bluestein Family 112
Bob Skiles and His Skyrockets 100, 120
Bob Wills and the Texas Playboys 6, 73, 100, 120
Boswell Sisters 116
Bothy Band 32, 39, 96, 110
Boys of the Lough 13, 32, 95, 96, 98, 113
Breakfast Special 106
Breaux Brothers 121
Buck Robers and Johnny Gimble 120
Buddy Duhon and Harry Choates 120
Burnett and Rutherford 94
Byrd Moore's Hot Shots 120

Cambridge Folk Orchestra ?35
Campbell Family 111
Canray Fontenot and the Carriere Brothers 118
Canterbury Country Dance Orchestra 32, 122
Captain Fiddle Band 36
Carolina Tar Heels 120
Carroll County Boys 120
Carter and Young 90
Cat Mother and the All Night Newsboys 112

Central Park Sheiks 108
Chieftains 3, 7, 32
Claude Casey and the Pine State Playboys 99
Cliff Bruner's Texas Wanderers 99, 100, 101
Cobb and Underwood 92
Coon Creek Girls 118
Corn Dodgers 115, 116
Country Cooking 106
Country Gazette 106
Country Ham 118
Critton Hollow Stringband 117, 118
Crossroads 119
Crystal Springs Ramblers 99, 120
Cuerteto Monterrey 120
Curley Williams and His Georgia Peach Pickers 99

Dakota Dave Hull 118
Darby and Tarlton 120
David Bromberg Band 112
David Grisman Quintet 105
De Danann 32, 97, 109, 117
Delmore Brothers 89
Delta Sisters 116
Dickie McBride and the Village Boys 100
Double Decker Stringband 112
Dutch Cove Old Time String Band 123

Eaglebone Whistle 111
Earl Johnson's Clodhoppers 116, 120
Earth Opera 105
East Texas Serenaders 88
Eddie Adcock and Martha 119
Evangeline Playboys 107

F and W Stringband 32
Fairport Convention 124
Falls City Ramblers 118
Farr Brothers 99, 120
Felice and Boudleaux 119
Fennigs All-Star Stringband 122
Fiddle Fever 32
Fiddlin' Arthur Smith and His Dixieliners 89
Floyd County Ramblers 88
Fly by Night String Band 111
Foggy Mountain Boys 119
Fuzzy Mountain String Band 93, 94

Geoff Stelling's Hard Times Bluegrass Band 115
Georgia Yellow Hammers 90, 93, 116
Geranium 124
Golden Eagle String Band 118
Grant Street String Band 117
Grayson and Whittier 120
Guerrero y Garcia 120
Gypsy Gyppo String Band 114, 115

Hackberry Ramblers 120
Hammons Family 97

Hatton Brothers 92
Heights of Grass 119
Herschel Brown and His Washboard Band 120
Highwoods String Band 13, 32, 88, 91, 93, 94, 114
Hill Billies 93
Hodges Brothers 121
Hollow Rock String Band 89, 93
Home Folks 123
Hot Club of France 31, 32
Hotmud Family 118
Hot Rize 6
How to Change A Flat Tire 32, 122
Hoyle Nix and His West Texas Cowboys 100
Hoyt Ming and His Pepstepper 90
Hutchison Brothers 118

Incredible String Band 98

Jack Rhodes with Al Petty 120
Jim and Jesse 119
Jimmie Revard and His Oklahoma Playboys 99, 100
Jimmy Bryant and Speedy West 120
Jimmy Johnson's Boys 90, 92
Joe Val and the New England Bluegrass Boys 35
Joe Venuti's Blue Four 108
Johnny and Jack 123
Johnny Gimble and the Texas Swing Pioneers 119
Johnny Tyler and his Riders of the Rio Grande 99
Johnson Brothers 93
Johnson Mountain Boys 118
Johnson's Clodhoppers 116, 120
Joseph Falcon with Clemo and Ophy Breaux 120
Jones Brothers 119
Josh Graves with Bobby Smith and Shiloh 118, 119

Kentucky Colonels 32, 106
Kentucky String Ticklers 92
Klezmorim 120
Knock-Na Shee 109

LA Fiddle Band 84
Landreneau Band
Last Chance String Band 35
Leaford Hall and His Texas Vagabonds 100
Leake County Revellers 90
Leon "Pappy" Selph and his Blue Ridge Playboys 100
Light Crust Doughboys 99, 101, 120
Lilly Brothers 62
Lonesome Luke and his Farmhands 92
Lonestar Playboys 120
Los Alegres 120
Los Caporales De Panuco 120

Name Index

Afterword

PUTTING THIS BOOK TOGETHER has been a rewarding task. I have made every effort to make the information and its presentation as useful and accurate as possible. But, as with any major undertaking, errors are likely to creep in.

If you found the book engaging and informative, if it has given you some of the pleasure it has given me, I ask that you help make future editions more complete and accurate by sharing your special knowledge and observations with me in writing.

I would also be interested in photos, newspaper clippings, old letters, taped interviews, drawings and anything else related to fiddling. Any material that I use will be credited to the donor and will be greatly appreciated. If you have any questions about my interest in a particular item, please write me a note.

If you would like to be on my mailing list for more information on fiddling, please send me your name and address.

Ryan J. Thomson
4 Elm Court
Newmarket, New Hampshire 03857

About the Author

RYAN THOMSON, who often performs as "Captain Fiddle," is a freelance professional musician residing in Newmarket, New Hampshire. He was the Northeast Regional winner in the National Fiddle Contest in Weiser, Idaho, in 1977, and has won many other awards in fiddling. In 1983 he was hired on as fiddler for the Baked Apple Band which had won second place in the International Battle of the Bands in Nashville, Tennessee. Before returning to New England he successfully completed an eight state tour ranging from Rhode Island to Arizona.

He has studied violin and bow repair at the Violin Institute of the University of New Hampshire under bow maker and restorer Arnold Bone of Massachusetts and Carl Roy, Director of the State Violin Making School in Austria. Ryan's musical experience also includes a two year stint as a bluegrass radio show host and a year producing a folk music show for National Public Radio.

Besides teaching music privately, Ryan has led fiddle workshops at numerous folk festivals. He taught a college level course in the "Psychology of Music" at the University of New Hampshire where he has also taught several courses in "Folk Fiddling" through the Division of Continuing Education.